Migrant Workers in Asia

Migrant Workers in Asia provides rich and provocative comparative studies of South and Southeast Asian workers who migrate to other parts of Asia — ranging from Hong Kong, Macau, and Singapore, to Yemen, Israel, Jordan, and the UAE. Conceptually and methodologically this book challenges us to move beyond conventional area studies regional divides, proposing new ways of mapping inter-Asian connections. Rather than focusing on singular or binary sites of home and host destination, sending and receiving nation, one nationality and one location, the authors view migrant workers within a wider spatial context of intersecting groups and trajectories through time. Keenly attentive to the importance of migrants of diverse nationalities who have labored in multiple regions, this book examines intimate connections and distant divides in the social lives and politics of migrant workers across time and space. Collectively, the authors propose new themes, new comparative frameworks, and new methodologies for considering vastly different degrees of social support structures and political activism, and the varied meanings of citizenship and state responsibility in sending and receiving countries. They highlight the importance of formal institutions (state, local, familial, transnational, and capitalist) that shape and promote migratory labor, advocacy for workers, or curtail workers rights, as well as the social identities and cultural practices and beliefs that may be linked to new inter-ethnic social and political affiliations that traverse and also transform inter-Asian spaces and pathways to mobility.

This book contains articles previously published in two issues of *Critical Asian Studies:* Vol. 40, No. 4 (2008) and Vol. 41, No. 1 (2009).

Nicole Constable is professor of anthropology at the University of Pittsburgh. She is the author of *Christian Souls and Chinese Spirits: Hakka Identity in Hong Kong* (University of California Press, 1994), *Maid to Order in Hong Kong* (Cornell University Press, 1997, 2007), and *Romance on a Global Stage: Pen Pals, Virtual Ethnography, and Mail Order Marriages* (University of California Press, 2003), and the editor of *Guest People: Hakka Identity in China and Abroad* (University of Washington Press, 1996) and *Cross-Border Marriages: Gender and Mobility in Transnational Asia* (University of Pennsylvania Press, 2005).

MIGRANT WORKERS IN ASIA

Distant Divides, Intimate Connections

Edited by Nicole Constable

Routledge
Taylor & Francis Group

LONDON AND NEW YORK

First published 2010 by Routledge
2 Park Square, Milton Park, Abingdon, Oxon, OX14 4RN

Simultaneously published in the USA and Canada
by Routledge
711 Third Avenue, New York, NY 10017

Routledge is an imprint of the Taylor & Francis Group, an informa business

First issued in paperback 2011

This book is a reproduction of a two-part thematic issue of *Critical Asian Studies*: 40.4 (2008) and 41.1 (2009). The Publisher requests authors who may be citing this book to state, also, the bibliographical details of the thematic issues on which the book was based.

Typeset in Garamond in the USA by BCAS, Inc.

British Library Cataloguing in Publication Data
A catalogue record for this book is available from the British Library

ISBN 13: 978-0-415-57814-1 (hbk)
ISBN 13: 978-0-415-50949-7 (pbk)

Contents

Abstracts

1. On Sentimental Orientalists, Christian Zionists, and Working Class Cosmopolitans: Filipina Domestic Workers' Journeys to Israel and Beyond

Claudia Liebelt

Within a global gendered economy based on an international division of labor, Filipina migrants have become nannies, maids, and caregivers in affluent homes in numerous Asian and Middle Eastern countries. Filipina migrants who seek employment as domestic workers abroad have been described as "classical" transmigrants who keep in touch with family members back home and commute between their countries of origin and their destinations. In this article — based on ethnographic research in Israel, Palestine, and the Philippines between 2003 and 2008 — the author argues that Filipina migrants are transnational in a much broader sense than commonly discussed in studies on migration: engaged in border-crossing journeys through a number of nation states, many Filipina migrants move *on and on* rather than *back and forth*. They do so within a global hierarchy of desirable destination countries, ranked according to the differences between nation-states with regard to salaries and the legal entitlements migrants can claim, the costs and risks migrants have to take in order to enter, and these countries' overall subjective and imaginative attractiveness. By migrating on, Filipina domestic workers acquire an intimate picture of the Middle East "backstage." Some even become self-proclaimed Middle Eastern experts or politically active Christian Zionists or sentimental Orientalists, who, in spite of their Christianity, miss fasting on Yom Kippur or during Ramadan as they continue their journeys toward Western Europe and North America, where they have hopes of living and perhaps gaining citizenship.

2. High in the Hierarchy, Rich in Diversity: Asian Domestic Workers, Their Networks, and Employers' Preferences in Yemen

Marina de Regt

The Republic of Yemen, situated on the southwestern edge of the Arabian Peninsula, is the least economically developed country in West Asia. While it is well known that migrant domestic workers are employed in neighboring countries such as Saudi Arabia and the Gulf States, there is little awareness that most domestic work in Yemen is also done by migrant women. The majority of migrant domestic workers come from Somalia and Ethiopia, but women from Asian countries, such as the Philippines, Indonesia, India, and Sri Lanka also fill this role. These Asian women are positioned at the top of Yemeni employers' hierarchy of domestic workers: they have a high status, are employed by the upper classes, and receive the highest salaries. Ethiopian and Somali women have a lower status: they are employed by the middle and upper middle classes and receive lower salaries. Yet, women from Asian countries do not constitute a homogeneous category: important differences are evident among them and, as well, in the preferences of employers for particular categories of Asian women. This article analyzes some of these differences in respect to recruitment, employment, and living conditions, access to social support networks, and contacts with fellow countrywomen. The author argues that the shifting preferences of employers relate to the various recruitment and support networks available to Asian women. This article is based on anthropological fieldwork, interviews with fifteen Asian domestic workers, and interviews with employers in two cities in Yemen from 2003 to 2006.

3. Of Maids and Madams: Sri Lankan Domestic Workers and Their Employers in Jordan

Elizabeth Frantz

More than 100,000 Sri Lankan women leave their homes each year to seek employment as domestic workers in the Arab world. The oil-rich Gulf States remain the biggest recruiters, but demand has been rising sharply in Jordan, where few studies of the phenomenon have been undertaken. This article analyzes the social, economic, and political factors influencing the market for foreign domestic workers in Jordan and describes how demand there has been fueled by changes in class formation and kinship. It focuses on the largest group of domestic workers in Jordan — Sri Lankans — and draws on extensive fieldwork in Sri Lanka as well as Jordan. The article explores the dynamic relationships between domestic workers and the families who employ them, arguing that an essential strategy used by both groups involves the construction of relations of dependency. The article also chronicles Sri Lankan migrants' experiences, suggesting that there are meaningful cohorts, which are differentiated not by age, but length of stay and place of residence, that have distinct experiences, attitudes to the host country, and homeward orientations. The use of Christian worship and conversion as coping strategies are also described. The author argues that several factors relating to the ways paid domestic work are managed by the state, recruiting agencies, and employers have hindered collective action for workers' rights. In the absence of other forms of activism, faith-based networks fill the void, providing essential support to migrants in need.

4. Advocating For Sri Lankan Migrant Workers: Obstacles and Challenges

Michele R. Gamburd

Nearly a million Sri Lankan women labor overseas as migrant workers, the vast majority in the Gulf Cooperation Council (GCC) countries in West Asia.

They are poorly paid and vulnerable to a wide variety of exploitative labor practices at home and abroad. Despite the importance of worker remittances to Sri Lanka's national economy, and in spite of the nation's history of organized labor and active political participation, migrants have received only anemic support from the state, labor unions, feminist organizations, and migrant-oriented nongovernmental organizations. The article contextualizes Sri Lankan migration within larger-scale economic dynamics (such as global capitalist policies and processes) and local-level ideological formations (such as local political histories and culturally shaped gender norms). The author argues that political freedoms in destination countries have a significant effect on organizing activities in both host and sending nations. Comparing the Sri Lankan and Philippine situations, the author contends that the vibrant activism in the Philippines correlates with the liberal organizing climates in the European Union and in East and Southeast Asia, while the paucity of organizing in Sri Lanka correlates with the strict repression of guest workers in the GCC. Compared to other destinations, the GCC countries give workers (particularly women) less chance for autonomous activities, are less open to labor organizing, and are less responsive to political protest.

5. Transcending the Border: Transnational Imperatives in Singapore's Migrant Worker Rights Movement

Lenore Lyons

In the last five years, interest among civil society actors in the issues migrant domestic workers face in Singapore has exploded. Nongovernmental organizations (NGOs), informal networks, and faith-based groups have all formed to address the needs and interests of these workers. Most of these organizations are welfare-oriented, providing support services, training programs, and social networking opportunities. Some engage in advocacy and research activities. This latter group has lobbied successfully for important changes in how female migrant workers are recruited into and deployed within the domestic labor market. To date, their activities have been focused at the local level through their engagements with the Singaporean government, employment agencies, and employers. This orientation, however, has recently begun to change as they seek to develop transnational networks and support regional and international campaigns. This article examines the reasons behind this interest in cross-border organizing through detailed case studies of two advocacy-oriented NGOs, Transient Workers Count Too and the Humanitarian Organisation for Migration Economics. The article explains that although a "transnational imperative" has begun to shape the activities of these two NGOs, they have different motivations for engaging beyond the border. By revealing a diversity of forms and meanings associated with the processes of "scaling up," this article contributes to the broader scholarly understanding of the complex nature of transnational organizing and challenges earlier studies that assert that transnational activism is a necessary and natural outcome of migrant worker organizing.

6. The Making of a Transnational Grassroots Migrant Movement: A Case
Study of Hong Kong's Asian Migrants' Coordinating Body

Hsiao-Chuan Hsia

As capitalist globalization has intensified in recent years, academic studies of
international labor migration have gained significance. Studies have shown
how globalization has increased the extent of labor migration and how it has
greatly affected the lives of migrant workers. Few studies, however, have documented how migrant workers collectively resist capitalist globalization. By
collaborating with migrants from different countries, migrant workers have
created transnationalism from below, vehemently challenging capitalist globalization. This article focuses on the development of the Asian Migrants' Coordinating Body (AMCB) in Hong Kong to illustrate how grassroots migrant organizations resist capitalist globalization. Most studies of Hong Kong as a "site of
transnational activism" overlook the unique importance of grassroots migrant
organizations and their distinctions from migrant nongovernmental organizations (NGOs). The AMCB is particularly interesting and important not only because it is the first coalition of migrants from different Asian countries but also
because it is a coalition of grassroots migrant organizations from several nationalities. By focusing on the AMCB, this article analyzes how migrant workers
from the Philippines, Indonesia, Thailand, Nepal, and Sri Lanka have worked
together across nation-state, racial, and gender boundaries. This article describes the AMCB's origins and achievements and asks what makes the AMCB
possible and what lessons in grassroots transnationalism are to be gleaned from
the AMCB's efforts and its relationship with NGOS.

7. Migrant Workers and the Many States of Protest in Hong Kong

Nicole Constable

Migrant domestic workers rarely take part in — let alone organize — public
protests in the countries where they work. Public protests are virtually unheard
of among migrant domestic workers in Singapore, Taiwan, and Malaysia, and especially in the Middle East and the Gulf States. Over the past decade and a half,
however, migrant domestic workers in Hong Kong — mostly Filipinas and Indonesian women — have become highly active, organizing and participating in
political protests. Hong Kong's migrant domestic workers protest in a place
where they are guest workers and temporary migrants, denied the opportunity
of becoming legal citizens or permanent residents. Increasingly, these workers,
their grassroots activist organizations, and the nongovernmental organizations
with which they are affiliated frame their concerns in terms of global, transnational, and human rights, not merely local migrant worker rights. This article
takes the "Consulate Hopping Protest and Hall of Shame Awards" event — part
of the anti-World Trade Organization protests in Hong Kong in 2005 — as an
ethnographic example of domestic worker protest and as an entrée through
which to ask what it is about Hong Kong and about the position of women mi-

grant workers — whose mobility and voice is both a product and a symptom of globalization — that literally *permits* public protests and shapes their form and content. The article illustrates how migrant workers' protests and activism have been shaped by domestic worker subjectivities, by the dynamics of inter-ethnic worker affiliations, and by the sociohistorical context of Hong Kong as a post-colonial "global city" and a "neoliberal space of exception."

8. Undocumented Indonesian Workers in Macau: The Human Outcome of Colluding Interests

Amy Sim and Vivienne Wee

Presenting new research findings on undocumented Indonesian migrant workers in Macau, this article explicates the dovetailing arrangements between public and private sector interests that are systemically creating undocumented labor migration flows. It then shows how these arrangements are structurally inherent in the mutual competitiveness of globalizing nodes of wealth creation. Undocumented migration cheapens production costs and results in a flexible black market of vulnerable, right-less, and exploited workers. Contrary to illusions of an urbanizing Asia with expanding spaces for civil liberties, the development of globally competitive megacities, built and supported by low-skilled migrant workers, rests on a global underclass of transient workers who bear the human costs of transience and labor flexibility, enabling megacities to externalize such costs and enhance their global competitiveness. The article analyzes the vulnerabilities of undocumented Indonesian workers in the context of Macau's rapid economic development as an aspiring megacity. The Macau government's laissez-faire tolerance of such workers is grounded in its need for human labor that is abundant, cheap, marginal, and disposable. The flow of Indonesian migrant workers into Macau is linked to Hong Kong's exclusionary immigration policies, which aim at extricating surplus migrant labor. Meanwhile, the Indonesian government refuses responsibility for its migrant workers in Macau because Macau is not recognized as an official destination. The article shows how public and private interests motivate increasing numbers of migrants to become undocumented overstayers in Macau, as they try to avoid oppressive practices in labor migration from Indonesia and the exclusionary policies of Hong Kong.

❑

Preface

Distant Divides and Intimate Connections

Nicole Constable

IN MAY OF 2007 AN INDONESIAN WOMAN NAMED SAMIRAH[1] appeared at a Dunkin' Donuts shop in Syosset (Long Island, N.Y.), her face bruised, wearing only trousers, and wrapped in a towel. The police were called and, as the *New York Times* later reported in June, an investigation was then launched into the abuse of two live-in Indonesian domestic workers, Samirah and Enung, who were employed by an Indian couple who lived in Muttontown, a wealthy Long Island exurb.[2] The couple, Varsha and Mahender Sabhnani, had grown up in well-off families with several live-in servants, he in India and she in Indonesia. The article described them as successful immigrants who began their lives in the United States in the early 1980s with very little money and made their fortune in the perfume export business. As their wealth grew, their lifestyle became less modest and in 2002 Samirah, who had once worked as a maid in Saudi Arabia, was brought to the United States from Indonesia by Mrs. Joti, Varsha Sabhnani's mother. According to her travel documents, Samirah was coming as Mrs. Joti's "traveling assistant" for a three-month stay. She had previously worked for Mrs. Joti for two months during which time she had been trained to work for the Sabhnani family. In 2005 Varsha Sabhnani's sister brought Enung to New York.

The *New York Times* article, which was published on 23 June 2008, a few days before the Sabhnanis' sentencing, included interviews with the Sabhnanis' daughter, neighbors, and friends, all of whom expressed sympathy and disbelief that the Sabhnanis could be guilty of physical abuse, confinement, withholding food, underpayment, and a range of other abuses that have resulted in the labeling of the case in much of the popular media as the "Muttontown slave case." One of the Sabhnanai's Indian friends is quoted as saying, "There is no way on earth any Indian family in the United States could do what they were accused of…. The [Indian] people I know here all feel this way. Anybody from India who has come here comes from a very good family." Yet despite such expressed disbelief, the Sabhnanis were found guilty on twelve federal counts. Mr. Sabhnani was sentenced to over three years in prison and fined $12,500 on a federal indictment on charges "that included forced labor, conspiracy, involuntary servi-

1

tude, and harboring aliens." [3] Mrs. Sabhnani was sentenced to eleven years in prison, on charges ranging from torture to enslavement and fined $25,000. [4]

In a letter to the editor of the *New York Times*, members of Andolan: Organizing South Asian Workers, an activist empowerment organization for low wage immigrant South Asian women, voiced several criticisms of the *New York Times* article. They point to the missing voices of Samirah and Enung and to those of the wider community of domestic workers and domestic worker advocates (such as Andolan, Domestic Workers United, or Housecleaners in Long Island) who showed them support and had planned a protest outside of the courthouse during the Sabhnanis' sentencing. As the Andolan letter writers note, the article makes no mention of the wider plight of domestic workers or the growing activism by and in behalf of domestic workers in New York, such as the effort to pass protective legislation and a domestic workers' bill of rights. Whereas the Sabhnanis are depicted in some detail as a well-liked family who lived the "American Dream" — an immigrant success story — humanized by the testimony of family and friends, the stories of Enung and Samirah, the letter writers remind us, are largely glossed over. The *New York Times* article cites Dilip Ratha, an economist for the World Bank, who is said to have referred to the case as fitting "a common template for the many women who leave countries like Indonesia, the Philippines and Malaysia for wealthier nations." [5] Yet the letter points out that Enung and Samirah are not merely "templates"; they are individual women immigrants who also struggled to attain the American dream despite the great obstacles they faced and their undocumented immigration status. As members of Andolan write: "We are concerned that not only were the voices of the two women silenced by the Sabhnanis', but the article offered no insight into the plight and activism of domestic workers." [6]

Domestic worker activism, slowly growing in the United States during recent years, reflects the influence of and lessons learned from migrant workers elsewhere in the world. Domestic Workers United, a New York City-based organization of Latina, Caribbean, and African workers who labor as nannies, housekeepers, and elderly caregivers, for example, traces its origin in 2000 to the activism of Filipina domestic workers, members of Kalayaan/Women Workers Project of CAAAV, in collaboration with Andolan. [7]

The story of Enung, Samirah, and the Sabhnanis encapsulates and illustrates many of the themes and concerns of the collection of articles that appear here and are forthcoming in the March 2009 issue of *Critical Asian Studies* (see facing page). In particular, it illustrates the intimate connections and the distant divides that characterize the lives and experiences of migrant domestic workers, often rendering the workers isolated among intimate strangers and vulnerable to abuse, but also offering possibilities for sources of support and advocacy. As live-in workers Samirah and Enung were unequal but "intimate" members of the Sabhnani household. Their intimacy was built upon geographically distant ties — in this case through Varsha Sabhnani's mother and sister in Indonesia — through which domestic workers often enter households that are far away from their home countries. Back home, Samirah and Enung's family members depended on their meager earnings, which were far below U.S. minimum wage.

Samirah and Enung's story also reveals a growing intimacy — or at the very least a collaboration — that has developed in the New York City metropolitan area among domestic workers of different nationalities; growing connections between activist and grassroots organizations, some influenced by Filipina activists, resemble the patterns we describe in the articles in this collection.

The story of Samirah, Enung, and the Sabhnanis suggests that many of the issues that we have chosen to explore in depth within the context of Asia broadly defined apply to Asian and other nationalities of domestic workers in and well beyond Asia. Although we focus on Asia, it is important to note that domestic workers in North America and Europe are not immune from the problems and experiences faced by domestic workers in Asia and the Middle East.[8] And needless to say, their employers need not be "Asian" for the workers to experience abuse and exploitation.

We argue that there are broad generalities and lessons to be learned from case studies, common experiences, and difficulties faced by many domestic workers, situated within a broader context of global capitalism and neoliberalism. But we also point to the critical importance of local specificities and variations in experiences, patterns, and practices in different locales, among different ethnic groups and nationalities, and at different stages of migrant workers' lives and employment trajectories. As Elizabeth Frantz observes, a woman's degree of "dependency" on her employer varies according to her "cohort," whether she is a live-in or live-out domestic worker, and her length of stay in Jordan. As Amy Sim and Vivienne Wee will show in their forthcoming article, the flow of undocumented Indonesian domestic workers from Hong Kong to Macau is part of a wider pattern of feminized labor exportation, but each context offers unique challenges for workers and for researchers.[9]

The articles in this collection aim to move away from static depictions of domestic workers in individual locations, highlighting instead connections between groups and nationalities, through time, and across borders. We look at change within the context of larger ongoing processes of networking and organizing, formations of intimate connections across distant divides, and possibilities and examples of subtle and overt forms of activism that have affected policies and individual lives. In the broadest sense, we point to a wide range of contexts in which the sources of support and advocacy for workers vary greatly. On one extreme are Yemen and Jordan, where foreign domestic workers are relatively isolated in individual homes with very few sources of social support to draw on. On the other extreme is Hong Kong, where grassroots and nongovernmental organization (NGO) activism by and in behalf of migrant domestic workers has grown and spread phenomenally over the past two decades.

Inter-Asian Connections

The eight articles in this book are written by nine authors who hail from a range of social science disciplines (anthropology, sociology, political science) and specialize in regions of Asia that are not typically grouped together. All of the authors share a topical interest in migratory labor and gender and an ethnographic and qualitative methodological research orientation; all employ firsthand ethnographic field research and close textual analyses. These articles draw on stories and voices of domestic workers; they are also informed by the varied perspectives of government officials, employers, employment agents, NGO staff, activists, and family members, among others. Although each article stands alone, as a group they highlight a comparative perspective.

Over the past two decades scholars have produced many single-nationality studies of migrant domestic workers within the social and recent historical context of a single receiving region. Nicole Constable's 1997 edition of *Maid to Order in Hong Kong*, for example, focused almost exclusively on Filipina workers in Hong Kong. Given radical shifts over the past decade, the 2007 edition — a decade later — necessarily considers the increase in Indonesian domestic workers and burgeoning transnational coalitions of workers in and beyond Hong Kong.[10] Some scholars such as Rhacel Salazar Parreñas and Pei-Chia Lan have gone beyond the single-destination, single-nationality model, focusing for example on sending and receiving countries; others such as Michele Gamburd have examined the impact of migrants' remittances and their absence on their place of origin and on the family members who are left behind.[11] Two important comparative edited volumes on Asian domestic workers have also been published, and much more work is currently underway.[12] Up to now, less attention has been paid to comparisons or connections between groups of domestic workers in different host regions, to interconnections between domestic workers of various nationalities within and beyond state boundaries, to the ways in which individual receiving locations influence the work trajectories and life experiences of migrant workers of various nationalities, and to the links between workers, employers, and advocacy groups of various sorts. The articles in this collection take steps to fill this gap.

This two-part series includes articles by scholars and scholar-activists who have focused on migrant domestic workers in a wide range of regions, but whose regional foci usually preclude their coming together for productive intellectual exchanges. The regional divides between those who study domestic workers who migrate to labor in East and Southeast Asia and those who study domestic workers who migrate to labor in what is variably referred to as West Asia, the Middle East, or the GCC (Gulf Cooperation Council) countries make little sense, but it often follows an older conventional disciplinary divide that artificially separates East and Southeast Asia from the Middle East, West Asia, and the Gulf.[13] Overall these articles suggest new ways of thinking about what constitutes "Asia." They challenge conventional subregional divides and offer critical theorizing about migrant workers' citizenship, rights, and most significantly the factors that promote or prevent improvements in working conditions.

By providing empirically grounded studies that move across and beyond conventional area studies regional divides, these articles challenge us to think about differences and similarities in the experiences of domestic workers (who themselves have little regard for academic disciplinary boundaries) and about the varieties of distant divides and intimate connections that exist within and beyond the borders of Asian nation-states, as migrant workers perform intimate labor in the private homes of their employers. This collection provides new themes and comparative frameworks for considering vastly different degrees of social support structures and political activism and for the varied meanings of citizenship and state responsibility in sending and receiving countries. Collectively, the authors consider the effects of globalization on both family and economy, examining how migration can affect household relations and organization, expressions of political activism, and the forms of transnational social movements.

Collectively, these articles indicate the importance of understanding the roles of formal institutions (state, local, familial, transnational, and capitalist) that shape and promote migratory labor and work conditions. They point to ways that social identities and cultural practices and beliefs relating to gender, religion, class, race, and nationality are linked to affiliations, divides, and transformations that traverse and also transform and create new and unique experiences and sites of interaction, new inter-Asian spaces, new pathways of mobility, or new inter-Asian-scapes.

Divides and Connections in "Asia" Broadly Defined

Over the past three decades, inter-Asian connections have become both more distant and more intimate. They are more distant in the sense that hundreds of thousands of women domestic workers migrate each year from evermore far-flung regions of South and Southeast Asia, to regions of East Asia, Southeast Asia, West Asia, and other parts of the world.[14] Our examples focus primarily on migrant domestic workers from the Philippines, Indonesia, and Sri Lanka and the destination counties or regions of Hong Kong, Macau, Taiwan, Singapore, Malaysia, Yemen, Jordan, Israel, and the United Arab Emirates (UAE). We consider women's experiences, their relationships, and the advocacy (or lack thereof) provided by sending states and receiving states, NGOs, grassroots organizations, and other community or faith-based groups.

Inter-Asian connections as seen through the experiences of migrant domestic workers have covered greater distances and have also become more "intimate" in certain ways. Connections between domestic workers and their employers have always been intimate in the sense that the workers live and labor in the very private spaces in the homes of their employers. As such, they gain personal knowledge of family dynamics, religious practices, and the everyday lives of their employers, developing — in the case of employment across national and cultural borders — what can be seen as a sort of "working class cosmopolitanism," a double vision or an awareness that is, according to Edward Said, "contrapuntal."[15] As Claudia Liebelt describes in her article, evangelical Christian Filipina domestic workers develop intimate knowledge of the religious practices and beliefs of their employers as they work in Arab countries and in Israel and Palestine, the so-called Holy Land. Their intimate knowledge makes them Middle East "experts" of sorts, and their working class cosmopolitanism, Liebelt argues, "fosters an understanding of transnational (migrant) subjectivities beyond both ascription of victim-hood and an uncritical celebration of cosmopolitanism."[16]

In turn, such intimacies often require mechanisms that distinguish workers from employers and maids from madams and that maintain distance. Requiring workers to wear uniforms or to dress differently from their employers, for example, makes distinctions of nationality and race plain to see, while enforcing restrictions on household spaces that are off limits to domestic workers underscores status distinctions. As Marina de Regt describes, Yemeni employers' preferences for foreign domestic workers are "not based only on essentialist notions of, among others, class, race, and culture, but also on employers' search for an intimate balance of social, cultural, and religious closeness and distance."[17] As others have demonstrated, employers often go to great lengths to differentiate themselves from domestic workers who seem uncomfortably close to them in terms of appearance, class identity, or education, requiring clothing, behavior, and spatial regulations that serve to highlight desired or perceived differences.[18]

As the articles by Hsia, Sim and Wee, Lyons, and Constable in this volume illustrate — and as the example of Domestic Workers United cited in the beginning of this introduction also shows — cross-national intimacies between domestic workers and worker advocates of different nationalities are of critical significance. Cross-national relations between domestic workers have intensified over the past fifteen years as in the case of the growing cooperation and collaboration between Filipina and Indonesian domestic workers in Hong Kong and Macau, who exchange knowledge, promote political organizing, and share support networks.[19] Such cross-ethnic/national connections are often carried forward, expanding to new locations as women migrate onwards or return home to work for activist organizations in the Philippines or Indonesia. Although such alliances are markedly less developed or appear to be largely nonexistent in other settings such as Singapore, Yemen, Jordan, Israel, and the UAE, they might eventually develop or alternative sorts of organizations and structures (e.g., religious ones) will serve in their place.

Each host and sending country is clearly part of the current global economy as manifest in inter-Asian connections that have their own unique histories and trajectories. Many factors propel labor migration. Chief among them is globalization. The shortage of domestic labor in wealthier and more developed regions and "neoliberal spaces of exception" in the so-called global North are satisfied by workers from the poorer and less-developed countries of the so-called global South that suffer from high rates of unemployment and underemployment.[20] "Sending nations" must ensure the steady flow of migrant workers if they wish to compete successfully in this market of human labor export. Sending countries depend on maintaining a flow of workers as profitable "resources," generating the supply through growing rural landlessness and urban unemployment and poverty. As Constable shows in chapter 7, with a twist on David Ricardo's nineteenth-century concept of comparative advantage, in such situations migration becomes one of few viable alternatives, offering a comparative *dis*advantage to the exported workers. In an even more striking example, Sim and Wee describe, in the context of their exploratory research among undocumented Indonesian domestic workers in Macau, how host countries meet local labor demands by creating structures that perpetuate the availability of undocumented (and therefore especially cheap and highly vulnerable) workers to meet the local labor demands. As their groundbreaking study reveals, Macau takes a "don't ask, don't tell approach" and does little to enforce rules against undocumented Indonesian domestic workers who take refuge in Macau after their Hong Kong visas expire. Building on Ong's ideas about neoliberal spaces of exception, these articles demonstrate how migrant domestic workers are themselves excluded from the protections of citizenship, but serve instead as one of the fringe benefits for neoliberal elites.

As these articles suggest, broad patterns of globalization alone do not adequately account for the motivations behind migration, the wealth and variation of migratory experiences, or the vastly different degrees of activism in different locations. Gamburd's article (chapter 4) queries the apparent lack of activism among or in behalf of Sri Lankan migrant "housemaids" in the Middle East or GCC countries, highlighting the myriad factors that might explain the degrees of activism by and in behalf of Filipino versus Sri Lankan migrant workers in different locations. As she points out, the varied relationships between the migrant worker sending and receiving states warrant attention. Whereas Sri Lankan government officials in the UAE express their sense of impotence in advocating for the well-being of Sri Lankan workers abroad (lest wider economic and political state concerns be jeopardized), the Philippine government — given the activism and growing political power of Filipino migrant workers — must more subtly balance the avowed protection of its workers against their growing reputation as spoiled and demanding.[21]

Central Themes

Collectively these articles raise fresh and important insights on seven interrelated topics and themes, pointing to important new avenues for further critical inquiry and research.

Patterns of Mobility and Immobility

Particularly important in examining migration, as cultural geographer Doreen Massey reminds us, is not only who moves and who does not, but who controls mobility.[22] The authors consider who migrates, where they go, why they go where they go, where they go next, and the factors that propel or deter mobility. Another important question we raise is who does not move and why some migrants sometimes remain in one place. As Liebelt's study of Filipina workers in Israel reminds us, in contrast to many binary models of migration, migrants often move *on and on* through a hierarchy of destinations rather than *back and forth* in a binary pattern between sending and receiving country. They often move on in search of better and more desirable destinations such as the United States, Canada, or Western Europe.[23] Workers move for several reasons: in search of better employers, higher wages, to seek new experiences, to see the world, or to reach the "Holy Land." State laws and regulations, quotas, restrictions, and the lack of restrictions are also factors as undocumented workers or overstayers seek new destinations.

As Sim and Wee's research illustrates, most undocumented workers in Macau once worked legally in Hong Kong, opting to go to Macau as a response to Hong Kong's "two-week rule," which requires them to return to their home country within two weeks of the termination of a work contract. Most Indonesian overstayers in Macau would prefer to remain and work there despite the exploitative conditions they face, rather than have to return to Indonesia and stay in the required training camps before emigrating again. Recruitment agencies and employers' desires are also relevant to the patterns of migration, as de Regt has shown in the case of Somali, Ethiopian, Filipina, Indonesian, and Sri Lankan domestic workers in the relatively poor and usually labor-sending country of Yemen.[24] Far from reiterating a simple binary pattern of South–North migration, these articles demonstrate a multiplicity of patterns of mobility, influenced or propelled by many factors, as migrant domestic workers choose and move between different countries of destination, reflecting the influence of personal networks and familial connections, profit-oriented recruitment agencies, and national level labor import and export policies.

Gender, Family, and Household Institutions

All of these articles contribute to the rapidly growing literature on the feminization of migrant labor throughout Asia. Several articles (Gamburd, Lyons, Frantz, Liebelt) point to the continuing importance of interrogating patriarchal institutions of family in relation to the position of domestic workers, and all of the articles implicitly or explicitly point to the importance of gender in relation to every aspect of migration, work, and activism. All of the domestic workers we have studied work in households doing tasks such as child care, care for the elderly, cooking, and cleaning that are widely considered women's responsibilities. Yet in each setting the definitions of family and household, and the delineations of domestic space and gender roles differ. As Frantz and de Regt illustrate, not only are the opportunities for women's activism greatly curtailed in receiving counties with greater sex segregation, but greater degrees of sex segregation and isolation within households also promote a greater dependency on employers, often at the expense of rights discourses. This in turn helps to explain why the articles focusing on regions in which women experience relative freedom of movement outside of the home, such as Hong Kong (Hsia, Constable), Macau (Sim and Wee), or Singapore (Lyons), stress activism, whereas those focusing on regions with greater sex segregation and relative exclusion of women from the public sphere, such as Jordan (Frantz) or Yemen (de Regt), and the Gulf Cooperation Council countries, observe little or no activism and query instead the absence of activism (Gamburd) or focus on other sorts of support groups and networks (Liebelt, de Regt).

Comparative Hierarchies

The articles in this collection reveal several hierarchies: hierarchies of nationalities of workers as in the case of Filipino, Indonesian, Indian, and Sri Lankan domestic workers in Yemen, who are more highly prized by their employers than Somali or Ethiopian workers (de Regt); hierarchies of employers, such as Hong Kong employers who allow workers greater independence, making it possible for them to participate in political activism (Hsia, Constable); and hierarchies of destinations wherein Canada is ranked by many Filipino workers above Israel, and Israel by many workers as more desirable than Hong Kong and Taiwan (Liebelt). What factors promote or justify comparative hierarchies of domestic workers and employers in different settings within a context of neoliberal globalization? What qualities characterize "good" workers or "good" employers in different regions and contexts? What role do class, race, and nationality play in relation to such hierarchies and subordinations? As Parreñas has written, Filipinas often experience "contradictory class mobility" upon migration.[25] These articles point to further paradoxes of class mobility in which workers gain new visions (Liebelt), new political roles (Hsia), and new routes to mobility. Such hierarchies change through time and vary across locations. Filipinas, for example, were the most popular workers before the Asian financial crisis of the late 1990s, but they are now deemed to be too haughty, spoiled, demanding, and knowledgeable in Hong Kong, Taiwan, as well as in Yemen. Employers in these locales — if they can afford "Asian" workers — increasingly prefer Indonesian women who are widely considered more subservient and obedient, and who have been more actively promoted, throughout Asia broadly defined, as ideal workers by the Indonesian government since the 1990s.[26] States play different roles in promoting their workers. And — perhaps most significantly — we must continue to ask how workers themselves participate in the "othering" of groups of a different nationality, and how they reproduce or oppose rights discourses that may deny the rights of others.

Transnational Framing and Activism

Collectively we ask how East and West Asian receiving countries empower or delimit the ability of domestic workers to improve their circumstances. The first four articles in this collection (Liebelt, de Regt, Frantz, Gamburd) point to the lack or alternative sources of support that exist in Israel, Yemen, Jordan, and the UAE in the absence of overt grassroots or NGO activism. The rest of the articles, including Gamburd's, deal more explicitly with forms, expressions, articulations, and limitations of overt activism. Whereas Gamburd points to many factors in the GCC receiving countries — especially the UAE — that deter activism, Constable asks what it is about Hong Kong — particularly in the post-1997 era — that allows and even promotes migrant worker protests and activism. Several articles (Lyons, Hsia, Constable, Sim and Wee) provide examples of cross-national affiliations of domestic workers and worker advocates.

Lenore Lyons raises critical questions about the factors that "promote or inhibit activist links between organizations based in different locations, as well as the challenges and contradictions faced by organizations that attempt to address the rights of female domestic workers within a transnational frame." In Singapore's case, the state tightly controls civil society, where migrant worker organizations are notably missing and where all organizations must be registered and are prohibited from taking part in "political activity." Lyons draws on her case studies of two advocacy-oriented NGOs in Singapore, Transient Workers Count Too (TWC2) and the Humanitarian Organisation for Migration Economics (HOME), pointing to the challenges and limitations the organizations face, as well as to important conceptual distinctions between *trans-ethnic*

Asian Migrants' Coordinating Body (AMCB) demonstration in support of migrant worker rights, Hong Kong, 2006.

solidarity and activism, *cross-border* organizing, and *transnational framing*. As Lyons argues, these concepts highlight subtle but critical differences between processes and relationships that are often simply glossed and reified as "transnational." Hong Kong organizations involving Indonesian, Filipina, Thai, and other nationalities of workers and Singapore-based NGOs, with members from Singapore and other countries, are examples of trans-ethnic affiliations. Examples of cross-border organizing include the Asian Migrants' Coordinating Body's activities in Hong Kong, Taiwan, and the Philippines (described in detail by Hsia in chapter 6) and anti-WTO protestors from many international organizations and countries joining together in protest (described by Constable in chapter 7). Transnational framing, by contrast, the key focus of Lyons's inquiry, refers more to the conceptual and discursive notions of globalization and how they are linked to and build on awareness of power relations and inequalities across and between nation-states and nationalities.

In turn, Hsia urges us to pay close attention to the roles and relationships between organizations that are often glossed as "NGOs" and to distinguish carefully between grassroots migrant worker organizations and NGOs of various sorts and to examine critically the varied roles and relationships between them as she does in analyzing the formation of the Asian Migrants' Coordinating Body. The distinctions Lyons and Hsia point out reveal subtle dynamics of activism or advocacy by or in behalf of migrant domestic workers in Hong Kong and Singapore. Growing solidarity (as well as competition) between groups, the development of cross-border affiliations, and the rhetoric of transnationalism are all relevant as workers, activists, NGOs, and governmental organizations grapple with issues related to the well-being of migrant domestic workers. Indonesian state policies, capitalist interests, and the "debt bondage" employment agencies impose all fuel the vulnerability of Indonesian workers and the sense of competition between them and workers of other nationalities. Yet, as Hsia describes, the Indonesian activism that has developed over the past fifteen years has been strongly influenced by Filipino activists, and their work has yielded some success in terms of work conditions.

State–Citizen Relationships

State–citizen relationships are central to our discussions of migrant domestic workers, and through these studies we reveal how meanings of citizenship and state responsibility for and obligation toward citizens have been transformed and eroded in the face of neoliberalism. Migrant workers call the notion of "citizenship" into question in unique ways. What are the obligations of the state in relation to the rights of its citizen subjects at home and abroad? Sending states differ in their relationships with host states, and the interests of workers are often subordinated to the sending state's desire to maintain diplomatic relations and to glean economic benefits from its relationship with the wealthier and more powerful receiving country. Representatives from sending states such as Indonesia (Sim and Wee) and Sri Lanka (Gamburd, Frantz) are often unable or unwilling to advocate for their citizens abroad. As Frantz argues, the state-required *kafala* (sponsorship) program in Jordan legally binds domestic workers to their sponsors, thus producing relations of dependency that prevent workers from seeking new or better employers. As Sim and Wee demonstrate, receiving countries compete for workers. Macau, they argue, perpetuates a system by which undocumented overstayers are unofficially tolerated because of the benefits they provide; with this setup the government provides no social services or support and workers are at the mercy of their own resources, personal relations, or activist organizations. These articles explore the question of what roles NGOs, employers, and grassroots activists might play in different contexts and what circumstances galvanize states to act. They also call for further analysis of the forms of and claims for citizenship among migrant workers. Constable argues that migrant domestic worker protests in Hong Kong are facilitated in part by a sort of "flexible noncitizenship" and by human rights claims, in contrast to the legal citizenship and the flexibility that having multiple passports provides to the elite Chinese transnational entrepreneurial families Ong describes.[27]

Religion and Faith-based Groups

Religion is an explicit topic of discussion only in the articles by Liebelt, Frantz, and de Regt; yet it is significant to the opportunities and experiences of most domestic workers. Religion influences employer and worker preferences as in the case of Muslim employers who prefer Muslim or Christian workers, or Jewish employers who prefer Christian maids to Muslim ones. Religious experiences in different regions, moreover, contribute to the intimate knowledge and the "cosmopolitanism" (Liebelt) of migrant workers. In countries that prohibit explicit organizing and activism, faith-based groups may serve as a primary source of identity and social support. Frantz's multi-sited project focuses on Sri Lankan workers in the receiving country of Jordan where there is little sign of overt activism. Yet in this highly restricted context, churches and Christian religious groups are sources of social support. Such religious groups do not promote or speak in a language of "human rights," but use instead the language of "love, compassion, loyalty and sacrifice." Collectively, these articles suggest that faith-based groups might have greater potential for affecting change in contexts where overt activism is prohibited, in contrast to other areas (such as East or Southeast Asia) where certain religious groups are seen as an impediment to political awareness and activism. Overall we ask what are the varied roles and possibilities for religious institutions and faith-based groups to benefit or obscure the rights of migrant domestic workers.

New Mappings

Finally, these articles indicate ways to move beyond the single space/single nationality of worker approach, and point in new directions for comparison, contrast, and accountability. Collectively we identify the need for new longitudinal, multi-sited, and multi-perspective methodologies to fully appreciate the constraints faced by transnational domestic workers and also the opportunities for improved conditions. As noted above, a central contribution of this volume is to challenge conventional definitions and delineations of Asia. Methodologically we utilize and promote new ways of mapping inter-Asian routes and connections. Rather than adopting the singular or binary sites of home and host destination, or one nationality and one location, these articles view workers in a wider spatial context on crosscutting and intersecting trajectories through time. We are keenly aware of the importance of workers who have labored in more than one country and who have established ties and networks that reach across multiple nationalities of workers in several countries. We therefore call for more such studies that map the lives and the locations of migrant workers across time and space and for paying greater attention to the movement and interconnections of recruitment agencies, NGOs, grassroots organizations, and political and religious groupings.

ACKNOWLEDGMENTS: Eight of the authors (Constable, de Regt, Frantz, Gamburd, Hsia, Liebelt, Lyons, Sim) jointly participated in a workshop entitled "Distant Divides and Intimate Connections: Migrant Domestic Workers in Asia," as part of a Social Science Research Council Conference on Inter-Asian Connections, held in Dubai, UAE, in February 2008. I am indebted to Seteney Shami, Srirupa Roy, and Shabana Shahabuddin at the SSRC for providing us with an ideal context in which to reflect on each other's work and build on the range of insights that arise from a broader regional and disciplinary comparative framework. I am most grateful to the contributors for all of their hard work and insight, and to Sami Hermez, Mehraj Jahan, and Habibul Khondker, participants whose contributions added much to the workshop but did not fit well into this collection.

❏

1. On Sentimental Orientalists, Christian Zionists, and Working Class Cosmopolitans

Filipina Domestic Workers' Journeys to Israel and Beyond

Claudia Liebelt

WITHIN A GLOBAL GENDERED ECONOMY based on an international division of labor, Filipina migrants have become nannies, maids, and caregivers in affluent homes in numerous Asian and Middle Eastern countries.[1] Filipina migrants who seek employment as domestic workers abroad have been described as classical transmigrants who keep in touch with family members back home and commute between their countries of origin and their destinations. In this article — based on ethnographic research in Israel, Palestine, and the Philippines between 2003 and 2008 — I argue that Filipina migrants are transnational in a much broader sense than commonly discussed in (anthropological) studies on migration. My research shows that Filipina migrants are engaged in border-crossing journeys through a number of nation-states and that many of them move *on and on* rather than back and forth. They do so within a global hierarchy of desirable destination countries, ranked according to the differences between nation-states with regard to salaries and the legal entitlements migrants can claim, the costs and risks migrants have to take in order to enter, and these countries' overall subjective and imaginative attractiveness.

Within this global hierarchy, Israel holds a middle position, above most Asian and Middle Eastern destination countries, but clearly below Western Europe and North America. By overcoming multiple hardships and restrictive migration policies and border regimes, by intimately confronting culturally foreign practices as domestics in private homes in the Asian countries in which they once worked, and by collectively claiming rights and belonging to the country they currently inhabit (in religious communities, for example), Filipina migrants acquire an intimate and comparative picture of the Middle East "backstage." They may even turn into Middle Eastern experts or become politically active Christian Zionists or sentimental Orientalists, who in spite of their Christianity express nostalgia for fasting on Yom Kippur or during Ramadan as they continue their journeys beyond the Middle East. As "working class cosmopolitans," to borrow an expression from Pnina Werbner,[2] Filipina serial migrants, I argue, transcend the divide typically drawn in the literature between parochial migrants and bourgeois cosmopolitans. Following Stasiulis and Bakan's understanding of citizenship as a negotiated relationship between social actors and the state, Filipina migrants' moves can be seen as a way of negotiating political, economic, social, and legal rights across nation-states and on the global level.

Drawing from scholarly literature and statistical material, I first address the historical patterns of Philippine migration. On the basis of interviews with Filipina domestic workers in Israel, I then go on to describe the global routes that take many women from the Philippines to the Middle East and beyond. Taking into account their everyday and political practices as well as following their narratives, I describe Filipina domestic workers as women who throughout their stay in Israel and other Middle Eastern countries have acquired much cultural knowledge. They often adopt local practices and beliefs that allow them to symbolically "claim" the land collectively, through domestic work or as Christians who engage in missionary work or pilgrimages. As an example of this, I draw from research among a church group of Filipina born-again Christians in Israel, Jesus Is Lord.

Filipina Migrants' Routes to the Middle East and Beyond

Filipina domestic workers belong to an increasing number of female migrants who move from the so-called Third World to the centers of global capitalism in order to take jobs at the bottom of the social hierarchy within a highly gendered economy.[3] The Philippines today is among the world's largest exporters of temporary contract labor, and Filipinos are living and working abroad in more than 190 nation states.[4] Originally designed as a temporary measure by the Marcos regime in the early 1970s, the Philippine government's labor export policy became a permanent national development strategy during the global economic recession of the 1980s. Overseas employment has long been a major pillar of the Philippine economy.[5] In spite of a change in state rhetoric after the execution of Flor Contemplacion, a Filipina domestic worker in Singapore — which led to much outrage in the Philippines and to international criticism — the Philippine government's labor export policy remains essentially intact.[6]

In recent decades, migration flows from the Philippines became increasing feminized — contributing to the global feminization of migration — and major destination areas have changed. Thus, at least since the 1960s women have been playing an ever-increasing part in international migration flows and today comprise approximately half of migrants worldwide. The Philippines is no exception: while in 1975 over 70 percent of Filipino contract workers were male, the male–female ratio changed in the late 1980s. Ever since, approximately half of Filipino emigrants are female, even according to official statistics.[7] In this process, Filipina migrants headed first toward domestic urban centers, especially the capital, Manila,[8] and then, most especially after the adoption of a state labor export policy by the Marcos regime in 1972, they took up work as professionals or domestic workers in the United States,[9] East and Southeast Asia, and the GCC (Gulf Cooperation Council) countries. Now they migrate to practically every nation-state in the world.

According to statistics of the Philippine Overseas Employment Administration (POEA), about one-third of the newly hired and rehired land-based Overseas Filipino Workers (OFW) worldwide sought employment in the Middle East annually from 1998 until 2003.[10] Out of the fifteen Middle Eastern countries where Filipinos engaged in contract labor in 2003, the major destinations were Saudi Arabia (169,011 individuals); United Arab Emirates (49,164); Kuwait (26,225); Qatar (24,344); Bahrain (6,406); and Israel (5,094). These countries vary consider-

Michele R. Camburd

Sign posted outside a migrant workers recruiting office in Ajman, UAE, 9 November 2004. About one-third of new Filipino workers worldwide sought employment in the Middle East annually from 1998 until 2003.

ably in the legally and illegally charged sums migrants have to pay to recruiters in order to be employed, the salaries and labor rights migrants can claim, as well as the kinds of work they engage in and the lifestyles they can lead. As an example, the average broker's fee collected by Filipino and/or foreign recruiters from migrants to Israel was US$4,256 in 2005,[11] while interviewees reported that it was US$500 to $1,000 for Saudi Arabia and the GCC countries. Salaries in the GCC countries were reported to range from US$150 to $400 in 2007, while at the same time legally recruited caregivers in Israel typically earned US$500 to $900.

Migrants take up work in the Middle East in spite of the rather bad image this region has as a destination for Filipina domestic workers, due at least in part to highly publicized cases like that of Sarah Balabagan, a 15-year old Filipina domestic worker in the United Arab Emirates, who in 1995 was sentenced to death for killing her employer, who had raped her.[12] On its website, the POEA describes Saudi Arabia and Kuwait in a gloomy tone, stating that "Kuwaitis treat their household workers as slaves," and listing maltreatment and "sexual harassments/abuses and rape cases" as problems workers commonly face.[13] Even though Filipina domestic workers in Israel suffer many of the adversities listed for Kuwait and Saudi Arabia — delayed or unpaid salaries, maltreatment, rape, sexual harassment, and detention, for example — Israel remains a clearly favored destination within the Middle East because of the relatively high salaries workers can obtain there, its active recruitment of migrant caregivers for the sick and elderly, and its imagined attractiveness as the "Holy Land" for predominantly Christian Filipinos.[14] Yet, the large fees Filipinos must pay to enter Israel deter many from taking up employment there. Those who do gain entry typically had to work elsewhere first in order to be able to afford the high entry fees, especially migrants from rural areas or from an "urban poor" background.[15]

During my research, I found that for many of those who managed to enter and be employed there, Israel soon became yet another "stepping stone country." This was especially the case after Israel introduced a far-reaching deportation campaign in late 2002 that adversely affected Filipinos, the majority of whom had been made illegal by an exclusionary citizenship regime and a "binding arrangement" that ties workers' legal status in the country to a specific employer.[16] Accordingly, an increasing number of Filipino migrants prepared to leave Israel. They either returned to the Philippines or paid recruiters to arrange employment elsewhere, where they hoped they could earn more, be granted more encompassing rights, and eventually acquire citizenship in a Western nation.[17]

Moving On and On (rather than Back and Forth)

Much recent research on (transnational) migration has treated bidirectional moves of migrants, typically between a third world country of origin and a first world country of destination.[18] By contrast the experiences and practices of migrants who move on and on rather than back and forth have received far less attention. One major exception is Aihwa Ong's research on Chinese transnationalists, who, as she shows, migrate toward a multiplicity of geographical destinations. Ong shows how the transnationalists she writes about develop culturally infused norms of globality, move within global family networks, "playing off one nation-state regime against another, seeking tactical advantage — knowing that it is easier to become a citizen here rather than there, that there are more legal and political rights in country X than in country Y."[19]

The following account will show that Filipina migrants similarly move between nation-states, seeking foreign passports, and sharing sophisticated knowledge of various national incorporation regimes, legal regulations, and strategies of playing these off against one another. Nonetheless, they lack some of the important resources of the economic elite Ong describes: Rather than collecting several passports and easily jetting off around the world, Filipina women — who are far less economically privileged than the Chinese transnationalists Ong writes about — typically labor hard and long in order to move around.

The findings of a questionnaire survey conducted during three one-day organized bus tours in Israel and Palestine that took place between September and December 2007 detail the number of serial migrants among Filipino workers and the routes they have traveled. Twenty-seven out of eighty-one survey respondents (33.3 percent) stated that they had worked abroad prior to entering Israel. Of these, seventeen had worked in one country; seven, in two other countries; and three, in three countries before coming to Israel. The most frequent destination countries mentioned in this context were Taiwan (ten cases),

Hong Kong (seven cases), Singapore (five cases), Cyprus and Saudi Arabia (three cases each), as well as Kuwait and Dubai (two cases each). Moreover, most of the respondents dreamed of leaving Israel or had already made plans to do so in order to work elsewhere. Thus, more than half of the respondents (fifty-eight out of eighty-one, or 58.0 percent) stated that they thought about or planned to "continue to another country to work," mentioning Canada in twenty-seven and Europe in six cases.

Among my interviewees in Israel, the life stories of Marietta, Romelyn, and Lyna illustrate best the global routes of many Filipina women and the complexity of their experiences.[20] Thus, Marietta, a college graduate from a middle-class family in Cebu (southern Philippines), left in 1985 to work in Abu Dhabi, where she was employed as a housekeeper and nanny in the ruling family's household. She returned to the Philippines after her work contract expired and left shortly thereafter for Jordan, where — due to her knowledge of Arabic and the high status of her former employer — she was hired by a wealthy and high-ranking politician of Palestinian origin. After several years, Marietta was transferred to work with an extended relative of his in Ramallah (situated in the Palestinian West Bank, occupied by Israel). There, she lived in a luxurious villa close to the Muqataa, the headquarters of the Palestinian Authority, and took care of the family's disabled son. On Sundays, her weekly day off, Marietta typically left for Jerusalem, where she was the president of a Filipino organization within a Roman Catholic parish church. After the outbreak of the second intifada in 2001, life in Ramallah and entry to Jerusalem became increasingly difficult. Nevertheless, Marietta continued to sneak into Jerusalem illegally alongside other

Claudia Liebelt

Christmas in Bethlehem. Asian pilgrims celebrate Christmas in Shepherd's Field, adjacent to Bethlehem, 25 December 2004.

Filipino and Palestinian workers. Later she managed to secure employment and living arrangements in Jerusalem, first as the live-in caregiver for an elderly (Jewish-Israeli) person, then as the housekeeper for a U.S. diplomat. In 2006, she left Israel in order to become a live-in domestic worker in the United States, following her only daughter there. She hoped that soon she would be able to secure permanent legal status in the United States and then be able to "bring over" her husband, who had followed her into Israel as a domestic worker, but in the meantime had been forced back to the Philippines because of his illegal status in Israel.

Romelyn, the eldest of a family of farmers in the Mountain Province (northern Philippines), arrived in Israel in 2000, after having worked as a housekeeper and nanny in Hong Kong and Dubai for many years. In Dubai, a family of Palestinian migrants employed her as a nanny for their small child. After six years there, she returned to the Philippines, but soon thereafter left for Hong Kong, realizing that — having no children and being too old to get married, so she said — nothing kept her there. When her Filipino friends in Hong Kong applied for employment in Israel, she decided to join them. In 2006, she left Israel after the death of her employers — an elderly Jewish couple of Eastern European origin whom she had taken care of as a "live-in" for six years —and the expiration of her work permit. In contrast to many other domestic workers in Israel, who stay on illegally, Romelyn decided to return to the Philippines "voluntarily" (rather than risk being deported). She hoped that doing so would better her chances of being granted a "Schengen visa"[21] entry into Western Europe.

Lyna, the last of the women to be portrayed here, had been employed as a nurse in Libya and Saudi Arabia for many years prior to her move to Israel in 1996. In Israel Lyna was unable to practice her profession as a nurse; she worked instead as a live-in caregiver for several elderly persons in an old people's home. Nevertheless, she claimed that she loved the country and she managed to stay there more than two years after her work permit expired in 2005. In December 2007, after several unsuccessful attempts to obtain a visa for the United States or Italy, she decided to return to the Philippines. In the meanwhile, she had "invested" in the college education of her daughter in nursing. Therefore, Lyna argued, even if she could not be hired in the United States, her daughter certainly could and she would then bring Lyna over later on.

While both Marietta and Lyna were married and — apart from their own efforts to move on — had initiated intergenerational migration projects ("investing" in the migration of their daughters to the United States, that is), many others who moved on and on, or wished to do so, were unmarried or separated single mothers. Often, they had relatives elsewhere abroad and had been in Israel for longer than those who were (still) planning to return to the Philippines. As in Romelyn's case, and similar to what Nicole Constable has described for Filipina workers in Hong Kong, "home" has become an ambivalent category: they claim to miss it, but soon after they return they often leave again (to take up "just one more" labor contract), or they are not sure they really want to return at all, so they stay abroad.[22] As Parreñas has pointed out, "[w]omen hesitate to go back home not just because of poverty."[23] Rather, they stay abroad because migration — especially if it results in a permanent legal status in a Western nation-state — represents a move toward independence, a career. All the more so if the move away implies escaping the social control of an over-protective family, abusive husbands, and a life confined by traditional gender roles and expectations.

The Middle East according to Filipina Migrant Workers

In Israel, Lyna, Romelyn, Marietta, and other serial migrants frequently talked about their lives in other (Middle Eastern) countries, all reflecting their particular historical, economic, social, cultural, and religious orientations and circumstances. Most of all, they compared these situations with Israel and the countries they hoped to one day reach. Thus, Lyna told me:

> I came to Israel also because I want to see the place of Jesus Christ. That's why it's also nice to change the country, non-Arab. And then, Israel is much better....The people — also in Libya, some are nice. But they are not modern. Like in Saudi [Arabia], I have to wear the *baya* [abaya], the black cloth. Then, when we go to the hospital, we have to be all covered...we have to work only in pants, no skirts. And they don't want us to talk to boys, even Filipinos. In the hospital, we have uniforms, but outside we use the *baya*. As if we are Muslim. But here [in Israel], even though it is still the Middle East, [it is] modern. When I arrived, I was very surprised.

Like Lyna, most Filipina domestic workers who work in Israel came after earlier employment in other Middle Eastern countries (they "changed the country," according to Lyna) and they all stressed the fact that Israel was more liberal and ostensibly more modern than the others. Those who worked as nannies, housekeepers, and helpers of employers they described as "good," were quick to list the more positive aspects of work elsewhere, such as the fact that in contrast to Israel, employers in other Middle Eastern countries would finance annual vacations to the Philippines or give their Filipina nanny gold jewelry that parents typically receive for newborn children. As former nurses, caregivers, or housekeepers/nannies of families in Middle Eastern countries, Filipina migrants in Israel typically spoke Arabic, had tasted hummus,[24] and were familiar with Islam and the political views (on the Middle East conflict) of their former employers, colleagues, or patients. They often spoke about their experiences in the fashion of what could be called "sentimental Orientalism." They claimed to "know" the Middle East inside out, judging it to be backward and unmodern, but at the same time they stressed its magic exoticism. Edward Said (1978) defined Orientalism as Western cultural discourse that viewed Arabs, Islam, and the Middle East from an assumed superior status. I found (Christian) Filipino representations of the "Orient" to be similarly prejudiced. Once in Israel, Filipinos encountered a comparable, yet significantly different reality: While Arabic was helpful for learning Hebrew and hummus was still available — to put it in a starkly simplified way — the experiences, religious orientations, political views, and ethnic prejudices in Israel often contrasted sharply with what they had encountered elsewhere.

This is clear in Romelyn's case. Romelyn frequently talked about the years she had worked in Dubai. She deeply missed the small child she had cared for,

Claudia Liebelt

Mount of Olives, Jerusalem. Filipinos posing for the camera during a pilgrimage to Jerusalem and Bethlehem, 30 December 2008.

and she nostalgically recalled waking up with the muezzin's call to morning prayer, the relaxed lifestyle in the large, luxurious house of her employer, and what she described as the "exotic" and "magic" moments of religious or familial celebrations she had taken part in. In this family of Palestinian refugees from what became Israel in 1948, it was clear to her that Israel was created by "Zionist colonizers" who were responsible for Palestinian suffering and the ongoing tragedies of the Middle East conflict. As Romelyn told me, back then she shared this view without reflecting on it, since she said she "knew nothing about the history." When I interviewed her in Israel, Romelyn was employed by an elderly Jewish couple who had lost many family members in the Holocaust. Talking to them and experiencing their ongoing trauma of persecution during World War II (by comforting them when they awoke from nightmares, for example), gave Romelyn quite a different view on the political situation in Israel and the Middle East.

From her position as a domestic worker, more precisely a caregiver — first of a child, then of elderly persons — Romelyn, like other Filipina domestics, came to understand cultural practices, took part in the everyday routines, and had access to the intimate private spheres of the employers whose countries she worked in. It has to be emphasized here that domestic work — most especially caring — is affective labor, being deeply relational and typically implying emotional intensity between the caregiver and the person in need. Notwithstanding the typical problems that live-in domestic workers face — such as conflicts with extended family members, nonpayment of wages, or illegal confiscations of passports — I found that in situations of intimate encounters and continuous presence, Filipina caregivers developed intensive affective bonds and a great deal of knowledge and understanding of — if not the societies they worked in, then at least — the personal histories of their employers. Alongside their employers, some Filipina domestic workers fasted during Ramadan or on the Jewish holiday of Yom Kippur. In religious households, they learned to cook kosher or halal food. In Israel, numerous Filipinos through their work with elderly immigrants came to understand Yiddish or Ladino (Judeo-Spanish) — languages of the Jewish diaspora that even their employers' children rarely knew.

Romelyn's case also draws attention to the change of political "frontlines" often experienced by Filipina domestic workers who were first employed in Muslim Middle Eastern countries and then in Israel. This often created (inner) tensions, moments of reflection, or a change of political views, as I was told. Nevertheless, and not surprisingly, Filipina women, from the position of structurally dependent domestic workers, generally refrained from taking sides too openly and avoided discussing politics altogether within the private confines of their workplaces. In spite of the sympathy and compassion with which she cared for her Israeli employers, Romelyn, for example, nevertheless felt that they were heavily, and negatively, prejudiced toward Palestinians or the "Arab world," of whom they "knew nothing," as she put it. Still, she preferred the neutral position of a listening learner to that of arguing with her employers.

This does not mean, however, that Filipina domestic workers generally refrain from taking sides, engaging in political debate and action, or using their knowledge as well as the social capital they gained along their migratory routes. A look at Filipina domestic workers' religious communities in Israel makes this clear.

Domestic Workers for a (Global) Cause: Filipino Christians in the "Holy Land"

Even though live-in Filipina domestic workers in Israel are separated from one another in geographically dispersed households for six days a week, they are not as isolated, docile, or immobile as one might assume. A rich community life of Filipinos and other so-called "foreign workers" (Hebrew *'ovdim zarim*) has developed most especially in the southern neighborhoods of Tel Aviv, Israel's large coastal city. There, Filipino migrants, most of whom are employed in the affluent and densely populated coastal strip around Tel Aviv, typically come together on their weekly day off, which in Israel generally stretches from Saturday night until Sunday night. Within the urban space of some specific southern Tel Aviv neighborhoods, a large infrastructure has developed that caters to migrants' needs and itself employs numerous Filipinos, who succeeded in leaving restrictive (yet state-sanctioned) live-in arrangements, typically by either getting married to an Israeli citizen or by giving birth in Israel.[25] In addition to internet cafes, laundromats, Asian food stores, karaoke bars, local newsstands with Filipino magazines, and shared weekend apartments, this infrastructure includes over a dozen independent churches established by Filipino migrants.

As the "Holy Land" of Christian believers worldwide, Israel and Palestine attract a large number of devoted Filipino Christians, among them many evangelicals, so-called born-agains.[26] Thus, while Filipina domestic workers in Israel are predominantly Roman Catholic (attending local parish churches alongside mainly Arab Israelis), a large and arguably overrepresented number belongs to evangelical churches. This, I suggest, is due to the fact that (1) evangelical churches often proclaim pro-Israeli attitudes and emphasize the Jewish roots of Christianity — making Israel especially attractive as a destination country for born-again Christians, and (2) many Filipinos convert to evangelicalism in the course of the migration process. As typically tight-knit social groups, these evangelical churches function not only as a space of belonging for potentially lonely and vulnerable migrant women — in keeping with the

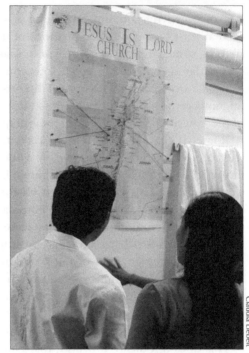

Jesus Is Lord (JIL) map of Israel/Palestine showing sites of JIL congregations.

dominant pattern in much of the literature on migrant churches[27] — but also serve as platforms for collective claims, supporting and organizing migrants' global routes as a way of expanding their global mission.

One of these groups in Israel is the full-gospel Jesus Is Lord (JIL) movement. JIL was founded in 1978 in the Philippines.[28] In Israel, the movement developed as a bible study group of Filipina domestic workers during the second half of the 1990s. Today, it has nine places of worship in Israel, with its main church located in Tel Aviv's large central bus station, a major meeting place for Filipina domestic workers. Here, church activists distribute flyers among Filipinos inviting them to join the church. Each weekend the Filipina pastors — all of whom engage in domestic work throughout the week — welcome newcomers during the Saturday night and Sunday morning church services.

Within the church administrative structure, JIL-Israel is part of JIL-Europe, whose center is situated in Milan, Italy, which also has large concentrations of Filipina domestic workers. Jesus Is Lord has established churches and conversion centers in practically every country where Filipinos are employed in large numbers. Through the on-migration of church members, these different locations are frequently connected by strong personal as well as institutional social ties. Thus, many Filipina domestic workers who attend the church services in Tel Aviv were once part of JIL or similar Filipino evangelical congregations and bible study groups in Hong Kong, Dubai, and Malaysia.

Congregation members who leave Israel for Western Europe and North America or who return home to the Philippines typically enjoy high status within church communities due to their being former residents of the Holy

Land, speakers of Hebrew, and "experts" in Jewish practices and religion, which are appreciated as "authentic roots" within evangelical Christianity. As globally oriented missionary Filipino Christians, they are thus integrated into a large global network of believers, within which those who were employed in Israel turn into — to borrow an expression from Rebeca Raijman and Adriana Kemp on Latin American migrants in Israel — "Ambassadors of Zion."[29] In Israel itself, those with experience in Arabic-speaking countries become crucial within the congregation's aim to spread their mission among Palestinians, arguing that if they become Christian, peace will reign in the Middle East. Thus, JIL Israel hopes to be able to "conquer" Gaza City in the near future (that is, establish a congregation there). Within the narrative of Filipino believing Christians, domestic work — most especially the caring for and serving of Jews — the people of God, as is typically emphasized in this context — becomes much more than an economically rewarding job, but a spiritually rewarding act agreeable to God. Entering the intimate sphere of private homes as domestic workers also gives them the opportunity, so they hope, to spread the mission "one by one." Thus, Filipino evangelical Christians frequently told me that they tried to "share the Word" with their (Jewish) employers and often took the fact that these joined them in watching Christian TV channels as a sign of approval or even missionary success. The six days of domestic work, for which they are legally recruited to work in Israel — so preachers and members of the congregation frequently proclaim — are nothing but a "sideline." Their major purpose, they say, is to be in the Holy Land and reach out to the Jews.

This can be illustrated by a speech of Marissa Albert, a well-known Filipina preacher among evangelical Filipinos in Israel. Speaking to a crowd of more than one hundred Filipino JIL congregants, who for this regular, quarter-annual meeting had gathered from all over Israel in a ("worshipping") tent on the top of Jerusalem's Mount of Olives, she said:

> Prepare the way for the King by having a people who know how to move in those kingdom places.... And the Lord said, "When there's already Israel, I will send Filipino caregivers to Israel!" [*laughter from the audience, shouts:* "Amen!"] Alleluia! [*Thunderous applause, more shouts:* "Amen!"] If there's already Israel, He said, I will give them tents of meeting on the Mount of Olives! [*Applause; shouts:* "Amen!"] Praise the Lord! [*switches to Tagalog*] They're only one race but it's they I will use to bring the word of God to the whole of Asia! [*Applause; shouts:* "Amen!" *switches back to English*] Praise the Lord and the God of Israel. That's how important we are to God.... We are written in the Bible! [*Applause; shouts:* Amen!"] Alleluia! [*in Tagalog:*] Do you want to see that? [*in English:*] You want that verse? Okay, we'll look for it very quickly [*in Tagalog*] because those verses are really exciting. [*In English*] Read Deuteronomy 16:13–16, also Deuteronomy 31:10–13. It's specified there, "aliens, maidservants, menservants." We're listed in the Bible! Alleluia! [*shouts:* "Amen!"] Then maidservants, menservants, aliens who live in Jerusalem, Israel, the Holy City. — That's us! We were not even born yet [when] we were already written in...! Alleluia![30]

In Pastor Albert's preaching, Filipinos become a chosen people, those who as "aliens" and "maidservants" have the mission to bring "the word of God to the whole of Asia." From the Mount of Olives, overlooking the lit-up Temple Mount within the old city of Jerusalem, Pastor Albert continued to explain that an agreement, which Israelis and Palestinians were about to make and which would lead to the division of Jerusalem and the land promised by God to the Jews, was "wrong." Moreover, she announced the meeting of several Philippine senators with Filipino Christian representatives in Israel in the following month, which all Filipinos in Israel were invited to attend.

As Filipino Christians experienced that night, their engagement in a church community made them part of a global movement, a movement — so they are being told by Christian activist leaders such as Pastor Albert — that was continually growing and would come to change the face of Asia, the Middle East, and the world. By giving their tithes, that is 10 percent of their monthly salaries, to the church, Filipino Christians actively support this movement. By studying in the training seminars offered in the ministry, many manage to rise within its hierarchy and during their time in Israel turn into missionaries, preachers, or even "certified" pastors. As globally mobile domestic workers, who in many cases "know" both the so-called Arab World and the Holy Land from inside out, they form an important part in this movement's global mission, as especially honored cultural brokers back in the Philippines or in other destination countries.

Finally, communities of belief such as JIL give Filipina domestic workers a chance to become publicly visible and active groups. During pilgrimages, large gatherings or worshipping events like the one I have described, they come to experience the Holy Land by physically relating to, praying at, and claiming the land as Christians and Filipinos. Within these groups, migrants develop practices, strategies, and narratives that contradict societal stereotypes and processes of social, economic, and political exclusion in Israel. There they not only formulate claims of political and social inclusion, but re-narrate the hardships of domestic work into a position of power. By working in the confinement of Israeli/Middle Eastern private homes, Filipina domestic workers may be largely physically excluded from public visibility and space, yet they are changing Israeli society by raising the children of their employers or sharing "the Word" with the elderly. Due to their marginalized legal, economic, and social status, they need to do so from "below" and "beneath" public visibility. Christian Filipinos' narrative of this hidden power functions to restore dignity and social recognition, which their social status as women, domestic workers, and foreigners from an apparently poor country within more affluent ones often denies them.

Filipino Working Class Cosmopolitans in Search of Greener Pastures

In their niche in the international division of labor, Filipina migrants move predominantly as domestic workers. Through their employment in the private sphere, often as caregivers, they acquire intimate and affective knowledge about the societies and cultures in which they work. As they move on to other destination countries, from Muslim/Arab countries to Israel, for example, they acquire a more differentiated picture of the Middle East, as in the case of Romelyn, or they move toward a more ideologically motivated activism, as in the case of evangelical born-again Christians. In either situation, through their knowledge and understanding, migrant women become highly esteemed cultural brokers within the migrant community or, so first research impressions on the topic have shown, as they return to the Philippines. In contrast to those who stay behind, migrants may develop a "plural vision," as Nicole Constable, drawing from Edward Said's work on exiled people, has analyzed it in regards to Filipina domestic workers in Hong Kong.[31] They are, it can be argued, "working class cosmopolitans."

Pnina Werbner coined the expression "working class cosmopolitanism" in 1999 in an article on transnational Pakistani Sufis. Werbner argued against the divide typically drawn in the scholarly literature between parochial migrants and bourgeois cosmopolitans. Werbner's term also criticized the lumping together of migrants, refugees, and tourists in Ulf Hannerz's work and Hannerz's failure to analyze class formations. One might argue, of course, that Filipina migrants are not working class subjects at all. Like the college graduates Marietta, Romelyn, and Lyna, many migrants are of middle-class background, and invest in small businesses or else acquire economic, social, and cultural capital that deeply effect processes of class formation in the Philippines. Upon migration, though, they often experience what Parreñas calls a "contradictory class mobility,"[32] that is, engagement in socially devalued low-wage labor as workers, in spite of their typically high educational attainments and middle-class status "back home." Moreover, within global capitalism's international division of labor, Filipina migrant domestic workers are part of a relatively new and highly gendered global-proletariat-in-the-making, whose subject, as Pessar and Mahler put it, "tends to be female, a person of color, and a resident in the Third World."[33]

In Werbner's definition, cosmopolitanism is not an absence of belonging, but the possibility of belonging to (and, one might add, through local knowledge, claiming) more than one cultural location simultaneously.[34] Moreover, it is a willingness to engage with the Other. Given this definition, I argue, Filipina migrant workers who practice serial migration clearly develop cosmopolitan subjectivities. As the normative debate on a new cosmopolitanism shows,[35] the notion often functions to evoke promises of personal autonomy beyond individualization on the one hand and restrictive communitarian arrangements on the other, as well as of a cosmopolitan morality as opposed to ethno-nationalism and racism. The account of Filipina migrants' forms of a longed-for belonging to, understanding of, or claim to other cultural locations nevertheless points to the fact that cosmopolitanism may also (and simply) be a (business) strategy: for the successful business person trained in intercultural communication jetting off around the globe as well as for Filipina domestic workers largely excluded from social, economic, and cultural belonging and citizenship in the centers of global capitalism — in the case of Filipina domestic worker Christian activists claiming to "know" the people they wish to convert. Understood in this complexity and based on ethnographic material, the notion of working class cosmopolitanism, I argue, fosters an understanding of transnational (migrant) subjectivities beyond both an ascription of victimhood and an uncritical celebration of cosmopolitanism.

Concluding Remarks

As North America and Western Europe — typically the ultimate dream destinations for Filipina domestic workers — adopt ever-stricter border controls, legal regulations, and requirements for entry and acquisition of citizenship rights, Filipinas' global movements take on an increasingly dangerous, time-consuming, and cost-intensive form. Due to the practical impossibility of entering the European Union, the United States, or Canada straight from the Philippines, most Filipinos are forced to follow global routes through a number of nation-states, in order to reach the most desirable destinations. Lyna, who was described as having worked in Libya and Saudi Arabia before going to Israel, told me in 2005 about her recent interview at the U.S. Embassy in Israel, where she had applied for a visa: "I told them: 'Only I will just see America, to fulfill my dream.' Because that's why I chose to be a nurse, to fulfill my dream, to see America."[36] This not only illustrates what has been called Filipinos' "education for travel" — one of the most blatant examples of which is doctors in the Philippines who return to college in order to take up nursing, because Filipino nurses are more sought after in the global market[37] — but also hints at the immense importance of the imaginative factors of migration. Thus, destination countries are ordered along a global hierarchy of desirability, within which Israel as the "Holy Land" for Filipino Christians is more desirable than most Asian and Middle Eastern destinations, though less so than Western Europe and North America, where Filipinos hope to achieve economic success and Western citizenship rights. Through their moves toward the global North, Filipina domestic workers thus actively "negotiate citizenship."[38] Apart from doing so in the country they currently inhabit — as Stasiulis and Bakan have shown for domestic workers in Canada — at least some of them also do so on a global scale, by migrating on and on, rather than back and forth. Transnationally organized institutions like church groups often play a crucial role in fostering and organizing migrants' global routes, as the example of the evangelical Jesus Is Lord group in Israel has shown. As cross-culturally informed, politically engaged, or zealously religious women rather than mere victims of global capitalism, Filipina domestic workers are part of an ever-growing global-proletariat-in-the-making, trying to both make sense of their marginalized position, and striving to overcome it.

ACKNOWLEDGMENTS: I thank Pnina Werbner for her detailed comments on this article. An earlier version was presented at the workshop "Distant Divides and Intimate Connections: Migrant Domestic Workers in Asia" of the SSRC Conference on Inter-Asian Connections, Dubai, February 2008. Thanks go to the workshop participants for their insightful comments. I remain deeply grateful to my Filipino interview partners for having shared their life stories, thoughts, and dreams with me and for integrating me into their everyday lives in Israel and beyond.

❏

2. High in the Hierarchy, Rich in Diversity

Asian Domestic Workers, Their Networks, and Employers' Preferences in Yemen

Marina de Regt

URING MY RESEARCH AMONG MIGRANT DOMESTIC WORKERS IN YEMEN I met Maria, a Filipina in her late forties who had lived for more than twenty years in Yemen's capital city of Sana'a. I knew that Filipinas were working as domestics in this Arab country, but locating them was not easy. My earlier research had focused on Ethiopian and Somali women, who constitute the majority of domestic workers in Yemen and are relatively easy to contact. The number of "Asiyawat," as women from South and Southeast Asia are commonly called in Arabic, is much smaller and because they are employed mainly as live-in domestic workers they are more difficult to approach. They live with the families of their employers and often have no day off. Within the Asiyawat category, Filipinas seemed to have the most freedom of movement. They are also able to move from live-in to live-out domestic work and from Yemeni to expatriate employers.

Maria was one of these live-out domestic workers and I was very pleased when she agreed to be interviewed. Maria was very friendly on the phone, but arranging an appointment to meet was difficult. She worked six days a week at the residence of the Italian ambassador, and although she returned home to her own apartment every day around 6:00 P.M., she had a very active social life. In the evenings she visited friends and went to religious events at the homes of other Filipinas. On Friday, her weekly day off, she attended the Roman Catholic Church[1] and once every two weeks her husband, who lived in another town in Yemen, visited her. When we finally met, she welcomed me warmly, waiting for me at the balcony of her four-room apartment in Sana'a. She was wearing trousers and a t-shirt, her hair uncovered, and I wondered whether she also dressed this way when going outside the house.[2] Maria introduced me to her 24-year-old daughter, explaining that she had persuaded her to come to Yemen because she could not find work in the Philippines. Maria hopes that her daughter can find an administrative job instead of becoming a domestic worker, a job that Maria has been doing for the past twenty-two years.

Maria is one of the seventy-four Filipinas registered as domestic workers at the government's labor office in Sana'a and a member of the small and close-knit Filipino community in Yemen. The majority of Filipinos living in Sana'a are women, who are employed as nurses, domestic workers, and administrative staff. Filipino men work mainly as technicians in factories outside of the capital city. The Filipino community is one of the many migrant communities in Yemen.

Yemen, situated on the southwestern edge of the Arabian Peninsula and the least economically developed country in West Asia,[3] is primarily seen as a sending country in migration. During the oil boom in the early 1970s, thousands of Yemenis migrated to Saudi Arabia and the Gulf States as cheap and unskilled laborers. As a result foreigners coming from a wide variety of countries filled the need for specialized skills, especially in former North Yemen, but also to some extent in former South Yemen.[4] Chinese road workers, Egyptian and Sudanese teachers, Indian nurses, Russian doctors, Filipino technicians, and Western development workers became part of Yemen's immigrant population. The unification of North Yemen and South Yemen in 1990 nearly coincided with the downfall of President Mengistu in Ethiopia and of President Siad Barre in Somalia in 1991. Since that time the number of Somalis and Ethiopians coming to Yemen as refugees or as labor migrants has risen; they now form the largest groups of immigrants in the country.

While Somali and Ethiopian men have difficulties finding paid work because of the high unemployment rate among Yemen's male population, Somali and Ethiopian women are often employed as domestic workers for middle and upper-middle-class families in urban areas. Whereas the large-scale employment of migrant domestic workers in the "rich" countries of the Arabian Peninsula is well known, there is little awareness that migrant women are also hired as domestic workers in an economically underdeveloped country like Yemen. Yet, the demand for migrant domestic workers in Yemen's urban areas has increased rapidly in the past two decades. Urbanization has resulted in changing family structures, with nuclear families increasingly replacing extended families. As a result domestic tasks can no longer be handled by several adult women living together in one household, but fall instead on the shoulders of one woman. In addition, a growing number of urban women have taken up professional or voluntary work. These women find combining their activities in and outside the home a challenge and employing domestic workers offers them a solution. Moreover, employing migrant domestic workers has increasingly become a new form of social distinction.[5] Whereas urban middle and upper-middle-class families employ Somali and Ethiopian domestic workers, upper-class families in the cities make use of Filipinas, Indian women, Sri Lankan women, and more recently also Indonesian women.

Migrant domestic workers are thus ranked in a clear hierarchy, with Asian women at the top and Ethiopians and Somalis following next in order.[6] Asian women are employed by the upper classes and receive the highest salaries; Ethiopian women are employed by the upper middle classes and Somali women

The old city of Sana'a, Yemen. Most domestic work in Yemen, the least economically developed country in West Asia, is done by migrant workers.

work for the middle classes. The tasks for which Asian and African women are employed also differ. African women typically do cleaning tasks, while Asian women more often cook and take care of children and the elderly. "Asian domestic workers" is not, however, a homogeneous category. Significant differences among Asian women are based on, amongst other things, nationality, religion, ways of recruitment, employment conditions, access to social support networks, and work trajectories. Moreover, preferences of employers for particular nationalities of Asian workers also vary.

Whereas Ethiopian and Somali women are quite visible in Yemen's urban landscape because of their larger numbers, Asian women are rarely seen on the streets of Yemen's main cities. Those Asian women who are visible in public are often employed as nurses. The invisibility of Asian domestic workers can be attributed to their lower numbers but also to the fact that they mainly work as live-in domestic workers for upper-class families and are not allowed to leave the homes of their employers. This is particularly the case for Indian and Indonesian women, while Filipinas seem to have more freedom to come and go. Furthermore, Filipinas in Yemen appear to have access to much larger support networks that enable them to improve their living and working conditions during their time in Yemen.

Maria is an example of a Filipina who came to Yemen as a live-in domestic worker and gradually improved her situation thanks to her social network. In this article I present the stories of Maria and two other domestic workers, one an Indian woman and the other an Indonesian woman, and analyze the differences and similarities in their experiences, paying special attention to the unique recruitment and social support networks available to them. How and why do different nationalities of Asian women come to an economically under-developed country such as Yemen? What are the different ways of recruitment? To what extent does the way in which workers are recruited affect their access to social support networks? And what is the relationship between the recruitment networks, social support networks, and employer preferences for particular groups of workers?

The article is based on anthropological fieldwork in two cities in Yemen (Sana'a and Hodeidah) from 2003 to 2005.[7] The main data collection methods consisted of in-depth interviews and informal conversations with domestic workers and employers and observations in the homes of employers. I inter-viewed fifteen Asian domestic workers — seven Filipinas (five live-out and two live-in), five Indonesian women (all live-in), two Indian women (both live-in) and one Sri Lankan woman (live-in) — and seven employers of Asian domestic workers. Although the number of interviewed women is relatively small, the long period of fieldwork and the high quality of the interviews ensure the reli-ability of the data. The interviews with Filipinas were done in English, the other interviews, in Arabic. In some cases I made use of a translator. Almost all inter-views were recorded and fully transcribed.

High in the Hierarchy

The Yemeni market for paid domestic labor has changed rapidly in the past two decades. In the 1980s few foreign women were hired by the upper classes as do-mestic workers. These were principally Asian, Filipinas, Indian, and Sri Lankan women in particular. Beginning in the early 1990s more and more foreign work-ers — many Somali and Ethiopian — began to be hired to perform paid domes-tic labor.

Confident that they will be given refugee status, many Somalis flee to Yemen in smuggling boats, often intending to travel later to richer countries in the re-gion, or if possible, to the United States, Canada, or Europe. Yemen is the only country on the Arabian Peninsula that has ratified the 1951 UN Convention re-lating to the Status of Refugees and its 1967 Protocol and Somali refugees are thus accepted on a prima facie basis. According to the UN High Commissioner for Refugees (UNHCR), approximately 90,000 Somali refugees were registered in Yemen in 2004, but the actual number is much higher because many are not registered. Most Somali women are employed as domestic workers by middle-class families who can afford their salaries (around US$50 per month). The women rarely live with their employers, performing cleaning tasks only (not cooking or care-giving) on a part-time or full-time basis. Somali women occupy the lowest position on the migrant domestic labor market in Yemen. One rea-son is because they have their own family responsibilities in Yemen and there-fore are not available for live-in domestic work; another reason is that they are stereotyped as "unclean" and "unreliable."[8]

Ethiopian women occupy a higher position in the hierarchy of domestic workers. They come to Yemen via (illegal)[9] recruitment agencies or via relatives and friends who are already residing in the country.[10] According to the Ethiopian Embassy in Sana'a, there were around 8,000 Ethiopian women in Yemen in

2004, but reliable statistics are not available because not all of the women are documented. Ethiopian women are employed as live-in and live-out domestic workers for cleaning, cooking, and caretaking tasks. Their salaries (between US$100 and $200 per month) are affordable for middle and upper-middle-class families. The majority of Ethiopian domestic workers are unmarried and Christian, but small numbers of married women and Muslim women are also employed. Ethiopian women are regarded as "honest" and "clean," and they therefore occupy a middle position in the domestic labor hierarchy.

Asian domestic workers have the highest social status in the hierarchy of domestic workers. They receive the highest salaries (on average between US$150 and $250 per month) and are employed mainly by Yemen's upper classes. Indonesian, Sri Lankan, and Indian women work exclusively as live-in domestic workers for Yemeni families, performing tasks such as cooking and caretaking for children and the elderly. Filipinas may also be employed as live-out domestic workers by expatriate families living and working in Yemen.[11] The total number of Asian domestic workers employed in Yemen is hard to estimate because not all of them are registered at the Ministry of Social Affairs and Labor. This applies particularly to Filipinas and Indonesian women.

Elsewhere, I have argued that the preferences of Yemeni employers for domestic workers of particular backgrounds and nationalities are not based only on essentialist notions of, among others, class, race, and culture, but also on the employer's search for an intricate balance of social, cultural, and religious closeness and distance.[12] Employers prefer to hire domestic workers who are not too similar to themselves with regard to class, race, or culture.[13] Yemeni employers therefore prefer to employ foreign women of a different nationality or ethnicity. Because Ethiopian and Asian women are socially more distant than Somali women, they are preferred as domestic workers. They are not part of the local community, they do not speak the language, and they do not share the same cultural values. In addition, unlike Somali domestic workers, they often leave their families behind in their home countries and are therefore available as live-in domestic workers. Moreover, because they come as temporary labor migrants they accept the hierarchical relationship inherent to domestic labor more easily, and they do not claim citizenship rights.

Another important factor explaining the preference for Ethiopian and Asian women is that their employment as live-in domestic workers strengthens class status. In the past, only elite families had permanent servants.[14] They were in most cases women from the rural areas who were brought to the city at a young age and who stayed with the family until they married. Nonelite families occasionally made use of domestic workers, employing them for particular domestic tasks and paying them in money or in kind.[15] With the rapid social, economic, and political changes that have taken place in the past forty years, Yemen's hierarchical system of social stratification has altered and social status is now no longer dependent only on descent. With the large out-migration of people of various social status backgrounds and the subsequent monetarization of the economy, economic success is no longer restricted to people from high social status groups. A new urban middle class has emerged of people actively involved in trading, business, and the professions. For these new urban middle classes, employing migrant domestic workers has become a strong sign of social status.[16]

In general, middle- and upper-middle-class families employ Ethiopian women whereas upper-class families employ Asian women. The main reason is that recruitment costs and salaries of Ethiopian women are lower than those of Asian women. Ethiopia is geographically closer to Yemen and plane tickets are consequently cheaper. In addition, Yemen and Ethiopia have a close historic relationship, and many Yemenis are acquainted with Ethiopia through relatives or friends. Middle- and upper-middle-class families sometimes explain their employment of Ethiopian domestic workers with reference to cultural closeness: "We know their culture and they know ours; that is why we like them."

Yet, preferences of employers of different social classes vary and change. In the past five years an increasing number of middle- and upper-middle-class families have started to employ Asian domestic workers, particularly Indonesians. One factor that may explain this shift is the high social status attached to employing Asian domestic workers. Indonesian women receive the lowest salaries among the different nationalities of Asian domestic workers and are thus affordable as domestic workers in middle- and upper-middle-class families. In addition, Indonesian women are Muslim and an increasing number of Yemeni employers express a preference for employing Muslim domestic workers. Yemen is a Muslim society and religious values are important in many parts of daily life.[17] Yet, religious closeness is not automatically a positive value in paid domestic labor.

Gender relations in Yemen are to a large extent based on practices of gender segregation, regulating contact between nonrelated women and men. The fact that performing paid domestic labor challenges practices of gender segregation is one of the reasons why Yemeni women are unwilling to perform this type of labor; their respectability is at risk if they are in contact with nonrelated men. Somali women, who are also Muslim, sometimes also have difficulties accepting their work as domestics because they do not accept the hierarchical relationship with their Yemeni employers, a reluctance that may be related to the emphasis placed on equality in Islam. I argue that religious closeness is an asset only when other forms of social and cultural distance are ensured. In my view the increasing preference for Indonesian domestic workers has therefore less to do with religious closeness than with the extent to which employers can maintain distance and assert control and authority. As Muslims in an unknown (Muslim) country, Indonesian women workers more easily accept being confined in the domestic space; it is harder for them to go out and establish contacts with fellow countrywomen than for domestic workers of other nationalities. Social support networks are extremely important for migrant domestic workers, particularly in a country like Yemen where organizations supporting domestic workers are scarce.

At the start of my fieldwork in 2004, there were no governmental or nongovernmental organizations defending the rights of domestic workers. Domestic workers, whether local or foreign, are explicitly excluded from the Yemeni labor law. Thus no legal framework is available to protect their rights. Migrant domestic workers who encounter problems have only their embassies to turn to for assistance. Since 2004, public awareness about the situation of domestic workers has increased, resulting in the establishment of a nongovernmental organization protecting the rights of migrant domestic workers, more attention for domestic workers within the Yemeni Ministry of Social Affairs and Labor, and better protection measurements of the respective embassies.[18] Informal support networks remain highly important, however, especially in a country like Yemen where government control of recruitment agencies, employers, and workers is relatively weak.

The Importance of Social Networks

Maria, the Filipina domestic worker who was introduced at the beginning of this article, came to Yemen in 1982. She was twenty-two years old, married with two children, when her sister encouraged her to go abroad:

My elder sister worked in a travel agency. She knew a Filipina who worked as a tailor in Yemen and who was looking for someone to work for her. So my sister arranged my passport and found work for me.... Actually, I did not want to go abroad but my sister convinced me. She said that it was a good opportunity for me.

Her sister also spoke to Maria's husband, who was a construction worker with a low salary, saying: "Think practical, if you really want to set up a family you need money." Maria was going to earn US$300 per month in Yemen, which was a huge amount of money compared to what her husband earned. Maria left the Philippines when her youngest child was two years old, expecting to work as a tailor's assistant. She was surprised when she found out that she was going to work as a domestic:

My sister didn't tell me that I will work in houses. She told me that I would work as a seamstress, because the lady that recruited me is a tailor here in Yemen. She is earning a lot of money. When I came here I was really shocked, because I didn't have any experience.... Every day I cried because I was thinking about my daughters, I left them there and they were the same age as the children I was taking care of. So I was taking care of somebody's child and I didn't see my own children. It was a very big sacrifice.

At the time of our interview, Maria had been in Yemen for twenty-two years,[19] returning to the Philippines only for holidays. She worked for several families, and shifted from live-in domestic work to live-out work. The path her "career" followed shows the importance of social networks:

The family I worked for was very nice. They taught me everything and gave me a day off. I went every Sunday to my friend's place and slept there. The first month was very difficult, I used to cry a lot and when they saw me crying they told me not to cry and said that my children were in good hands. They took me with them when they went outside.... After two years I went home for a month but I had renewed my contract and worked another year and nine months for the same family. But they decreased my salary from [US]$300 to $200 because they had less money, so I took another job.... There were a lot of Filipinos working in Yemen whom I met through the woman who recruited me first. One of them told me that someone working for UNDP [UN Development Program][20] was looking for a maid. They interviewed me and accepted me. Because I was still under contract with the other family I could not start working for them immediately and I told the new employers that they had to recruit me from the Philippines.... I told the first family that I had an emergency at home and I went back to the Philippines. I paid my own ticket and they let me go. Three weeks later the new employer sent me the visa and I returned to Yemen. I worked two years for them and when they left I returned to the Philippines for a month. When I came back I did not have work, but a friend of mine told me that the Italian embassy was looking for a maid. She said that I was qualified to work there. My employer had talked to the wife of the Italian ambassador and had told her, "If you ever need a maid, my maid is good." She also introduced me to her but at that time they did not need a maid. So when my madam left I went to the Italian ambassador, and his wife spoke to me and asked me where I worked before. I told her that I worked for Miss Azaz and her husband, who worked for UNDP, and she said "OK, I know her" and she employed me.

Maria was still working for the Italian ambassador at the time of the interview. Her salary had increased from US$300 per month in 1982 to $800 in 2004. As she explained: "I don't tell people about my salary. Everybody says I am lucky.... I feel that my luck is here in Yemen, I didn't have any problems with my bosses." Maria's two daughters grew up with their grandmother and Maria lost contact with her first husband. She married again in Yemen, to a Filipino who is working as an engineer in a factory in another city. They have a six-year-old daughter who they recently sent to the Philippines for schooling. Maria is an active member of the Philippine community in Sana'a; she goes to church regularly and has many friends.

There is no Philippines embassy in Yemen, but there are two community organizations that regularly organize activities and parties. Prior to the civil war in May–July 1994, a few thousand Filipinos were living in Yemen.[21] By 2004, the number had decreased to around six hundred. The large numbers of Filipinos who left during the civil war never returned because Yemen's economic situation had deteriorated and Yemenis could no longer afford to employ Filipinos. Nevertheless, Filipinas and Filipinos still bring their relatives to Yemen in the hope that they will find a job as a domestic worker or preferably in administration. Maria, for example, brought her daughter to Yemen. Another Filipina I interviewed had brought at least fourteen relatives and friends to Yemen over a ten-year period. Some of them came on contracts and others on tourist visas, with the latter hoping to obtain a residence permit as soon as they found work.[22]

Maria's story shows the importance of recruitment and support networks for migrant domestic workers. As noted above, she obtained her first job through her sister, who knew a Filipina who was working in Yemen as a tailor. The fact that from the very beginning she was in touch with other Filipinos helped her a lot. She found better-paid jobs through her social networks, and even met her present husband in that way. She then moved from live-in domestic work for a Yemeni family to live-out domestic work for expatriates. She later remarried and lives now by herself. Maria facilitated her own daughter's migration. Networks of relatives and friends often play a role in determining migrants' destinations, facilitating their migration and arrival in the destination country, and easing their access to housing and work.[23] Migrating via relatives or friends has important advantages. First, women might be better prepared for their work and life abroad. Second, the presence of relatives or friends facilitates women's adjustment to a new living and working situation.

Networks of relatives and friends are very important for migrants' well-being in general and for domestic workers in particular because they often work in isolated situations.[24] The fact that friends or family members have selected the family a woman is going to work for increases her chances of being treated well. Relatives and friends can also offer support and protection in times of trouble.

Moreover, the availability of support networks determines to a large extent whether women can be upwardly mobile and improve their living and working conditions. As Hondagneu-Sotelo states in her study on Mexican housecleaners in Los Angeles, "a domestic worker's position within the occupation is not static. It is subject to change and may improve as she gains experience, learns to utilize the informational resources embedded in the social networks, and estab-

Arda Nederveen

Villas in a residential area of Sana'a, Yemen.

lishes a number of *casas* (houses) to clean."[25] While Hondagneu-Sotelo's article focuses on women doing part-time cleaning tasks for a number of families, her statement is also applicable to migrant domestic workers employed by one family and even to live-in domestic workers. Finding a job abroad, leaving this job for a better (paid) job with another family, shifting from live-in to live-out domestic work, and leaving domestic work altogether are to a large extent dependent on access to social networks. Access to social networks depends in Yemen, however, on the way in which women are recruited. This may not necessarily be the case in other countries, where in some cases all workers are required to go through recruitment agencies, but in Yemen women who come via relatives and friends tend to have greater access to social support networks than women who come via (illegal) recruitment agencies and often do not know anyone in the country of migration.

Filipinas who migrate as domestic workers are supposed to do so via private recruitment agencies registered at the Philippine Overseas Employment Administration (POEA) in Manila. In addition, they have to go through pre-departure training to prepare them for their work abroad.[26] The Philippine government actively promotes women's migration as domestic workers,[27] but Yemen is not considered a country where women can earn a decent income and the Philippines government has little or no relationship with Yemen on migrant labor issues. No bilateral agreement exists between the two countries concerning domestic workers labor migration, for instance, and there is no embassy of the Philippines in Yemen. Filipinos in Yemen are represented by the consulate in Jeddah and the embassy in Riyadh. When I visited the POEA in Manila in October 2007 and inquired about agencies that recruit women for the domestic labor market in Yemen, I found only two. According to the POEA, these two agencies had sent a small number of "domestic helpers" and "babysitters" to Yemen in the past three years. This small number coupled with the fact that all of the Philippine women I interviewed in Yemen came via networks of personal contacts and not through a recruitment agency shows the weakness of government policies of both sending and receiving countries and illustrates the blurred line between legal and illegal migration. In addition, the small number shows that regulated migration (migration according to the rules and regulations of sending and receiving countries) is not necessarily in the best interest of migrant domestic workers.[28]

As we have shown, migrating via relatives and friends has many advantages over migrating via recruitment agencies, not in the least because women who migrate to Yemen via recruitment agencies often lack a social network. In the following sections I present the stories of two women, one, Indian, and the other, Indonesian. As is the case with most Indian and Indonesian migrant workers, these two women were recruited for work in Yemen by agencies. They, like Filipina domestic workers, are employed mostly as live-in help, but they have less freedom of movement and therefore only limited access to a social network.

Women without a Social Network

In Hodeidah, Yemen's port on the Red Sea, I interviewed Ayesha, an Indian domestic worker who came to Yemen in 1994. During the more than four years I lived in Hodeidah,[29] I had never seen Asian women in the city, with the exception of the wives of Asian technicians and managers working in the port or in one of Hodeidah's factories. According to the Labor Office in Hodeidah twenty-seven Indian women worked as live-in domestics for the small number of wealthy, factory-owning families in the city 9n 2005. I tried for several weeks to get access to these families, but was only able to meet and interview Ayesha, whom I met via a friend whose daughter's schoolmate had an Indian domestic worker. Nadia, Ayesha's female employer, did not mind me interviewing Ayesha. She told me that she had previously employed two Sri Lankan women and another Indian woman, but they never stayed as long as Ayesha (more than ten years).[30]

Ayesha arrived for our interview dressed in a colorful Yemeni dress. The fluent Arabic she spoke bolstered her resemblance to a Yemeni woman. We sat down in the guest room and she openly told me her life story. Coming from a poor Muslim family in Mumbai, she finished primary school, but her family could not afford to pay for her continuing education. She married her cousin when she was thirteen years old, had her first child when she was fourteen, and her second child when she was fifteen. Her husband was an unemployed mechanic.

> I wanted to leave because I had children and my husband was unemployed. And when my children grow up they will have to go to school so they need money. Now they both go to school…. I want to educate my children so that they don't work in people's houses like I do. I want their life to be better than mine.

Prior to coming to Yemen, Ayesha had worked two years as a domestic in Saudi Arabia and two years in Kuwait.[31] Initially the recruitment agency did not want to arrange her migration because she was too young. Unable to acquire a passport before she became twenty, she convinced the agency that she desperately needed work and she eventually migrated to Saudi Arabia with a false passport.[32]

Back in India her agent put her in contact with Nadia, who was on holiday in India and looking for a domestic worker. Ayesha had never heard of Yemen, but she liked Nadia and accepted the job. This was the first time she would be traveling on her own passport. She explained that the security of having proper documents was one of the reasons why she has stayed in Yemen for more than ten years. Ayesha has an air-conditioned room on the roof, but she may also spend her spare time inside the house, watching television in one of the rooms. She feels at home but realizes that her situation is not ideal. She never leaves the house by herself and does not know her way around Hodeidah: "I only know the walls of this house, when I need something the driver takes me to the market and I can buy what I want." She has no friends although there are other Indian

women living in Hodeidah: "How can you make friends when you don't go any-
where?"

The number of Indian domestic workers in Yemen is relatively small. In 2004
only seventy-three Indian women were registered as domestic workers in
Sana'a and twenty-seven in Hodeidah. These workers came to Yemen on contracts arranged via the Yemeni embassy and the Yemeni Ministry of Labor.[33] In
contrast with Filipina domestic workers, who often have a close community life
and a network of contacts, Indian domestic workers have much less contact
with fellow compatriots even though the Indian community in Yemen is much
larger than the Filipino community.[34] The fact that Ayesha does not know any
other Indians or any of the other twenty-six Indian domestic workers living in
Hodeidah is telling. Although she is treated well, her world is very small and she
has no friends. She has lived with the same family for more than ten years, and
has not been able to change employers or shift from live-in domestic work to
live-out work because she lacks contacts and information that a social network
might facilitate or provide.

The same applies to the majority of Indonesian women working in Yemen. I
had heard about the increasing number of Indonesian domestic workers at the
start of my fieldwork,[35] but locating them was difficult. Because they often come
to Yemen on a contract arranged by an illegal recruitment agent or an individual
employer, and work as live-in domestic workers for upper-class families, they
are hardly visible in the public sphere. Occasionally Indonesian women can be
seen in one of the large supermarkets, accompanying their employers' family
when they are shopping, but those occasions are not the most suitable to approach them. I was told that there was one particular supermarket that used to
be in Indonesian hands, where Indonesian women sometimes went to shop by
themselves. But at the times that I visited the supermarket I failed to meet any
migrant women. During one of these visits, however, I met Fadl, a man of mixed
Yemeni-Indonesian descent and one of the managers of the supermarket.[36] Fadl
told me that upper-class families approached him regularly, asking for help in
finding Indonesian domestic workers, and that he sometimes recruited Indonesian women to work for them. He was willing to arrange an interview with
Faridah, one of the Indonesian women he had brought to Yemen.

I interviewed Faridah in the restaurant of the supermarket in the company of
Fadl, who sometimes had to translate because Faridah's Arabic was very basic.
Faridah came to Yemen in 2000, after having worked for ten years in Saudi Arabia. A friend who was working at the Yemeni Embassy advised her to go to Yemen: "She told me that you could walk freely in the streets, that you were not
locked up in a house, and that there was more freedom. I thought, I have seen
Saudi Arabia, now I want to see Yemen." Faridah is working as a live-in domestic
worker for an upper-class extended family that employs many other domestic
workers. There were eight Ethiopian, three Indonesian, and four Yemeni domestic workers employed by the same family. Faridah takes care of one of the
older women in the family and shares a room with the other two Indonesian
women, whose main task is child care. She does not have a day off but she may
leave the house with permission, but for no longer than three hours. Faridah

said that she liked working in Yemen and prefers it to Saudi Arabia: "The people are nicer; they are like Indonesians; they are nice and good-hearted."[37]

While Faridah says that she is satisfied with her job, other Indonesian women feel deceived and disappointed by their living and working conditions in Yemen. The Indonesian embassy is increasingly confronted with Indonesian domestic workers who have run away after conflicts with their employers. Strenuous workloads, not receiving their salaries, and mental and physical abuse are their main complaints and reasons for running away. Because of the increasing number of Indonesian runaways the Indonesian Embassy has opened a shelter for runaway women to stay. The Indonesian Embassy is the only embassy in Yemen with such a facility. During the time of my fieldwork, small groups of women were living in the shelter, and there I interviewed two of them. Ella and Salma had both worked in Saudi Arabia and Kuwait before coming to Yemen. They told me that they had arrived three and a half months earlier by means of the services of an agent. Upon arrival they were immediately taken to the house of their employer. They not only had to clean her house but also a private school. They hardly had time to sleep, were working continuously, and were permitted no time off. In addition, their employer delayed paying their salaries and regularly called them names. When things became unbearable they decided to run away and left the house in the middle of the night. A Yemeni taxi driver took them to the Indonesian Embassy, where the guard let them in. While the women wanted to leave Yemen immediately, they had to stay in the shelter for months because the employer refused to pay their salaries and return their passports. This happens not only to Indonesian women but also to domestic workers of other nationalities who have entered the country via illegal agencies.

The Indonesian Embassy finds it difficult to resolve the problems of Indonesian domestic workers because many of them came to Yemen via illegal agents who provide them with tourist visas, but never followed up to arrange for residence permits and work permits. The lack of a bilateral agreement regulating labor migration between Indonesia and Yemen also makes it hard to protect the rights of Indonesian migrants.

The Indonesian government discourages labor migration to Yemen because of the country's low standard of living, and the subsequent low salaries domestic workers receive (US$50 to $100 per month), but in the deteriorating economic situation in Indonesia since the Asian financial crisis of the late 1990s, overseas migration has been one way to make a living. Large numbers of Indonesian women migrate as domestic workers to other countries in Southeast Asia (such as Malaysia, Singapore, Hong Kong, and Taiwan) and to the oil-producing countries on the Arabian Peninsula (such as Saudi Arabia and the Gulf States). A much smaller but increasing number of Indonesian women migrate to Yemen, preferring to work in a Muslim country.[38] Indonesian agents recruit women from rural areas, in particular from Java, to work in Yemen. Telling potential recruits that the market for domestic workers in Saudi Arabia and the Gulf States is essentially filled, the agents convince the women that it is easier and cheaper to get visas for Yemen than to apply through the official channels for work permits for Saudi Arabia and the Gulf States.

Indian and Indonesian women almost always come to Yemen on individual contracts arranged by brokers and agencies and most are employed as live-in domestic workers. Live-in contract workers are seen as the most underprivileged group of domestic workers worldwide because they live with their employers and their freedom of movement is often restricted. Some employers give their domestic workers a day off but in most cases the women are not allowed to leave their employer's house unaccompanied, and these restrictions affect their ability to build a social network.[39] In the worst case they may be locked inside the house when the employers go out in order to "protect them" and in order to prevent them from running away or meeting compatriots. The women may also be denied basic human rights such as a good place to sleep and wholesome food, and they may work under exploitative conditions, facing physical, mental, or sexual abuse.[40]

Contract workers, as we have seen, are not, however, an undifferentiated category of workers: their freedom of movement and access to social networks depend on how their contracts are arranged and on how the individual employers treat them. Contracts are arranged via the Yemeni Ministry of Social Affairs and Labor, but government control of the implementation of these contracts is nonexistent. In addition, no licensed recruitment agencies exist in Yemen and the Yemeni Ministry lacks the facilities to systematically control the activities of illegal recruitment agents. Domestic workers whose contracts are arranged via relatives and friends, as is often the case with Filipinas in Yemen, run less risk of being isolated and exploited than domestic workers whose contracts are arranged via agencies. Women who migrate in small numbers via impersonal recruitment agencies to countries in which there is less freedom and mobility for women, such as Yemen, are less likely to have a social network in the host country and are likely to have much more difficulty gaining access to fellow countrywomen because of the isolated nature of the work they do in private homes. They are therefore dependent on their employers and agents to meet fellow countrywomen.

Changing Preferences?

Maria came to Yemen in 1982, Ayesha in 1994, and Faridah in 2000. The times of their arrival in Yemen are to a certain extent representative of the changes that have taken place in the Yemeni domestic labor market. Although reliable statistics are lacking,[41] my interviews with staff employed at the government labor offices in Sana'a and Hodeidah and at several embassies, as well as with employers and domestic workers, all confirm that the numbers of Filipino employees has decreased while the number of Indonesian domestic workers has increased. The number of Indian women working as domestic workers has remained stable, but there are now fewer Sri Lankan women working in Yemen than in the past.[42] What are the reasons behind these shifts? Are preferences of employers changing or are other factors playing a role? How important is women's access to social support networks and what is the relationship with religion?

One reason why the number of Filipina domestic workers has dropped is the deteriorating economic situation in Yemen. After the civil war of 1994, the structural adjustment program imposed by the World Bank and International Monetary Fund slashed the purchasing power of Yemen's population. The rise in inflation has made it too expensive to employ Filipinas, who typically demand the highest salaries. Their professionalism, their long history of domestic work in Yemen and elsewhere, and their "strong mentality" have almost priced them out of the market in Yemen: "Their salaries are far too high, they have been spoiled and think that they are the ones in charge," one ambassador complained to me. This is the case in other countries as well. Bakan and Stasiulis describe how the positive image of Filipinas in Canada as "frugal and ambitious" has changed into a stereotype of the "greedy Filipino, selfishly exploiting the Canadian immigration system, as a result of the collective strategies of Filipina domestic workers to challenge exploitative work conditions."[43] Similarly, Constable shows how Filipinas in Hong Kong from the mid 1980s onwards have been depicted as "far too savvy, assertive and contentious."[44] As a result, by the mid 1990s Indonesian women were gaining popularity among employers in Hong Kong.[45] In her study on Filipinas and Indonesian domestic workers in Taiwan, Lan describes similar stereotypes. While Filipinas were portrayed as "outgoing, individualistic, opinionated, smart and hard to manage," Indonesians were described as "obedient, born to be hardworking and thrifty" or "emotionally stable, living a simple life, [with] no days off."[46]

Salary issues are thus not the only explanation why upper-middle-class families in Yemen (as in Hong Kong and Taiwan) prefer to hire Indonesian women as domestic workers. Jamila, an upper-class-woman who employs the only two Filipinas still working as domestics in Hodeidah, cites a second reason: people think that they are too open-minded and outspoken.[47] "People prefer to employ Indonesian women," she explains, "because they are quiet and obedient, but also because they are Muslim and do not go out." Jamila's two domestic workers have every Thursday evening off, which they spend with male Filipinos who work in factories in Hodeidah, and go to church on Sunday afternoon. Her backdoor neighbors also employed two Filipinas, but they forbade them to be in touch with Jamila's workers, afraid they would adopt their behavior and start dressing "indecently" and going out.

Interestingly, I heard similar comments about Sri Lankan women, who are not regarded as having very strong social networks and who are not positioned very highly in the hierarchy of domestic workers in other Middle Eastern countries.[48] According to stories I heard, Sri Lankan women workers had an active social life and went outside on their day off. Halima, the wife of a merchant in Hodeidah, said: "Everybody had Sri Lankan domestic workers [in the late 1980s and early 1990s]. Our maid was very nice in the beginning but then she began to go out a lot and married a Sri Lankan here. We did not like that and that is why we dismissed her." She now employs two Ethiopian Muslim women as live-in domestic workers. They are not allowed to go outside. Radiya's family also employed a Sri Lankan domestic, but dismissed her because "she behaved as if she was the boss, and treated the children as if they were her own children." The fact that she was Hindu also played a role: "They worship cows and we did not like that." Ahmed Shamsan, the owner of a large company in Hodeidah and employer of two Indonesian women, said: "The Sri Lankan women we employed were not clean and they went out and things like that."

I referred above to the role of religion in the employment of migrant domestic workers in Yemen. Based on my interviews with Yemeni employers, I argue that religious closeness is not automatically a positive value in domestic work but only becomes important when other forms of social and cultural distance between employers and domestic workers are ensured. I encountered employers who stated that religion did not play a role in their preference for certain domestic workers. "It doesn't matter if she is Christian or Muslim, as long as she is God fearing" was a common answer. Others explicitly preferred Christian women as domestic workers, stereotyping them as "honest" and "clean." They sometimes had bad experiences with Muslim domestic workers who did not accept the hierarchical relationship between themselves and their employers. A third group of employers expressed a preference for Muslim women as domestic workers: "I feel more at ease when I work with a Muslim woman. I understand her and she understands me," explained a young employer. My research shows that this last group is growing and the number of Muslim domestic workers employed is increasing. Filipinas and Sri Lankan women, once the preferred domestic workers of upper-class families in Yemen, are now being replaced by Muslim workers, especially Indonesians and Ethiopians.

Yet, I argue that the preference for Muslim domestic workers has not so much to do with the fact that they are religiously close as with the fact that employers can exert more control and authority over them. Muslim women stereotypically accept being kept inside the house, especially when they are living in an unknown country where they do not speak the language. They do not request a day off and they accept leaving the house only in the company of their employers. "Indonesian women are quiet and obedient, and that is why Yemenis like them," was a statement I often heard. This perception about the character and mentality of Indonesian women should be understood with reference to the way in which Indonesian women are recruited and employed. Indonesian women are attractive as domestic workers because they come to Yemen via recruitment agencies — as opposed to utilizing informal or personal networks of domestic workers — thus restricting their access to other workers and the support structures that a ready-made network of workers might provide. This is particularly the case because an increasing number of middle- and upper-middle-class families are employing Indonesian domestic workers as status symbols, although they cannot really afford them. These families make use of informal recruitment agents, and often neglect to arrange the domestic worker's residence and work permits because of the costs involved. Some employers underpay their workers or postpone payment because they are short of money. These employers explain their preference for Indonesian domestic workers with reference to their Muslim identity, but my interviews lead me to conclude that they prefer them because they are cheaper and easier to control.

Conclusion

Although the number of migrant domestic workers in Yemen is relatively small compared to other countries in the Middle East, and the number of Asian domestic workers even smaller, their stories give interesting insights into the multiple ways in which they are positioned. This is particularly important because the dominant discourse on migrant domestic workers in the Middle East tends to present them as a homogeneous category, suffering from exploitation and abuse. Notwithstanding the fact that migrant domestic workers in Yemen also suffer human rights violations and few organizations have been established to defend the rights of this particular group of workers, the case of Asian domestic workers in Yemen shows how important it is to emphasize the varied experiences of migrant domestic workers.

As we have seen, Asian women are considered the top of the hierarchy of foreign domestic workers in Yemen, above women from Somalia and Ethiopia. This is because they are socially and culturally distant and because their presence strengthens the social status of their employers. They tend to be employed as live-in domestic workers and thus have limited freedom of movement. Practices of gender segregation and a relatively strict division between public and private spaces facilitate the exclusion of live-in domestic workers in the private sphere. Yet, there are important differences between Asian domestic workers in Yemen. Their patterns of mobility, their contacts with fellow countrywomen, their access to social support networks, and the possibilities they have to improve their living and working conditions differ greatly. In addition, employer preferences differ and change.

Migrant domestic workers come to Yemen in various ways. Filipinas often come via networks of relatives or friends who are already residing in the country. Some enter the country on a tourist visa and look later for work; others arrange for a contract and work permit prior to their arrival. Indian and Indonesian women almost always enter the country via (illegal) recruitment agencies. These agencies arrange women's migration with the assistance of "brokers" both in the country of origin and in Yemen. Indonesian women, in particular, enter Yemen via illegal recruitment agencies.

Women who come to Yemen via (illegal) recruitment agencies have no social network, and their chances of building one are slim because they are not allowed to leave the house of their employers unaccompanied. Women who enter Yemen via networks of relatives and friends benefit from the start from these networks and may become involved in community and religious activities. In addition, they often succeed in moving from live-in to live-out domestic work thanks to their social network. The increased demand for Indonesian domestic workers, my research demonstrates, is inspired not so much by a desire for religious closeness between employer and domestic worker as much as by the larger extent to which employers can exert control and authority over them. With no social network in Yemen Indonesian migrant women more easily accept their limited freedom of movement. The fact that they are Muslim is an additional advantage for employers, but not the main reason for their preference.

ACKNOWLEDGMENTS: Research was made possible with grants from the International Institute for the Study of Islam in the Modern World (ISIM) and WOTRO Science for Global Development in The Netherlands. The research was part of the research programme: "Migrant Domestic Workers: Transnational Relations, Families and Identities" (ISIM/University of Amsterdam). An earlier version of this article was presented in the workshop "Distant Divides and Intimate Connections: Migrant Domestic Workers in Asia" organized by Nicole Constable as part of the SSRC-Conference on Inter-Asian Connections held in Dubai (21-23 February 2008). I would like to thank Annelies Moors for her support throughout the research and Reinhilde König, the participants of the workshop, and especially Nicole Constable, for their valuable comments on earlier versions of this article.

❏

3. Of Maids and Madams

Sri Lankan Domestic Workers and Their Employers in Jordan

Elizabeth Frantz

FROM THE PALATIAL ABODES OF THE ULTRA-RICH in Amman's Abdoun district to modest apartment blocks in its middle-class neighborhoods, foreign domestic workers have become ubiquitous in the homes of well-to-do Jordanians. The Sri Lankan, Filipina, and Indonesian women who migrate to take up these jobs are part of an exodus triggered by the burgeoning demand for domestic workers in the Arab world since the mid 1970s. The Gulf States remain the most frequent destinations, but in recent years demand has boomed in Jordan, where at least 70,000 foreign domestic workers are now employed.[1] Based on this figure, at least one in every eleven Jordanian households employs a foreign domestic worker.[2] For the Jordanian elite, foreign housemaids have become socially indispensable.

The tiny desert kingdom of Jordan is less wealthy than its oil-endowed neighbors.[3] It has traditionally been thought of as a labor source country and home for Palestinian refugees rather than as a destination for migrant workers. But for the past three decades, it has maintained relatively relaxed policies toward the entry of guest workers, who have flocked to the country in increasing numbers to work in agriculture, the garment industry, construction, and domestic service.[4] The steady stream of Arab and Asian workers that cross Jordan's borders each year have received scant attention from scholars, and little is known about these migrant groups. This article aims to fill at least part of the gap by exploring the reasons for the increase in demand for foreign domestic workers, which is the most important type of employment for women migrants in Jordan and throughout the region.[5] Thereafter, it investigates Sri Lankan migrants' lives in Amman, suggesting that there are meaningful cohorts differentiated by age, length of stay, and place of residence that have distinctively different experiences of the host country. Next, the article discusses working conditions for Sri Lankan domestic workers and the politics at play in relationships between housemaids and the Arab families who employ them. Relations

between domestic workers and their masters are often described in terms of patron–client ties. However, I suggest that given the context of Jordan's *kafala*
(sponsorship) system, which legally binds foreign workers to their local sponsors, migrant housemaids and their Arab employers may be better understood
as having relations of dependency. In the final section, religious conversion
and the popularity of Christian holy sites among Sri Lankans of various faiths
are described. Given that migrants have limited legal protections and few opportunities for activism, faith-based groups play an important role by providing
vital support to migrants in need.

This article is based on ethnographic fieldwork in Jordan and Sri Lanka conducted between July 2006 and August 2008. The research involved semi-structured, in-depth interviews with employers and domestic workers. Life histories
were collected from Jordanians and Palestinians in Amman as a way of learning
about popular understandings of historical changes associated with household
work and family structures. Individual migration histories were elicited from returned and current Sri Lankan migrants in order to gain a deeper sense of their
lives prior to departure, motivations for migrating, experiences in Jordan, and
aspirations for the future. Interviews were also conducted with recruitment
agencies, embassy staff, labor ministry officials, lawyers, and nongovernmental
organizations (NGOs). The bulk of the research time, however, was spent doing
participant observation, consisting of house visits, sharing meals, attending social gatherings and religious services, and generally passing time with people in
their homes as regularly as possible.

Historical Perspectives on Domestic Service in Jordan

While migratory links between the Arab world and South Asia are long-standing,
massive labor migration to the Middle East did not begin until the mid 1970s,
when rising oil prices triggered a rapid influx of capital. Wealthy yet sparsely
populated Gulf States began recruiting large numbers of foreigners to work in
the construction and services sectors. As demand for male workers gradually at-
tenuated as oil revenues became less stable, the foreign workforce became increasingly feminized due to a growing demand for housemaids and nannies.
Migrants to the Middle East from Sri Lanka, Indonesia, and the Philippines are
now predominantly women domestic workers.

The Sri Lankan exodus to the Middle East was part of a deliberate labor export strategy promoted by the Sri Lankan government to generate foreign exchange. By the mid 1970s, facing declining export revenue, escalating inflation,
and rising unemployment, Sri Lanka's failing economy had grown increasingly
dependent on foreign aid and commercial borrowing. Following the election of
the economically liberal United National Party in 1977, overseas migration was
encouraged to alleviate the country's economic problems and reduce unemployment.[6] Sri Lankan labor gained a comparative advantage in the Arab world
because many other sending states, including Pakistan, Bangladesh, and India,
restricted female migration.[7] Sri Lanka is now one of the largest migrant exporting countries in the world, with an estimated 1.5 million Sri Lankans employed
abroad, 60 percent of whom are women domestic workers.[8]

In comparison with the many historical studies of servants in European and North American contexts, domestic workers are an under-researched topic in the scholarship of the Arab world. The genealogy of domestic service in the area that now comprises Jordan is difficult to trace due to a lack of source material. As Zilfi noted with reference to the Middle East from the sixteenth to the early nineteenth centuries, historical sources on women's work in general, let alone domestic employment, are few and far between, and most of what is known of servants derives from shari'a court registers.[9] Previously, paid domestic workers in Amman were predominantly poor Arab women from rural households and Palestinian refugees from the camps.[10]

Interviews with older residents of Amman suggested that the employment of women from the refugee camps and the Jordan Valley (Ghor) to assist with domestic work and child care, while common in the 1950s and 1960s, has since become rare. Two reasons are generally given for this. One is that it became harder to find women willing to do this type of work; the other is that once foreigners became available for domestic work, employers preferred them. Unlike locals, they were willing to work on a live-in basis for less pay.[11] Foreigners were also easier to control. A woman in her late sixties recalled her experiences employing domestic workers from the Jordan Valley.

> The women from Ghor were inconvenient. They'd want two or three days off. When they went, they'd take sugar and milk and olive oil and all sorts of things from the home back to their families. You have to spend like twenty JD [Jordanian dinars] on all of this stuff and pay for their transport. Her people would come with her when she came back to the house. So, people would rather have a Sri Lankeeyah. It's also very difficult to find girls from Ghor nowadays who are willing to do this work.[12]

Significant changes in the paid domestic workforce occurred as the Jordanian economy grew increasingly intertwined with the oil-based economic boom in the Gulf. Beginning in the early 1950s and throughout the following two decades, hundreds of thousands of Palestinians and Jordanians sought employment in the Gulf, furnishing the kingdom with a steady stream of remittances. Jordanian labor migration to the Gulf peaked from 1973 to 1985, and during these years the new revenue permitted Jordan to begin recruiting Asian workers. Men from Asian countries were sought to work in construction while Sri Lankan and Filipina women were hired as domestic workers. The total number of migrant domestic servants in Amman in 1984 was estimated at 8,000.[13] The number has grown considerably since then. The Ministry of Labor reports that there are now 70,000 domestic workers in Jordanian households, including 35,000 from Sri Lanka, 20,000 from Indonesia, and 15,000 from the Philippines.[14] Given that many migrants enter through unofficial channels and stay beyond the legal residence period, the actual population is certainly much greater. Interviews with recruiting agents and employers suggest that Sri Lankans and Filipinas were the first groups to begin coming to Jordan in the late 1970s and early 1980s but that greater numbers of Indonesians have been recruited in recent years, partly in response to employer demand for Muslim housemaids and because they are willing to work for lower salaries than Filipina workers, who now command a minimum monthly wage of US$400. In interviews, recruiting agencies regularly reported that they were unable to satisfy even half of the demand for domestic workers in Jordan because there were not enough applications from the three main source countries: Sri Lanka, Indonesia, and the Philippines. According to one agency, lower salaries and living standards in Jordan meant that many migrant domestic workers preferred to work in the Gulf States.

Understanding Employer Demand in Jordan

Recruiting agencies play an important role in shaping employers' perceptions of domestic workers. Agents often advise employers about which nationality of domestic worker would best suit their family based on stereotypes. They maintain that Filipinas are the best educated and most efficient, and they speak the most English, making them suitable for parents who would like their children to learn English. Sri Lankans and Indonesians, on the other hand, are reputed to be harder workers, suitable for large homes with lots of work, and are less apt to demand independence and push for certain rights, for example, to have a mobile phone or to go out on weekends.[15] One agency owner shared his observations about the nature of employer demand:

> Families without much money, who have little resources, always want someone with no experience. They think, "She'll take what she gets." The most common problems with Filipinas are about a day off and a mobile. They want these things. Indonesians, because they are Muslim, don't believe in a day off. They have the same culture as the employers. With very conservative clients, I don't recommend that they get Filipina girls because in the Philippines, they have a Western life[style] and have a hard time adjusting to life here. Here, people's idea of a domestic worker is that I own you. You can sleep when I sleep. You eat when I tell you to eat. You cannot even open the window or go out unless I say so. So, I don't tell them to get a maid from the Philippines. One from Sri Lanka or Indonesia would be better. Although the contracts say that the worker should have a day's rest, that she is entitled to full payment, there is a very big gap in families' mentalities about these things. How a worker will be treated depends on where her dice fall. Some get lucky and are given gifts, clothes are bought for them, and they are taken out on their birthdays. Others are not even allowed to look out the window. So, we like to make good matches.[16]

Recruiting agencies also routinely recommend that employers confiscate workers' passports and prevent them from venturing outside.

The market for paid domestic workers in Jordan is partially underpinned by economic and social transformations linked to the spread of neoliberal economic models. While Jordan has fewer resources and historically has been more economically homogenous than many of its neighbors, an influx of petro dollars from the Gulf and International Monetary Fund–brokered structural adjustment programs introduced in 1989 have provided significant financial gains for some while increasing hardships for others.[17] The kingdom's growing integration with global capitalism has been accompanied by increases in the volume and forms of consumption. As Beal's work on Amman's upper classes illustrates, conspicuous consumption, particularly of items for the home, plays a crucial role in the construction and reproduction of elite status and identity.[18] Domestic service is part of this broader consumption pattern.

A number of changes in lifestyle among wealthier segments of society have led to a shift from the reliance on unpaid family labor to the employment of paid domestic workers. This is particularly evident at stages in the family developmental cycle when there is a need for child care and care of the elderly. Changes in household composition and cross-generational dynamics have meant that domestic workers are increasingly sought to perform work that members of the extended family might have done in the past. The average household size has shrunk by more than 15 percent over the past three decades, from 6.7 persons in 1979 to 5.4 in 2004.[19] This decline is a result of falling fertility levels as well as a greater incidence of nuclear household types. Examining changes in Jordanian family life from 1961 to 1981, Ghazwi suggested that although extended family households were once the norm, they are now rare, having been replaced by conjugal units.[20] The majority of respondents in his survey of 250 households in Irbid, Amman, and the village of Al Wahadna resided in nuclear households.[21] To explain this trend, Ghazwi cited new preferences for independence, an increasing tendency for married sons to establish separate homes, and a wider pattern of urbanization that contributed to the breakup of households as younger family members moved out of family homes to work in urban areas.[22]

A domestic worker in Amman, Jordan, holds one of the young twins she looks after.

The majority of employers interviewed for this research resided in nuclear households. This does not necessarily mean that people interact less with the extended family. As Othman has rightly pointed out, Jordanian families continue to have strong social and economic ties with wider kin.[23] Indeed, although many now live in nuclear family units, a strong preference for living near or next to extended family members remains. The ideal living arrangement traditionally has been and remains for a couple to build their home on the ground floor and gradually add stories vertically for their children as they marry and establish their own families. While the importance of the extended family should not be underestimated, there is an increasing preference for the privacy and independence that nuclear residential structures afford. Several young Jordanian women said in interviews that one precondition for a marriage proposal is a promise that the couple will have their own home, free from nagging and opinionated mothers-in-law. Interviewees also remarked that the ability to have a domestic worker care for children allows them to avoid having to live with their mothers-in-law, who in the past would have contributed to this task.[24] Hiring a full-time domestic worker, who may be paid as little as US$125 per month, also may be a more convenient and cheaper option than a private nursery, which typically costs well over US$150 per month.

A preference for privacy and independence is not limited to the young. Im Munzer, a widow in her seventies who employs a domestic worker from Indonesia, said she would never dream of living with her son.[25] His children make too much of a racket, and she would not be able to rest if they all lived in the same house. Beyond the issue of privacy, many elderly employers interviewed reported that they first decided to hire domestic help after a debilitating illness or accident. Even if their children lived nearby, they needed the sort of round-the-clock care that might prompt their European or North American counterparts to move into a retirement home. Although retirement homes exist in Jordan, they are generally unpopular. Hiring foreign caretakers is the preferred alternative.

Those Jordanians who are either too old or ill to take care of themselves are permitted to hire non-Jordanian domestic workers at rates subsidized by the government. The Ministry of Social Development exempts all elderly and/or disabled persons who are unable to care for themselves from paying work permit fees for domestic workers they employ. The numbers receiving these subsidies are surprisingly high. According to the Ministry of Social Development, 12,340 domestic workers were brought to the kingdom through these subsidies in 2006.[26] This is out of a grand total of roughly 30,000 domestic workers issued residence permits in Jordan that year. Thus, more than one-third of the domestic workers brought legally to Jordan in 2006 were in this category. The fact that the state facilitates the recruitment of foreign domestic workers through labor legislation and targeted subsidies effectively keeps child care and care of the elderly firmly within the realm of the individual family. The economic impact of this policy is schizophrenic: On the one hand, it encourages privatization by keeping care of the elderly and children within the family, yet at the same time the subsidies contradict the international financial community's mandate that Jordan reduce its social handouts.

Another factor contributing to the market for paid domestic work relates to women's employment. Studies from other locales have suggested that domestic workers fulfill a role that allows middle-class men and women to avoid conflicts surrounding the gendered division of labor.[27] Whether this is the case in Jordan is debatable. According to most informants interviewed for this research, housework remains unquestionably a woman's responsibility. Women's labor force participation rates remain low in Jordan compared to other lower-middle-income countries and even in comparison to the rest of the region. But increasing numbers of Jordanian women are taking up employment outside the home. According to World Bank estimates, female workforce participation rose from just over 10 percent in the 1950s to 27.8 percent in 2000.[28] While the ability to employ a domestic worker may not necessarily enable women to work who would not have otherwise, it appears that domestic workers do allow working women more time for leisure and to spend with their children.[29] Demand for domestic workers also reflects changing attitudes toward childhood and the importance of education. Children who a generation ago might have been expected to help with household chores are now encouraged to devote more time to studying and participating in after-school activities. Muna, a 38-year-old mother of six who is the principal of a kindergarten and in the evenings studies for a master's degree, illustrated these points when she explained her decision to hire a Sri Lankan domestic.

I have thirteen brothers and sisters. Growing up, everyone helped with all the responsibilities in the house. We took turns. We had shifts for the kitchen, the bedroom, doing the laundry, helping mom with everything so she didn't do all the work herself. And also the boys were helping. When I started my family, I was doing it the same way as my mom. But when the children got older, I thought these chores would distract them from their studies and even from having fun. I don't want to have arguments with them, to have misunderstandings, or to harm them by pushing them to help me. That's why we decided to have the maid. Because I thought it would be more relaxing for everybody…. I think that ten years ago, some had them [housemaids]. But now, everybody has them. Especially in the capital. The reasons are that women are working and they have money. If a woman works outside of the house, when she comes home, she must do the same work in the house whether she has a job or not. So, women think that if they work outside, they might as well pay for a maid from their salary so that when they come home they can be more relaxed. The mentality of the Arab or Eastern man is not to help in the house. So, she helps herself.[30]

Muna was one of several female employers who reported paying domestic workers out of her own salary. Interviews with employers suggest that when there are disagreements over hiring a maid, husbands are more apt to object. A number of mothers reported that their husbands and sons, some as young as eleven, refused to eat food cooked by a maid or to drink coffee or tea that she had prepared. For example, Im Leith, a 43-year-old mother of four, told me that although her family has employed a maid for more than seven years, her husband has never liked the idea.[31] He insists that the maid leave the room when he enters and forbids her to clean in front of him. When asked why she thought he felt this way, she said he had never gotten used to the idea of having a stranger in the house. A male interviewee commented that although his wife wanted to hire a maid, he refused. "I go out and work all day. Her job is to clean and put food on the table. What will she do if we get a maid?"[32] Such attitudes on the part of men may be an attempt to keep wives in traditional roles. But they also speak to a real sense felt by employers that inviting a foreign worker into the home entails an unwanted invasion of privacy. Since housework in Jordan is still considered women's work, it is logical that women are more willing to sacrifice their family privacy than men.

The "need" for domestic help also relates to the notion of leisure and heightened expectations about homemaking and hygiene. As Forte's work on the expansion of consumption among Palestinians in Israel and the West Bank shows, expectations for hospitality and cleanliness have escalated in recent decades. While women's labor in the home, cleaning and baking bread, used to play a central role in defining household status, that prestige is now connoted by women's ability to buy and use "modern" goods as well as by their enjoyment of leisure activities.[33] As Gill has noted of Bolivia, domestic workers help employers maintain an appearance of leisured gentility while also facilitating a convenient, "modern" lifestyle.[34]

Another important factor influencing the demand for foreign domestic workers in Jordan is the fact that migrants are available to work under conditions that are generally favorable to employers. Labor migrants in the Arab world are almost exclusively guest workers hired on temporary contracts through the kafala (sponsorship) system, in which migrants must have local sponsors in order to obtain entry visas, residence and work permits. The *kafeel,* or sponsor, who is also often the employer, assumes full legal and financial responsibility and must repatriate the migrant at the end of the contract period. Migrants are prohibited from changing employers without the sponsor's permission. Two practices augment the employer's power: they can threaten workers with deportation at any time, and they routinely confiscate workers' passports and other identity documents.[35] Thus, the kafala system effectively immobilizes the workforce, blocking the formation of a competitive labor market.[36] Most Arab states, including Jordan, Saudi Arabia,[37] Kuwait,[38] and Lebanon,[39] deliberately construct the household as a private sphere outside the scope of government regulation. This means that people who work within it have no legal recourse in case of mistreatment or nonpayment of wages. Domestic workers are specifically excluded from the labor law,[40] and all noncitizens are forbidden to strike or join unions.[41]

The right to freedom of association is highly restricted for Jordanians as well, and a large percentage of the local labor force, including public school teachers, lacks union representation. As I will argue later, it is within this context of limited legal rights that the ability to develop personalized relationships of dependency with employers becomes a key strategy.

Migrant Experiences in Jordan

Sri Lankan women who migrate to the Middle East are predominantly Sinhalese and Muslim (Moor and Malay), with fewer numbers of Tamils.[42] While in the late 1970s migrants originated primarily from the urban areas surrounding Sri Lanka's capital, Colombo,[43] they now come from all over the island, with the western districts of Colombo, Kurunegala, and Gampaha recording the highest numbers of departures.[44] Most are married and between twenty-five and thirty-nine years old.[45]

In Jordan, Sri Lankan domestic helpers can be divided into three main cohorts. These cohorts are differentiated not on the basis of age but by length of stay and place of residence (whether they live on their own or with an employer). They have distinctively different attitudes and experiences in the host country.[46] I prefer the term "cohorts" over the concept of a migrant "community" because it better explains the heterogeneity of working and living conditions, pay, outlook on life in Jordan, and homeward orientation. This framework is also better because the isolated nature of their work means many Sri Lankan domestic workers do not convey a sense of shared experience with other migrants.[47]

The first cohort is comprised of those employed on two-year contracts whose stay in the country is limited to one- or two-year stints. They reside with their employers and, as per employers' instructions, have limited interaction with the outside world. The vast majority are not allowed outside the home without being accompanied by a member of the employer's family, do not have a full day's rest each week, and are discouraged from communicating with other migrants or having romantic relationships with men. Trips outside of their employers' homes are usually restricted to running errands, escorting children to and from school, or attending social gatherings involving the employers' friends and family. Manoja's personal story reflects the broader experience of her cohort:

> Manoja is a 21-year-old woman from a village near Kalutara who worked for an elderly Palestinian woman in the district of Jebel Ashrafieh. Her mother had worked in Lebanon when she was growing up, and both of her parents are now unemployed. At the age of nineteen, Manoja came to Jordan in the hopes of earning money for her dowry. I first met her in Amman at a Christmas party for Sri Lankan migrants organized by a church group. Her employer had escorted her to the party and remained by her side until it was time to leave. This was Manoja's first interaction with other Sri Lankans in Jordan, and she knew none of the other migrants in attendance. I later visited her and her employer at their home in Jebel Ashrafieh, a lower-income neighborhood in Amman. Manoja told me she earned US$100 per month. Aside from her first two months' pay, which was deducted from her salary by the recruitment agency in Amman that placed her, she had saved all of her earnings and sent them to her mother. When I interviewed Manoja in early 2007, I asked how she felt about living in Amman. "I had a good experience," she said. "I am happy I came. When I

came, I didn't know any English. Now I can understand. I learned many things. How to clean such a big house, take care of money, take care of myself. But I want to go back and be with my family. I don't like being so far away."[48]

In June 2007, after completing her two-year contract, Manoja returned to Sri Lanka. I visited her at her parents' home near Kalutara in September 2007. Only weeks after she returned, her parents arranged a marriage with a man in her village. Manoja was excited for me to meet him and take a ride in the trishaw with which he earned a living. Much of Manoja's remittances had been spent on clothing, jewelry, and home furnishings for her husband's family, with whom she has lived since marriage. The fact that she had amassed these assets greatly enhanced her marriage prospects. Her limited mobility outside of her employer's home in Jordan had meant that Manoja was able to save considerably more than she might have otherwise.

The second cohort is comprised of domestic workers with longer periods of employment in Jordan, some for as many as twenty years, who also reside with their employers. They are typically fluent in Arabic or English and often have managed to win certain privileges from their employers by building trust over time. These perks may include higher salaries and being permitted to leave their employers' homes unaccompanied to attend church or migrant gatherings or to go on shopping trips. They have often developed friendships with other migrants in the same cohort but usually do not start conjugal relationships. Many of their social activities still take place in their employers' homes or those of their friends' employers.

Kamini is a 39-year-old mother of two from Panadura. When I first met her, she had been living in Jordan for eight years and had gone home to Sri Lanka only once in that time. Her husband, a former bus driver, had a hernia five years earlier and had not worked since, making Kamini the sole breadwinner. Her husband has a gambling and drinking addiction, so she sends her earnings to her daughter, who is twenty-two and spends the bulk of the money on the construction of the family's new home. The house that she has never seen is Kamini's life's work. When I interviewed her, she had spent US$6,000 of her remittance money to buy the land and lay the foundation. She had also borrowed an additional US$2,000 from the bank. She expects to work in Jordan for at least five more years to complete the house. Kamini earns US$250 per month working for an elderly Palestinian woman in the upper-middle-class neighborhood of Shmeisani. She also works one day a week for her employer's daughter, earning an additional $20 each time. Kamini accompanies her employer on all of her outings. She has two Sri Lankan friends who work in the same apartment block, and the three sometimes take short trips downtown to buy small gifts or cards to send back to their families in Sri Lanka. Otherwise, they rarely venture far from their employers' homes. Buying land and building a home is a primary reason many women decide to work abroad, and as Kamini's case illustrates, doing so often takes many years. Like Kamini,

A Sri Lankan nun visits a domestic worker and the elderly woman who employs her in Amman, Jordan.

many of the women in this cohort remain focused on their economic goals and their eventual return to Sri Lanka.

The third cohort is comprised of domestic workers who reside independently of their employers and are commonly referred to as "part-timers" or, in Sinhala, "*elli aya*" ("outside people"). They rent apartments or single rooms, often among other migrants in low-income neighborhoods. Some work full time for a single employer, while others work on an hourly or daily basis as housekeepers or office cleaners for multiple employers. Women in this cohort tend to have been in Amman for many years and speak fluent Arabic. They can make more than two to three times what live-in domestic workers earn in a month, particularly if they manage to secure coveted jobs with foreigners. The jobs are not always steady, however, and because they reside on their own, they have to pay for their own living expenses. Most of those who live independently initially came to Jordan on two-year contracts as live-in housemaids, but either decided to live on their own at the end of the contract period or ran away from their employers' homes prematurely. As many as 25,000 migrant domestic workers in Jordan live independently and work on a freelance basis.[49] Another source estimated that as many as half of the 40,000 Sri Lankan women working in Jordan fall into this category.[50] Employers and recruitment agencies regularly seize migrants' passports upon arrival, so those who abscond from their employers' homes often must leave their identity documents behind. According to the Sri Lankan Embassy in Amman, as many as one hundred Sri Lankan women run away each month, with approximately five per day seeking refuge at the embassy. Similar figures have been reported by the Philippines Embassy. The Indonesian Embassy receives an average of six to eight runaways per day.[51]

Other women in this cohort were helped to come to Jordan by family members or friends already working in the kingdom. Residence permits are regularly arranged for such family members or for migrants whose visas have expired by paying a Jordanian to act as a sponsor and complete the necessary paperwork. Doing so is expensive, costing at least 310 JD (US$440) for each year-long residence permit in addition to fees for the recruitment agency and for insurance and medical exams, plus an ample gratuity for the sponsor. It is also risky. I heard countless tales of migrants who paid large sums for visas that never materialized. The fact that their legal status in the country depends on having a local sponsor makes migrants vulnerable to such exploitation. Foreigners must pay the Ministry of Interior 1.5 JD (US$2) for each day they stay in the country past the period permitted by their visa, meaning that some migrants owe thousands of dinars in accumulated fines. While overstay fees are intended to deter workers from staying past the legal period of residence, they often have the opposite effect, keeping migrants in the country longer than they wish because they cannot afford to pay them. So, many migrants stay on, working until they are either too old or too sick to continue. If they need to return to Sri Lanka urgently, in many cases their only option is to turn themselves in to the police and wait in prison until they are deported.

Despite their precarious legal status, women in this cohort have more opportunities to socialize with other migrants. And while some felt trapped in Jordan due to the overstay fees, others had no plans to return to Sri Lanka anytime soon. Migrants in this cohort frequent stores in downtown Amman selling Sri Lankan music, clothing, and food. On Fridays, Sri Lankans in this cohort organize parties and outings to the Dead Sea and Aqaba. They also orchestrate musical shows, recruiting musicians from Sri Lanka to perform in front of crowds of hundreds of migrants, many traveling by bus from garment factories in the free-trade zones outside of the capital. Tickets for these events cost as much as 7 JD (US$10), making them lucrative ventures for their organizers. Many women in this cohort also operate informal revolving credit schemes ("*seetu*" in Sinhala) whereby members make monthly contributions toward a common fund. Once the fund reaches a certain amount, it is handed over to each member in turn. Such saving schemes are common in Sri Lanka and require a good deal of trust among the members. They don't always work, and stories of members disappearing with the money are common. Although domestic work is the chief source of income for most women in this cohort, many supplement their incomes with self-employment projects, such as making "hoppers," a Sri Lankan delicacy made of rice flour, and selling them out of their homes or at shops downtown. Gambling and prostitution are other sources of revenue for members of this cohort.

Women in this cohort have more romantic relationships than their live-in counterparts and often marry other Sri Lankans or men from Pakistan, India, Egypt, or Jordan, amongst other nationalities. These relationships can be controversial because they sometimes involve men and women who already have spouses back home. During the period of fieldwork, a Sri Lankan newspaper reporter came to Amman to write an article about Sri Lankan women who have relationships with men of other nationalities while working abroad. The article provoked an uproar in Amman, where many women with second marriages were furious that some of their friends had spoken to the reporter. In their eyes, such stories, while true, damaged the image of Sri Lankan migrants."

Delani is a 46-year-old woman from Ja-Ela who has been in Jordan for sixteen years. She lives in Muhajireen, an area named for its migrant population, along with her 25-year-old daughter, her husband, who is a hotel cook from Bangladesh, and her husband's son from a previous marriage, who works in a garment factory. Delani left Sri Lanka in 1991, when her two children, a son and daughter, were twelve and ten. She left, she says, because her husband drank heavily, was abusive, and was unable to support the family. She placed the children in the care of her husband's mother and came to Amman on a two-year contract to work as a live-in domestic worker. She worked for the same family for six years, but when they moved to the United States, leaving her jobless, Delani decided to stay in Amman and live on her own. When her daughter turned twenty, she brought her to Jordan and found work for her, also on a live-out basis. Delani returns to Sri Lanka every two years to visit her mother and son, for whom she has bought a track of land and built a small house. She has no contact with her first husband, whom she never divorced. She suffers from severe back pain and can no longer do the heavy cleaning required of a domestic worker. She makes a living as a seamstress, working several days a week in a shop sewing sequins and other decorations on blouses, and tailoring clothes on her own sewing machine at home.

One of the dangers in using the concept of cohorts lies in underemphasizing the diversity among members of the same cohort. In fact, there is a great deal of variation within the cohorts, particularly within the third cohort with respect to income and living and working conditions. Shiroma, for example, worked for several years as a nanny for a French family. When she lost her job, she asked for my help to find a new one. She had several conditions. She refused to do heavy work outside of the house, such as cleaning windows or washing cars. She would not work for a homeowner on a once-per-week basis because she might be expected to do a whole week's worth of cleaning in one day. She also preferred non-Jordanian, Western families and refused to work in homes with young children. Migrants in this cohort are able, far more than those in the first cohort, to refuse particular types of work and influence the terms of their employment. But their work is also more unreliable. Other part-timers I knew had not been as lucky as Shiroma and struggled to make ends meet, with daily wages barely covering their living expenses. They also tended to be more vulnerable in times of sickness than workers who lived with their employers and often had their medical care paid for by their employers.

Despite this variation, these cohort categories are relevant to the ways in which migrants identify themselves vis-à-vis other Sri Lankan domestic workers. Migrants in the third cohort emphasize the fact that they have more freedom than their "live-in" counterparts. Migrants in the second cohort, on the other hand, express a distrust of those living "outside." Many of those I knew said they

Elizabeth Frantz

Domestic workers enjoy a weekend picnic on Mount
Nebo, Amman, Jordan.

were willing to trade personal liberties for the financial rewards of living with their employers. They often invoked images of an idealized migrant who remains committed to her family and focused on her goals, does not spend money frivolously (e.g., on taxis, clothes, and jewelry), sends all of her earnings home, and does not have affairs with men. The discourse about "good" and "bad" behavior narrated by migrant women resembled patriarchal discourses of kinship common in Sri Lanka, with the idea of the sacrificial wife/mother/daughter who slaves away for her husband/children/parents as an important ideal.[52] Migrants also frequently reproduced Jordanian employers' discourses about "correct" behavior and propriety for housemaids when talking about other migrants. Those who ran away from their employers, lived independently, and had boyfriends were seen as disloyal and even dangerous. Gossip was frequently exchanged about part-timers indulging in inappropriate behavior, from prostitution and gambling to drinking alcohol and smoking cigarettes. Some members of the second cohort told me they avoided involvement with "part-timers" because they reminded them of the things they didn't have or tempted them to spend money or get involved in other migrants' financial problems. Members of the first cohort were generally isolated while migrants in the other two cohorts tended to form friendships with members of their own group.

There were, however, important forms of cooperation and interaction amongst migrants from different cohorts, particularly in times of hardship. Two Sri Lankan and one Indonesian domestic worker were interviewed at Prince Hamzeh Hospital in Amman after having sustained serious injuries falling from windows they had been cleaning. When other migrants learned of their situation, they formed an ad hoc support group, taking turns visiting the hospital to feed, bathe, and talk to the patients and help them call their families at home. In another instance of migrant solidarity, a group of women formed the Sri Lankan Christian and Buddhist Community Association, which consisted mainly of domestic workers who lived independently but also included some who lived with their employers. The group elected officers and met on a monthly basis to organize social and religious activities. If a member has to return to Sri Lanka urgently, the others donate or lend money to help with travel costs. Based on interviews and participant observation, it appeared that while friendships occasionally developed between domestic workers of different nationalities, such alliances were rare. Sri Lankan migrants tended to socialize with other Sri Lankans, and there were few signs of cross-national advocacy or organization.[53]

Mistress–Maid Relations and Dependency

With few exceptions, migrants in the second cohort were more economically successful than those in cohort three, who lived independently. This is in part because they didn't have to pay for their own accommodation and food, and therefore could save more. They also often chose to reside with their employers and to have fewer social ties within the migrant community, because they were focused on the goal of eventual return to Sri Lanka. But another important factor, as I outline in this section, is that housemaids who reside with their employers are better positioned to develop relations of dependency, which ensure greater financial security over time. These relations are constructed and maintained on the basis of highly affective, personal ties rather than contractual rights and obligations, but, as I will argue, are distinct from patron–client ties for several reasons.

A discourse of dependency is key to employers' understandings of domestic workers' rights and responsibilities. Employers demand deference and faithful service from domestic workers in exchange for material benefits. Protective, authoritative relations vis-à-vis housemaids are justified ideologically through the idiom of kinship. As has been described in accounts of domestic work in other locales, employers in Jordan claim fictive kinship with servants, referring to them as daughters and instructing them to call employers by the parental titles "baba" and "mama." This patriarchal discourse creates affectionate, familial relations that bind servants and employers, thereby naturalizing uneven power relations and affirming the employer's superiority.[54]

Domestic workers are often given detailed and strict rules about phone use, clothing, when and how often to bathe, and which food to eat when and where. One Sri Lankan interviewee expressed exasperation at being required by her "madam" to shampoo the living room carpet several times a week and wash the kitchen floor no less than three times a day. According to employers, such strict controls are necessary to keep domestic workers "in line." Employers say that when housemaids are treated too well or don't have enough work, they become lazy and start to transgress boundaries. One employer explains the need for stringent rules:

> One of the first Filipinas we had, I treated like a daughter. She had plenty of freedom, and I didn't ask questions. I was too easy with her. One day, we went to the pool, and she came along and wore this little bikini, and everyone told me, "What are you doing? What are you letting her do to your family?" I didn't understand what they meant. When she left, it was not on good terms. She had been lying to me…. Before, I didn't ask any questions if she was gone from the house. But starting in the last three years, I've been more strict with them….
>
> I used to think this was extreme — a friend of mine has so many rules for her maid. When the bus comes to pick up her children, if the maid isn't

outside with them, ready for the bus when it comes, she takes five dollars away from her. I used to think this was crazy. No way. You can't just have a contract on the one hand and then make up your own new rules when the girl comes to the house. But now I see. This makes some sense.[55]

Extreme discipline and behavioral control also result from the anxiety many Jordanian families feel about having a stranger in the home. Many talk about domestic workers as an endless source of problems, a burden that must be endured rather than a luxury. Disputes frequently arise as a result of cultural and linguistic differences that lead to misunderstandings between housemaids and their employers. Employers also express concerns that, as sponsors, they are legally and financially responsible if a migrant gets in trouble, for example if she becomes pregnant. Employers also have fears about domestic workers organizing robberies or revealing unflattering details about them. Finally, Jordanian employers typically pay 1,500 JD (US$2,118) or more in fees to bring a domestic worker to the country. These fees are paid to recruitment agencies before the worker arrives. If there is a dispute between the employer and domestic worker or if the domestic runs away, agencies usually do not return the money. These recruitment costs confer a sense of ownership and help the employer justify imposing a heavy workload. They also make employers reluctant to allow domestic workers to go out or communicate with other migrants, fearing that they may be tempted to run away or demand higher salaries. However, the forced confinement and heavy workloads often have the reverse effect, encouraging migrants to abscond.

One employer, Rana, employs a Filipina domestic worker whom she does not permit out of the house alone. She recalled her memories of the woman who worked in her family's home when she was growing up, noting that she had more freedom:

One of them stayed for seven years, starting from when I was four. I just loved her. She was so wonderful. She was a very hard worker. She used to have many privileges that we don't now allow our maids to have because she worked so well and we trusted her. She had a day off and used to go out of the house. She even had a mobile.[56]

When I asked Rana why the previous employee had these privileges while her current domestic workers do not, she responded:

Because she stayed with us for longer, and she had become one of the family. In the beginning, when the girls first come from the agency, we treat them as one of the family. If she is honest, doesn't lie, doesn't steal, is loyal, and if she prays.... You see, I'm not a very religious person, but somehow I like it when they are religious and pray. I can see that they have a belief in God. If someone doesn't believe in God, they will not do bad things because they have religious principles.

I then asked Rana why she had decided not to allow her current domestic worker to leave the house.

Because, *yaani* [I mean, um], I'm her sponsor. If she goes out and hurts someone, or kills someone, they'll come to me. If she gets raped, I'm responsible. She can't speak Arabic. I'm afraid of what could happen to her.

If she goes out of the house, for sure, I'll not have her in the house again, because if she did it once, she can do it again. There is a community of Filipina women who have been here for a long time. I think if she goes out and finds them, it will reflect badly on her attitude. The girl who was here before had an aunt here who is married to a Jordanian. I knew this aunt, and because I trusted the girl, I let her go out once a month to stay with her aunt. But this girl I have now has no family to visit. She doesn't know anyone in the country. She doesn't know how to take a taxi. Where will she go? If I let her go out alone, she could get raped. She could get ripped off at a store. She doesn't know how to do anything.

Rana's comments illustrate the fact that a housemaid's willingness to curtail her own personal freedoms is crucial to her ability to secure her employer's trust and, in turn, financial rewards.

They also suggest that developing trust is a lengthy process, and that basic privileges are not a right, but something that must be earned. Chandra, a Sri Lankan woman who has lived with and worked for a family in the Jebel Webdeh district of Amman for twelve years, told me, as many domestic workers did, of how she had to "win" her freedom from her employer.

When I first came, she didn't like my long hair and made me cut it. I cried and cried and was so ashamed. But time passed, and I got my way. I had to fight for things, like for them to pay for my toothpaste and shampoo and things. They didn't want to pay for these in the beginning. And I had to teach them, even though I am a housemaid, you must speak to me in a nice way. I am a human being.[57]

A year ago, Chandra's mother fell ill in Sri Lanka and her family pawned the deed to their home to pay for her medical treatment. As the interest compounded on their loan, the moneylender threatened to keep the deed, leaving the family with the possibility of becoming homeless. Despite her long time abroad, Chandra had continued to support her parents and felt obliged to help them. Her employer loaned her US$1,500, which she sent to her family to pay off the debt. Chandra's case illustrates how long-term, live-in service for a single employer can afford some workers the resources with which to respond to crises at home. Given that they are generally regarded with suspicion and mistrust, housemaids who prove themselves to be loyal and trustworthy become coveted commodities, and employers may be generous with salaries, gifts, and even loans in order to avoid losing them.

Such support is not guaranteed, however. Problems arise when employers fail to live up to their end of the bargain in the eyes of their domestics, as Arundathie's case illustrates. I met Arundathie in her village in Sri Lanka a year after she had returned from working in Jordan. Arundathie recounted her experience working for a military doctor and his wife, an English teacher. A year after Arundathie had begun working for them, the couple planned a trip to Australia to visit relatives. Arundathie wanted them to take her along, but they refused. "They were rich. It would have been nothing for them to take me. But they were greedy [lobai]. They wanted all their money for themselves," she said.[58] Arundathie asked to be sent to Sri Lanka while they were on holiday. They declined, instead placing her in the home of the husband's sister, who had recently had a baby. "That house was not familiar to me. The madam was rude. She expected me to look after the baby and clean. She wanted me to wash the stairs in the apartment building every day. Just taking care of the baby, I barely had time to eat. I started losing weight." In protest, Arundathie refused to do any cleaning, saying that she was unable to both care for the baby and do the housework. Her employers eventually returned from Australia, and Arundathie resumed her usual household duties in their home. At the end of her two-year contract, Arundathie returned to Sri Lanka. At her departure, they gave her the rest of her salary, which had been US$100 per month, in addition to an extra $50. Arundathie was furious. "I had to ask them for my salary in dollars. They weren't going to give me dollars at first. They didn't give me any gifts. No jewelry. No clothes. I gave them two years of loyal work. But they were heartless [*bengin netti,* or without feelings]. In vain I sacrificed everything for them." Arundathie expected *personal* gifts in exchange for her *personal* work and sacrifice. She felt betrayed at the end of her employment, but there was little she could do to influence the situation.

Employers, on the other hand, have greater power over housemaids who fail to meet expectations. The many cases reported in the media of migrant domestic workers who have been sent home without pay illustrate that employers have ultimate power.[59] As the numbers of "runaways" living independently in Amman suggest, migrant housemaids are not always powerless in rejecting the demands of their employers. But in most cases, their only recourse entails illegality.

Relationships between domestic workers and their employers have been characterized elsewhere in terms of patron–client bonds.[60] Following Scott, the patron–client structure can be understood as an exchange relationship "involving a largely instrumental friendship in which an individual of higher socioeconomic status (patron) uses his own influence and resources to provide protection or benefits, or both, for a person of lower status (client) who, for his part, reciprocates by offering general support and assistance, including personal services, to the patron."[61] This concept has some appeal given the interpersonal, affective, and dependent relations formed between domestic workers and their employers. However, the patron–client model has limited explanatory power for the situation of *foreign* domestic workers, particularly "guest" workers who are bonded to their employers by the kafala sponsorship system. Under this system, the worker's legal status is entirely dependent on the employer and she is restricted to the realm of the employer's household. She has no choice of patron. This system diverges from accounts of traditional patron–client relations in Latin America and the Mediterranean region in which the patron must bargain for the relations of the client within a wider political and economic arena, competing with other patrons to retain clients. The kafala system prevents such competition by prohibiting the free circulation of labor. Through it, employers are endowed by the state with enough coercive power over their migrant employees that the need for patrons to broker for their services is eliminated. Although the social ties that develop between Asian housemaids and their Arab employers often resemble patron–client relations, and domestic workers often seek and obtain patronage from their employers, the power imbalance is such that the workers may be better understood as captive labor, or temporary domestic slaves bonded for the period of their employment.[62]

Religious Activity and Faith-Based Networks

One of the ways many Sri Lankan migrants cope with the difficulties of life in Jordan is through religious activity. In 2006, an informal association of Sri Lankan Roman Catholics raised funds to bring a Sri Lankan priest to Jordan. He is the second Sri Lankan priest to serve in Jordan in recent years. The priest now holds bible study classes and says a Sinhala-language Mass each Friday. Between fifty and one hundred Sri Lankans attend the weekly services. Migrants also attend other churches throughout the city, including evangelical Christian churches. Others travel outside of Amman to a Greek Orthodox church with a shrine to the Virgin Mary in Madaba and to a church with a shrine to St. George in Salt. Buddhists, Hindus, and Catholics alike patronize these shrines, principally to make and fulfill vows. By performing a vow ("*bara*" in Sinhala), a person puts him or herself in the care of a particular saint, promising that if the saint fulfills a wish, the petitioner will repay them. Repayments typically come in the form of an offering of money, jewelry, or other valuable items, lighting candles, giving a *dane* (alms, often in the form of a large meal), or donating money or staples to the poor. The vows made by housemaids in Jordan are primarily petitions for help with mundane issues — to regularize one's visa status, obtain a good job, bring a relative to Jordan, cure an illness, or solve family problems in Sri Lanka. Repayments tend to be small and private, involving the lighting of candles, fasting for a few days, and/or giving a small amount of money or gold as an offering.

Several factors explain the popularity of Christian religious sites among Sri Lankan migrants of various faiths in Jordan. One is that prejudice against Buddhists and Hindus is common amongst employers. Many Jordanian employers express a distrust of Buddhists and Hindus and prefer to hire housemaids who are Muslim or Christian. Aware of the stereotypes, some migrants wear crosses around their necks and say they are Catholic in order to get jobs. A second factor is that many employers only allow domestic workers out of the house to go to church, assuming that they won't get into trouble there. Attending weekly church services provides migrants with a rare opportunity for free time away from work. Going to church is also an affordable way to socialize with other Sri Lankans. A third reason is that a Catholic organization called Caritas and several concerned priests and nuns provide some of the only humanitarian assistance available to migrant domestic workers in Amman. Evangelical missionaries also organize small-scale assistance for migrants. Faith-based networks collect money for migrants in need of medical care, for plane tickets to return to Sri Lanka in emergencies, or to regularize visas. In a number of cases, Caritas has been successful in persuading the government to forgive migrants' overstay fees so that they can return home. Caritas also provides medical care and legal advice to migrants. Affiliating oneself with these groups by attending church increases the likelihood of receiving aid. The final and most important factor is that the attendance of non-Christians at Christian holy sites is part of the syncretism and tendency toward devotional, personalized practices that are characteristic of contemporary Sri Lankan religiosity.[63] In Sri Lanka, Buddhists, Hindus, and Muslims alike patronize Christian churches and shrines to make vows. They also visit Catholic priests said to have healing powers. Against this backdrop, and given the absence of Buddhist and Hindu temples in Amman, the churches and shrines to the Virgin Mary and St. George act as stand-ins for shrines to more familiar saints and gods that Sri Lankans petition for help at home.

Distinct from saint veneration and attendance at Catholic churches is the remarkable way evangelical Protestant groups have taken root amongst migrants in Amman. Many of the members of the main evangelical Christian groups that meet in Jordan are foreigners, chiefly Sri Lankans and Filipinas, in addition to migrants from Korea, China, and several African countries. The exact number of Sri Lankans who attend evangelical churches in Amman is difficult to estimate. No central registration system or single umbrella organization covers all the groups, and many operate out of unmarked buildings or private homes and do not publicize their activities. Throughout my fieldwork in Amman, I regularly attended the services of two Pentecostal churches, both of which had between seventy and one hundred Sri Lankan attendees.[64] I was told of a handful of other churches with smaller congregations. This is part of a wider regional phenomenon: Evangelical churches with sizeable Sri Lankan congregations exist elsewhere in the Middle East, notably Kuwait, Israel, Lebanon, and the United Arab Emirates. Evangelical groups make a deliberate effort to reach out to migrant workers. This is partly because foreigners are easier to approach. Separated from their own social networks and lonely, migrants may be more easily persuaded to try new things. The fact that converting Muslims to another religion is

Live-in domestic workers gather for a social activity organized by Caritas, a Roman Catholic–sponsored organization that provides some of the only humanitarian assistance to migrant domestic workers in Amman, Jordan.

a criminal offense in Jordan also encourages these groups to target non-Muslims and non-Jordanians about whom the authorities would be less concerned and who would be less likely to inform on them.

Pentecostal churches appear to be attracting larger numbers of converts than the Catholic church.[65] Part of the reason may relate to differences in the process of conversion. To be baptized in the Catholic Church, one must be tutored for at least several months, whereas those ready to receive the Holy Spirit in many Pentecostal churches can take a one-month bible study course and be baptized more quickly. This is linked to the belief, which is one of the tenets of evangelical Christianity, that people can be "saved" through personal conversion at any time. Pentecostalism also entails beliefs in supernatural forces that are consistent with non-Christian beliefs prevalent in Sri Lanka, for example, spirit possession, faith healing, and other miracles. Part of Pentecostalism's appeal also may lie in the fact that Pentecostal ideas about sexuality and women's roles resemble patriarchal attitudes about women and the family that are widespread in rural Sri Lanka. Women who convert to Pentecostalism and are embraced by the church may achieve a respectability that provides a counterbalance to the common stereotypes about migrant housemaids being sexually promiscuous.

Pentecostalism also has inherent appeal. The services are intense, highly emotional, and uplifting, involving a large dose of singing, loud music, and bodily movement. Testimonials play an important role. Participants take turns verbally "testifying" to the good work God has done in their lives and the miracles they have witnessed. These testimonials have strong persuasive power. They center on several key themes: healing illnesses, fixing broken marriages, and bringing financial success. God is said to work at the level of human need to reveal Himself to the faithful. The message conveyed by the testimonials is that the faithful will be rewarded financially, among other ways. These stories, particularly when told by comparatively affluent missionaries, can be alluring to migrants, as they are intended to be. Beyond this, the missionaries connected with the Pentecostal churches I attended expressed sympathy and compassion for the plight of Sri Lankan domestic workers. They organized regular meals, outings, and other activities for members. This atmosphere of support and camaraderie provides comfort to migrants who are separated from their own families and feel downtrodden in Jordan. Rather than advocating for large-scale change to combat exploitation of domestic workers, however, the Pentecostal groups tended to organize assistance to individuals on a case-by-case basis in the form of personal prayer or limited financial aid. They very rarely mediated in disputes between housemaids and their employers.

Conclusions

Jordan prides itself as being at the forefront of initiatives to protect the rights of migrant workers. With support from the United Nations Development Fund for Women (Unifem), the kingdom introduced the region's first standardized working contract for non-Jordanian domestic workers in 2003. The contract forbids employers from withholding salaries or confiscating passports, grants workers a day off, and sets a maximum number of working hours, among other conditions. These are positive steps. But in the absence of a law governing domestic work or the political will to investigate and penalize employers, such reforms lack teeth. Among those domestic workers I interviewed, few were aware of the existence or contents of the contract. Interviews revealed that even the most basic labor rights — the rights to freedom from compulsory labor and to remuneration for work performed — continue to be violated, and errant employers are seldom held to account.[66] Moreover, the new working contract states that workers must have their employers' permission before leaving the workplace, thus reinforcing employers' control. While Jordan's contract has been touted as a model for the region,[67] its effectiveness at protecting workers' rights is questionable. Social attitudes about gender and domestic work as well as legal barriers continue to hamper the development of advocacy on behalf of migrant domestic workers. These problems are not specific to Jordan. Ultimately, migrant domestic workers in all countries in which the kafala system is in place are at the mercy of their employers.

The vulnerability of migrant women should be seen within a wider context in which the rights of local workers, and local women more generally, are inadequately protected. In Jordan, as in many other parts of the region, the rule of law is weak, and state–society relations are characterized by a lack of transparency and accountability, as well as a high degree of favoritism, known locally as the use of *wasta,* or personal connections.[68] Crimes against women, especially when they occur within the domestic domain, are often treated less harshly than those against men.[69] In this context, it is hardly surprising that migrant women, who lack the social networks, language skills, and respectability that might otherwise afford them some protection, are subject to abuses that go unpunished. As this essay has described, most migrant domestic workers in Jordan live under lock and key, isolated in private homes, and find few opportunities for socialization with other migrants. Lacking full integration in Jordanian society, some seek new forms of solidarity and social membership through faith-based activities. Many have also begun rejecting live-in jobs and now reside independently, working on a freelance basis. In so doing, they have begun creating increasingly visible Asian communities in the heart of Arab Amman.

ACKNOWLEDGMENTS: Research and writing time were supported by an Overseas Research Studentship, a London School of Economics Research Studentship, grants from the University of London Central Research Fund, the Council for British Research in the Levant (CBRL), an American Center of Oriental Research (ACOR)/Council of American Overseas Research Centers (CAORC) Postgraduate Fellowship in Jordan, and a Fulbright Fellowship to Sri Lanka. An earlier version of this essay was presented in the workshop entitled "Distant Divides and Intimate Connections: Migrant Domestic Workers in Asia," organized by Nicole Constable as part of a Social Science Research Council Conference on Inter-Asian Connections held in Dubai, UAE, in February 2008. I thank fellow participants for providing important feedback and insights. I am especially grateful to Nicole Constable for her comments on several versions of the essay. I am also grateful to Martha Mundy and Jonathan Parry for their constructive comments and encouragement throughout the research.

❑

4. Advocating for Sri Lankan Migrant Workers

Obstacles and Challenges

Michele R. Gamburd

AFTER THREE DECADES OF MIGRATION TO THE GULF COOPERATION COUNCIL (GCC) countries in West Asia, Sri Lankan migrants continue to face exploitative labor conditions abroad and anemic support at home. Despite the large number of transnational guest workers and the economic centrality of their remittances, migrants lack strong advocates among unions, nongovernmental organizations (NGOs), and government departments in Sri Lanka.[1] In this article, I argue that to understand the puzzling paucity of support at home requires an inquiry that encompasses not only the activities of Sri Lankan NGOs, unions, and government institutions, but also the wider economic and political context, particularly the international division of labor and the constraints that destination countries put on labor organizing and diplomatic activities.

Statistics highlight the importance of international labor migration to the Sri Lankan economy. The Sri Lankan Bureau of Foreign Employment (SLBFE) estimates the stock of overseas contract workers has increased steadily every year since this migration stream began in 1976, with about 1.2 million Sri Lankans working abroad in 2005.[2] Migrant laborers make up about 15 percent of the Sri Lankan work force, and their remittances contribute significantly to Sri Lanka's foreign exchange earnings.[3] In 2005, total remittances stood at over US$1.9 billion; over half of this total, roughly US$1 billion, came from the Gulf.[4] In generating foreign earnings, private remittances (29 percent) come second after Sri Lanka's large garment industry (47 percent).[5] Clearly, the country has a great financial stake in the remittances generated by migrant laborers, particularly those working in the Gulf.

Reflecting the increasing feminization of migrant work forces around the world, women make up two thirds of Sri Lanka's overseas contract workers. Domestic servants or "housemaids" alone constitute over half of Sri Lanka's migrants.[6] Each migrant woman supports an average of five family members; thus Sri Lanka's 800,000 female migrants support an estimated 4 million people, or a little over 20 percent of the nation's population of 19.5 million.[7] Despite the large numbers of women working abroad and the significant percentage of the population dependent on their remittances, however, little organizing around migration as a woman's issue has taken place in either the public or the private sector in Sri Lanka. What gender norms and political-economic circumstances explain this lack of support?

In neoliberal economies, market-driven logic has unsettled older relations between citizens and the state. Aihwa Ong argues that people with valued skills have entitlements all over the world, while unskilled laborers are excluded from rights both in their host countries and at home.[8] Because neoliberalism allows (even requires) the political liminality of some citizens, other ethical regimes (such as feminism, humanism, and religious traditions) and their representatives in civil society step in to protect individuals from the adverse effects of bare market forces. But to what extent can NGOs and labor unions protect workers in developing countries? In this essay, I explore what is happening, and, more importantly, what is *not* happening in Sri Lankan NGOs, labor unions and government administrative organs, traditional venues in which activists and state officials advocate for workers' and citizens' rights. I seek to identify the conditions that hamper state and civil society organizations in labor-sending countries from effectively advocating for guest workers abroad — from promoting, for example, higher wages, safer working conditions, and systematically honored contracts.

Explaining an absence or a lack is never easy, especially when examining an isolated case. Therefore I contrast the relative paucity of support in Sri Lanka's migrant sector with the well documented, energetic organizing in another labor-sending country, the Republic of the Philippines. I argue that a major source of difference can be found in the economic and political conditions of the destination countries in which Sri Lankan and Filipina migrants work. Labor dynamics in the Gulf (which receives 90 percent of Sri Lanka's transnational domestic workers) contrast with those in various countries in East and Southeast Asia (especially Hong Kong, Japan, Taiwan, and Singapore), which together receive 60 percent of Filipina workers. In short, I suggest that differences in the labor climates in destination countries influence how energetically sending-country governments and other groups will agitate for migrant rights. Above and beyond these political issues, however, looms the overarching economic reality of a global capitalist economy that disadvantages migrant laborers from the global South.

This essay begins with a discussion of the global economy and an overview of the role of gender in the international division of labor. I then explore the working conditions of Sri Lanka's transnational domestic servants, in the context of labor dynamics in the GCC (Gulf Cooperation Council) countries. Turning to the situation in the sending country, I consider activities undertaken by Sri Lankan NGOs, labor unions, and state institutions in support of migrant workers. To understand the transnational factors that constrain both labor and government in their activities and effectiveness, I compare labor-organizing climates in the GCC, Asia, and the European Union (EU). I then compare migration patterns in Sri Lanka and the Philippines to identify factors that promote and inhibit the support of migrant laborers. I conclude with a discussion of the challenges and obstacles faced by both labor and state actors in protecting transnational domestic workers in the global economy.

Globalization, Gender, and Migration

Since the end of World War II, theorists have struggled to explain the power imbalances between former colonies and former colonizers.[9] They discuss dynamics between the global North and South.[10] Despite different analytical perspectives, all agree that the concentration of capital and technology lies in the global North. Neoliberal economic policies have over the past twenty years polarized differences between countries and exacerbated the gap between rich and poor within countries.[11] This situation provides the context in which transnational migrants move from poor, less developed nations to developed ones.[12]

Although globalization affects the entire world, its dynamics are localized within regions and countries, thus research requires attention to ethnographic particulars. For example, modernization in the Gulf does not look entirely like modernization in North America and the EU, especially if the social, cultural, and political context is taken into consideration.[13] In the Gulf, strong states implement aggressive policies to marginalize migrants. Similarly, labor-sending countries occupy specific positions within the international economy and have unique histories of labor migration. To explain the paucity of support for migrant workers in Sri Lanka, I will examine labor conditions in the Middle East as well as the position that Sri Lanka holds in the international division of global labor and power.

Michele R. Gamburd

Hired domestic worker making sweets in a Sri Lankan home. Work opportunities available to poor women in their home villages in Sri Lanka are often temporary, poorly paid, and low-status jobs, thus the attraction of overseas employment.

All too often, explanations of transnational labor migration focus exclusively on large-scale demographic and economic factors. Anthropologists have argued that these explanations, while valuable, do not adequately account for other important influences, such as national politics, household relations, and gender norms, all of which affect the micro-processes of labor negotiations and in turn influence labor flows and work conditions.[14] Gender relations in both sending and receiving countries matter in terms of what sorts of freedoms and empowerment local and migrant women have.[15] Thus materials written about male migration do not necessarily apply to female migration, particularly when migrants go to the highly gender-segregated societies of the Middle East. In addition, women's mobilizing and organizing in their home and host countries take place within local contexts of existing gender norms and patterns.

In the past, scholars examining globalization have often assumed that women hold the fort at home while men migrate in the global economy.[16] The transnational migration of women who work as domestic servants radically upsets the association of "female" with "the local," and challenges Euro-American commonsense assumptions that women reproduce families in the home.[17] As part of their paid work, domestic servants take responsibility for care work outside the home (and country). As breadwinners, they earn money in the global economy, sending remittances to support their husbands and children back home.[18] Despite these objective changes in women's activities, older gender values persist in both Sri Lanka and the Middle East. In the United Arab Emirates (UAE) as of 2004, for example, the labor laws did not cover work that takes place within a private home, thus excluding all transnational domestic workers in the country from labor protections. Similarly, Sri Lanka has no national regulations on domestic service, a reality that hinders government and NGO efforts in behalf of women doing this job abroad. Both in Sri Lanka and in the Gulf, gendered norms affect the structures and attitudes within which labor organizing and government initiatives in migrant women's behalf take place, contributing to the lack of support for migrant women.

Women's Work Situation Abroad

Understanding women's work situations abroad provides some context for considering the lack of labor and other activism in Sri Lanka around transnational domestic workers' issues. The prevailing labor conditions limit women's ability to resist exploitation. One aspect of disempowerment pertains to living conditions. In the Gulf, most housemaids live in their employers' residences, as do many housemaids in Singapore, Hong Kong, the United States, and the EU. Research indicates that live-in housemaids have much less autonomy and freedom than do women with part-time or live-out arrangements.[19] Live-in workers make less money per hour than live-out workers do and find it more difficult to differentiate work time from free time. Their employers allow them little privacy and feel free to call on their labor at any time of the day or night, blurring the line between "workplace" and "home."[20] Live-ins depend on employers not only for employment but also for housing. In many cases, particularly in the Gulf, this arrangement is formalized with government regulations regarding residence and work permits; thus losing a job can jeopardize a migrant's right to stay in the host country.[21] In addition, compared to live-out workers, live-in domestic servants generally are more vulnerable to exploitation and have fewer backup safety networks.[22]

Other disempowering work conditions pertain to women's mobility and their social roles within their sponsor's families. Domestic servants working in the Middle East often describe extensive curtailment of their mobility. Sri Lankan migrants regularly report to researchers and human rights organizations that their employers confiscated their passports to keep them "safe" — an action illegal under international law and International Labor Organization (ILO) conventions, and one that causes great logistical difficulties for housemaids who flee untenable work situations but cannot leave the country without proper documentation.[23] Roughly half of the returned Sri Lankan migrants whom I interviewed stated that they never left their employers' houses during their entire two years abroad, or left only in the company of the sponsor's family.[24] Many of these same interviewees claimed to find this situation reassuring, saying that the sponsor treated them like a daughter of the family. Yet scholars report that migrant domestic workers joke that being considered "one of the family" is a justification for greater exploitation in the employers' household.[25] In addition, norms governing familial behavior often disadvantage young women, discouraging them from protesting against exploitative labor relations.[26] Gendered norms for familial deference, combined with restrictions on female mobility, limit women's abilities to resist exploitation or escape threatening situations.

State-level regulations governing labor relations also influence women's work situations and their ability to resist exploitation. In many GCC countries, labor laws cover male laborers but do not protect household workers.[27] The same situation occurs in Taiwan, where the Labour Standards Law does not apply to domestic workers.[28] In Hong Kong, labor laws do apply to foreign domestic servants, but are rarely enforced against middle- and upper-class employers.[29] Other state-level issues that affect women's work situations include the availability of health care, regulations surrounding bringing in family members, and the possibility of becoming citizens in the host country. For example, in Europe, migrant women can have relationships with local men, marry them, gain citizenship, and establish transnational families where members have different nationalities.[30] Women who work in countries with a strong discourse of human rights and an active civil society receive more support from the social system in their country of employment and have more opportunities to organize and mobilize. And women have greater control over their situations if they are free to leave their place of employment and seek other jobs — rights theoretically guaranteed in the few countries that have ratified ILO conventions C97 and C143.[31] Domestic servants who can change employers without losing their residence permits tolerate less exploitation and harassment at work and have more freedom to agitate and organize.

The reality of work situations reflects not only the laws but also their enforcement. Because few legal and organizational mechanisms support migrant domestic workers in the Gulf, women face an uphill battle with few allies and advocates.[32] Sri Lankan nationals working in the Middle East can obtain assistance from their recruiting agency, the local police, or the Sri Lankan embassy or consular office in their country of residence. But in their search for profits, labor recruiting agencies may not prioritize worker welfare, and many guest workers feel that the local police and job agents are more likely to support their employers.[33] And although they generally trust Sri Lankan diplomats to side with them, housemaids whom I have interviewed often find services at the embassy lacking, noting insufficient staff and Spartan accommodations. Rather than rely on formal institutions in times of trouble, women often turn to informal personal networks to help them out of difficult situations.

In sum, female domestic servants in the Gulf work long hours for low pay. Their live-in status, combined with local gender norms and familial expectations, constrain their sociability and mobility and limit their ability to separate home from workplace. Lack of legislation governing domestic service exacerbates this difficulty. In addition, other state and private institutions (for example, the police and the labor-recruiting agencies) stack the deck against the migrant housemaid.

Labor Dynamics in the GCC

Hardship, injustice, and exploitation often lead to organized resistance, but this has not happened surrounding the issue of foreign migration from Sri Lanka. The micro-politics of women's work situations unfold against a backdrop of larger-scale labor dynamics in the GCC. The techniques of governance employed in host countries illuminate the relative lack of activism for Sri Lankan migrant workers in both host and sending countries.

The history of labor migration in the Gulf sheds light on why these labor-receiving countries employ harsh and effective techniques in governing migrants. Following the oil boom in the 1970s, guest workers flowed into the Gulf and their labor soon became a crucial aspect of local economies. In 1981, six states (Saudi Arabia, Kuwait, Bahrain, Oman, Qatar, and the UAE) formed the Gulf Cooperation Council. Estimates vary, but sources suggest that guest workers make up the majority of the population in many small GCC countries.[34] Overall, foreigners make up 37 to 43 percent of the total population of the GCC countries and constitute 70 percent of the work force, with work force numbers significantly higher in the UAE (90 percent), Kuwait (82 percent), and Qatar (90 percent).[35] The high percentage of "foreigners" worries government officials in these small countries. Even giant Saudi Arabia strives to control its guest worker population, which makes up 65 percent of its work force.[36]

Not only do guest workers make up significant percentages of GCC work forces, they also occupy less desirable positions. Most GCC countries have a de facto dual economy, with well-paying, non-strenuous state jobs held by "nationals" and low-paying labor jobs performed by foreigners.[37] GCC governments have created public sector jobs with high wages and good benefits as a way to distribute oil wealth to their citizens. Foreigners, meanwhile, do the difficult, low-status jobs in the private sector. This situation has persisted for the past

Construction site, Dubai, 2008. "GCC governments have created public sector jobs with high wages and good benefits as a way to distribute oil wealth to their citizens. Foreigners, meanwhile, do the difficult, low-status jobs in the private sector." — Michele R. Gamburd

thirty years, but growth in the local population compounded with a halt in economic expansion and depletion of oil resources in certain countries, such as Bahrain, has created a need for change.[38] Government administration can no absorb large numbers of the citizenry, but locals still expect public sector jobs. Citizens have begun to resent guest workers' private sector jobs, but they themselves do not wish to work under foreigners since such jobs would diminish their status and bring much lower rates of pay.

The number, economic importance, and potential political volatility of guest workers concerns state authorities in the Gulf. In the late 1980s, many states implemented "nationalization" policies to replace the foreign work force with citizens.[39] These nationalization policies met with mixed results, succeeding in the public sector but not in the private sector. In addition, GCC governments crafted legislation to minimize the "threat" that these foreigners pose to the "native" population. Strict regulations on length of stay, difficult-to-meet criteria for bringing in family members, the sponsorship system, inability to own land and businesses, and the near impossibility of obtaining citizenship all work to keep guest workers' stays short, temporary, or informal, and to minimize their ability to organize.[40] Other circumstances also exacerbate the insecurity of migrant workers in the Gulf, including rampant discrimination, dependence on the whims of their sponsor, visa regulations that make staying in the country while changing jobs difficult, lack of legal rights, and the absence of unions.[41] These techniques of governance have functioned to make guest workers physically useful but politically docile.[42]

Despite oppressive political structures, workers retain a degree of agency. People choose tactically whether to resist or accommodate to undesirable labor conditions, weighing the current situation against other needs and goals. Writing of male migrants, Khalaf and Alkobaisi argue that in the GCC countries, "Given the inferior political, legal, economic and social status of migrants, they have opted to accommodate instead of entering into conflict situations."[43] Female migrants, with even fewer resources than male migrants and often with more pressing obligations at home, opt even more strongly for accommodation rather than confrontation. The policies of GCC governments effectively regulate foreign labor by keeping it temporary, docile, under control, and subject to deportation. These disciplinary structures strongly shape the choices individual migrants and their advocates make.

The labor market in the Gulf, bifurcated with the broad distinction of citizen vs. guest worker, is further stratified according to gender, ethnicity, and nationality. These divisions undermine class solidarity by enhancing competition between other groups. Leonard writes, "Foreign workers are ranked by place or origin, receiving differential payment and treatment."[44] Female domestic servants earn less than most other guest workers. In the UAE, for example, within the housemaid category, housemaids from the Philippines are paid more than those from Indonesia, Sri Lanka, Ethiopia, and Bangladesh in that order.[45] Racial, ethnic, religious, and national stereotypes predetermine wages.[46] Regional affiliation also plays an important role in guest worker recruitment. Over the past twenty-five years, the GCC states have employed fewer non–GCC Arab workers (e.g., Palestinians, Jordanians, Egyptians, and Yemenis) and more Asians (e.g., Pakistanis, Indians, Bangladeshis, Sri Lankans, Filipinos, and Indonesians).[47] Asians work for lower wages, leave their families at home, and are deemed (rightly or wrongly) by local governments to be less likely than co-ethnic Arab workers to engage in labor actions and spread radical ideas.[48] Identity politics inextricably intertwine with labor relations in the Gulf, undermining interethnic solidarity by emphasizing fragmenting categories of allegiance.

Identity politics within host societies also provide a key context for understanding migration. In discussing situations of migrant housemaids, one must note the degree of gender empowerment in various labor-receiving countries. In many GCC countries, women and men have separate spheres and different entitlements. For example, Kapiszewski notes, "Just granting Saudi women the right to drive cars alone should result in removing around one hundred thousand foreign drivers from the labor force," which illustrates how gender norms influence labor opportunities and mobility situations for male guest workers and female nationals in Saudi Arabia.[49] In most GCC countries, women are constrained in their freedom to socialize and move about, and few enter the work force.[50] Migrant housemaids are similarly constrained as women. Based on evidence presented below on differences in organizing activities in the GCC, Asia, and Europe, I suggest that in combination with GCC labor disciplinary techniques, these gender roles curtail migrant women laborers' ability to organize.

In sum, the GCC countries have extremely segmented labor markets, with the majority of workers coming from foreign countries and undertaking poorly paid, impermanent jobs in the private sector. Drawing on over thirty years of experience in regulating guest workers, GCC countries have developed effective techniques to control laborers' work, marginalize them from the dominant social structure, and reduce class solidarity across other categories of identity. These regulatory measures make labor organizing extremely difficult, particularly for migrant domestic workers.

NGOs and Labor Unions in Sri Lanka

I have argued above that women's work situations in their sponsors' homes abroad limit their potential to organize and that this disempowerment is reinforced by the larger governance structures by which the GCC regulates foreign guest workers. On the face of it, labor dynamics in receiving countries might appear to have little to do with activism in sending countries such as Sri Lanka. To the contrary, I argue that conditions in host countries directly influence migrant advocates' activities at home. In this section, I consider civil society and state organizations in Sri Lanka, examining the activities of NGOs, labor unions, and government institutions that support migrant workers. In subsequent sections, I argue that the activities of these Sri Lankan groups reflect transnational economic dynamics and the organizing climate in host countries.

Given the insecurity guest workers face while abroad, one might assume that vigorous labor organizations would arise in their home countries to protect their rights. But in Sri Lanka, despite the hard work and enthusiasm of the few activists who deal full time with migrant issues, civil society and the government have done surprisingly little for migrants. In stating this, I do not wish to denigrate the dedication and diligence of migrant labor advocates, only to point out that the several small organizations discussed below cannot and do not meet the organizing needs of Sri Lanka's migrant workers, who number over a million strong.

Several NGOs in Sri Lanka focus on labor migration. The American Center for International Labor Solidarity (ACILS), based in a modest house on a residential street in Colombo, Sri Lanka's capital, lobbies for migrant issues, works directly with government departments to support multilateral agreements with other labor-sending countries, and funds partner organizations that help migrants directly with social and legal difficulties.[51] In 1994, ACILS was instrumental in funding and establishing Migrant Services Center (MSC). With a staff number in the twenties, MSC ministers to worker needs and does advocacy work, lobbying, and campaigning.[52] In 2005, MSC had twenty-six affiliated Migrant Workers Associations (MWAs) scattered around the country, with a total of fifteen hundred members.[53] In addition to building leadership potential and dispersing information, the MWAs engage in activities such as reintegration and self-employment projects for returnees; savings, microcredit, and welfare schemes; the channeling of complaints from overseas workers to the SLBFE; and advocating for voting rights for citizens overseas.

Action Network for Migrant Workers (Actform) is another Sri Lankan NGO that focuses on migrant issues. Partially funded by the ACILS, Actform shares space with a feminist NGO in a suburban house and serves as an umbrella organization for other NGOs working on migration issues.[54] Many of their constituents are the MWAs affiliated with MSC. Actform is also affiliated with international migrant organizations, including the Philippines-based Migration Forum in Asia. Actform publishes informational handbooks and a vernacular quarterly newsletter, *Tharani*, which is distributed to MWAs, overseas embassies, and a small group of current migrant workers abroad.[55] Actform also organizes events on migrants' human rights, prints informational posters, and runs press and electronic media campaigns. In addition, they occasionally consult with the Foreign Ministry and the SLBFE.

The International Organization for Migration (IOM) is a third NGO focused on migration issues. The Sri Lankan branch of IOM, based in a stately colonial-era home, does capacity building with the SLBFE and other government branches.[56] True to their international missions, ACILS and IOM have hosted conferences to bring together labor ministers from Asian labor-sending countries to discuss mutual problems and come up with policy initiatives.[57] ACILS organizers do not feel that the conferences have brought about significant policy changes at the governmental level, but the organizers believe that their efforts on this front have brought wider pressure from international organizations and local civil society to bear on policy-makers in Sri Lanka and encouraged multilateral consideration of migration issues.

During 2004, when I conducted interviews to assess the effectiveness of NGO services in Sri Lanka, those with whom I spoke — NGO workers, government officials, and migrants alike — uniformly expressed their disappointment with these three local organizations on a number of fronts. They note that the migration groups are relatively small, the NGO movement lacks cooperation and coordination, and the movement has not been able to influence the government on significant policy issues.[58] In addition, barriers of language and locality hamper grassroots organizing. As one activist explained, class barriers have kept Colombo-based civil society groups from getting involved in migration issues most pertinent to unskilled rural women.[59] The issue of class differences that divide Colombo intellectuals and activists from the less-educated workers from Sri Lanka's rural areas has arisen in numerous contexts. For example, Jayawardena and de Alwis suggest that the accusations that Colombo women's organizations are led by Westernized, middle-class feminists who do not connect with local traditions and values are a backlash against feminist ideals.[60] Although I agree that one must examine the politics behind such a criticism, the gaps in world view, language, and locality between organizers and their intended constituents are clear, and these shortcomings undermine NGO labor organizing activities.

Like Sri Lankan NGOs, local labor unions have not taken up migrant issues with vigor — this despite the fact that Sri Lanka has a long history of labor organizing in other spheres, with unions organizing first against the colonial regime's labor extraction techniques in the plantation sector and then against post-independence governments and business entities.[61] Sri Lankan NGOs that advocate for migrant workers, such as ACILS and MSC, are nominally affiliated with local unions,[62] but NGO activists note that their union allies pay lip service to migrant issues but have not participated in related initiatives.[63] In addition, some strong unions, such as the plantation unions, are for historical reasons more concerned with the high prestige, masculine sphere of politics than with relatively low-prestige sphere of labor issues.[64] Showing solidarity with transnational domestic workers, even with women migrants from the plantation community, has not been a visible priority. Even the few garment factory unions that do recognize women's issues focus their attention on labor relations in Sri Lanka's free trade zones.[65] The relative lack of union attention to "women's issues" or domestic service, whether in Sri Lanka or abroad, no doubt reflects local gender relations, the difficulty of organizing workers isolated in separate houses, and cultural norms and values that obscure domestic service as a form of labor.

Despite the general paucity of activism around migration, the NGOs concerned with the issue *do* agitate for change. Recognizing the importance of raising political consciousness around migration, in early 2004 ACILS, MSC, Actform, and some affiliated NGOs and unions lobbied the government to provide a way for Sri Lankan citizens working abroad to vote in local elections. Earlier, in 1996, Sri Lanka had ratified the United Nation's International Convention on the Protection of Rights of All Migrants and Their Families (1990). This came into force in July 2003, when the twentieth world nation ratified the convention. Of interest for this discussion is the clause in the Convention giving migrant workers the right to absentee ballots while working abroad. Advocates felt that drawing attention to voting arrangements would raise the issue of citizens' rights.[66] By 2005, however, no government action had taken place on this front. In contrast, Kyoko Shinozaki notes that the Philippine state instituted absentee voting for overseas contract workers in 2003 as part of its effort to increase migrants' sense of national identity and belonging.[67] If Sri Lankan migrants voted while abroad, perhaps migrant workers associations would have more clout with politicians. And migrants' issues, particularly those of migrant domestic servants, might become significant campaign items. Here again, lack of forward movement on an important migrant issue proves puzzling — unless global economic issues and the organizing climate in the GCC are taken into account.

Government critiques of the way that the NGO movement and labor unions have dealt with migrant workers' problems highlight structural barriers at the national and international level. For example, L.K. Ruhunage, in 2004 the employment and welfare counselor at the Sri Lankan Consulate in Dubai, contends that unions and NGOs can be of little practical help to migrants. Jurisdiction, Ruhunage explained, is one contributing factor: local NGOs and labor unions have no authority to settle disputes that arise in foreign countries; the SLBFE and the consular offices have to take care of such situations. This Sri Lankan government official explains that even international human rights organizations turn first to the Sri Lankan Consulate to investigate and clear up problems. Ruhunage concludes that labor unions and NGOs have little authority abroad and he sees this lack of effective agency as a reason why these groups have dealt only tangentially with migrant issues.

The Sri Lankan government, then, seems to have a monopoly on the ability to administer to migrant labor. In addition to the administrative apparatus, the government would seem to have a strong economic and social motivation to support its citizens overseas. Migrant remittances provide valuable foreign exchange, and the protection of vulnerable housemaids and the families they leave behind receives a fair share of media attention and forms the basis for nationalist political rhetoric.[68] Migrant issues have seized the popular imagination, but that makes the lack of government will to strengthen support for migrants all the more puzzling.

Sri Lankan Politics and Diplomatic Activities to Support Migrant Workers

The discussion of the lack of NGO and union support for migrant workers leads inexorably back to the state. If the government indeed holds the sole power to ameliorate migrant workers' unstable employment situations abroad, why has it not done more in their behalf? I argue that government inaction reflects three main factors: Sri Lankan gender norms, women's lack of participation in national politics, and (above all) Sri Lanka's disadvantageous position in the international division of labor.

Lack of government focus on migrant housemaids mirrors the dearth of women and women's issues in Sri Lanka politics. One might think that national politics would favor women: women have voted actively in Sri Lanka since 1931 (as long as men have) and Sri Lanka elected a woman prime minister in 1960 and a women president in 1994.[69] In addition, women nearly equal men in educational qualifications.[70] But despite the fact that women vote regularly and enthusiastically in elections, they make up only a small fraction of elected legislative representatives, ranging from 2 to 5 percent.[71] Women vote, but they do not usually run for office. As in the rest of South Asia, women enter politics primarily through family connections, especially after the assassinations or deaths of their fathers or husbands. Although women receive respect once they obtain office, harassment, character slurs, and social restrictions on contact with strange men keep most women out of political campaigns and thus keep women's issues out of the political arena. There are few female legislative representatives and, except on International Women's Day, there is little political discussion of "women's issues" or female migration. Similarly, despite educational qualifications, women still lag behind men in employment, particularly in professional and managerial positions in both the public and the private sphere.[72] Women activists struggle against all these barriers, but in spite of the dedicated efforts of NGO leaders, the feminist movement remains small and marginal in Sri Lanka.[73] Thus women and women's issues play only a marginal role in Sri Lankan politics.

Even though women's issues have not dominated state policy on the social front, migration is of paramount importance for the nation's economy. In its state-to-state interactions with host countries in the Gulf, the government of Sri Lanka has historically balanced the interests of its laborers for higher wages and better working conditions against the need to maintain favorable diplomatic relations with a major source of employment. As a debtor and a developing nation, Sri Lanka has little status and power in the international hierarchy of nations and its diplomats operate within these preexisting power relations when crafting intergovernmental arrangements and protecting its citizens abroad.

Election posters, Southern Province, Sri Lanka. "If Sri Lankan migrants voted while abroad, perhaps…migrants' issues, particularly those of migrant domestic servants, might become significant campaign items."
— Michele R. Gamburd

Just as migrants accommodate to their labor conditions in the Gulf for fear of losing their jobs, Sri Lankan government officials in many cases accommodate to the wishes of the more powerful GCC governments for fear of losing valuable employment opportunities for its citizens. For example, in 2008 the Sri Lankan government negotiated a new minimum wage of US$180 a month for house-maids working in Kuwait.[74] But Sri Lankan government officials are also tasked with enhancing economic relations with labor-receiving countries in the Gulf — a goal that can conflict with the protection of workers' rights. For example, in 1998 four representatives from the SLBFE visited consular offices in Kuwait and the UAE. The following extract from a discussion of the aftermath of a labor dispute at Atraco Industrial Enterprises in the UAE illustrates the conciliatory atti-tude of the Sri Lankan officials:

> Very recently, a large number of factory workers were sent to Sri Lanka as they struck work demanding the removal of certain officers attached to the management of the factory. We had a discussion with the management of the factory and informed them that the purpose of our visit was to study la-bour requirement [*sic*] of the factory and the *shortcomings of our labour.* The management was very satisfied with the labour provided by Sri Lanka. However, they had a reservation on the behavior of some of our employ-ees. Notwithstanding the problems they assured continuation of using our labour and *we gave an undertaking to send more disciplined work-ers in future.*[75]

The delegation also found workers' complaints from another factory "base-less."[76] The content and tone of this report suggest that in future cases as in this one, Sri Lankan officials may hesitate to take up the labor cases of overseas workers, preferring instead to cement relationships with factory owners and employers. More generally, government representatives from labor-sending countries worry that if they support their guest worker population, a host country could hire laborers from elsewhere.[77]

Government officials have stepped in to help Sri Lankan workers when they have run into trouble abroad and diplomatic missions regularly aid stranded workers and support their citizens in court. In the Gulf countries, Sri Lankan welfare officers and labor attachés have taken up workers' causes with employers, job agents, and the police. But Sri Lankan embassies and consular offices face numerous challenges — including the understaffing of diplomatic offices — in doing so.[78]

In 2004, I visited the Sri Lankan Consulate in Dubai and shadowed its employment and welfare counselor, L.K. Ruhunage, for a week on his official rounds to job agencies, garment factories, police stations, the jail, the consular safe house, and the airport. This experience provided insights into the challenges of diplomatic work. As we traveled to the free trade zone in Ajman, Ruhunage remarked that the Sri Lankan consulate in Dubai needed one more diplomatic officer or labor welfare officer to handle correspondence and make field visits; at that time, only two field officers covered six emirates (Abu Dhabi has an embassy of its own).[79] Ruhunage suggested that the UAE limited the number of diplomats a country could place in its foreign mission. In addition, maintaining diplomats abroad is costly, particularly if a mission does not generate any income.

Even with additional staff, Ruhunage argued, the Dubai consulate would not be able to enforce labor conditions and wages for Sri Lankan workers. Enforcement rights lay instead with the government of the UAE. The Sri Lankan diplomats who handled labor issues could represent the interests of their citizens, but they had no official authority to inspect worksites and enforce standards. Instead, local labor officials held this authority. In Ruhunage's opinion, the UAE did not employ enough people to monitor the situations of its many guest workers. In addition, the Sri Lankan consular office covered accommodation for stranded workers; despite benefiting from cheap foreign labor, the UAE government bore no responsibility in such cases. In short, embassies and consular offices could bring only a limited number of staff into a host country, and the staff had only limited authority over local labor conditions.

Bilateral agreements in place between Sri Lanka and the UAE have allowed Sri Lankan diplomats to point out problems when high-ranking officials met. But Ruhunage suggested that if the Sri Lankan consular office complains too much, the UAE will reply that they should either stop sending workers or adjust to the current situation. Ruhunage thought that emphasis on labor issues needed to take place in other venues, including seminars, regional meetings, and academic research.

Activists and civil servants whom I interviewed agreed that the state apparatus (including embassies, consular offices, and governmental departments in Sri Lanka) could better serve migrants by providing additional informational coordination between various ministries in Sri Lanka, between the SLBFE and the

Sri Lankan embassies abroad, and between embassies of other labor-sending countries.[80] Hampered by lack of money and staff, and constrained by the laws of the receiving countries, governments of labor-sending countries in weak economic and political positions often fail to exert effective diplomatic pressure to protect the rights of their citizens.[81]

Given all of the conditions described above, it is fair to wonder whether any Sri Lankan organization can effectively apply pressure to improve the lot of migrant laborers. The preceding discussion of NGOs, labor unions, government initiatives, and diplomatic missions suggests a pervasive lack of political will and practical authority. Are states and civil society organizations in all migrant-sending countries equally hampered? If not, why not? What factors disproportionately disempower Sri Lankan organizations? The answer lies, I argue, not within Sri Lanka but in the nations where Sri Lankan migrants work. I illustrate this point with the following two comparisons: the first between labor organizing climates in the GCC, Asia, and Europe, and the second between migration in Sri Lanka and the Philippines.

Labor Relations Compared: Organizing Climates in the GCC, Asia, and Europe

As the activities of ACILS, MSC, and Actform show, labor activism and political agitation for migrant workers' issues is ongoing in Sri Lanka, but on a muted scale. The situation is even worse in the GCC — and, as I will argue here, inactivity in these two spheres is interconnected. In contrast to the situation in the GCC, organizing activities face less resistance in Europe and certain destination countries in East Asia. Staunch activism in countries that send labor to European and Asian destinations reflects these more favorable organizing climates. In this section, I explore labor relations in several of these destinations.

GCC government policies limit organizational activity. GCC countries have strict rules about civil society organizations established by their own citizens, not to mention those organized by guest workers, and they deport "troublesome" foreigners. Although the GCC governments generously grant their citizens many social welfare benefits (free education and health care; subsidized housing, water, and electricity; and well-paid government jobs with pensions and benefits), political rights have not kept pace. Khalaf notes, "Political life in the societies of the Gulf lacked and continues to lack the institutions of democratic representation."[82] For example, the Bahrain Centre for Human Rights lent help to migrants until its director was arrested in September 2004 for criticizing the government.[83] Volunteers reorganized, and the Society for the Protection of Migrant Workers' Rights received a license to operate in December 2004.[84] Other GCC countries are even stricter than Bahrain. In Dubai, "foreign" residents can organize "cultural" groups, but these cannot instigate political actions.[85] Because of the generous social benefits, local people support their governments even though they are not democratic or participatory. For foreign guest workers (who do not receive the same largess from the state) local political conditions limit opportunities for social organization or protesting work conditions.

In contrast to the Middle East, the organizing climate in Hong Kong and Singapore is more liberal. In addition, gender roles in these states are less restrictive for women. Although the state limits migrants' rights in many ways, Hong Kong offers foreign domestic workers a legislated (but still sub-poverty) minimum wage that, at US$470 a month, is nearly four times the going rate in the GCC countries.[86] Further, Hong Kong has various governmentally enforced contract requirements such as rest days, annual holiday, sick leave, and insurance protection. Moreover, Hong Kong has a political environment conducive to labor organizing: "Hong Kong has a vibrant civil society populated by lively labour unions, NGOs, media, religious groups and other organizations."[87] Wee and Sim argue that Hong Kong differs from many other labor-receiving countries in that it is "capitalist, liberal and governed by the rule of law."[88] This organizing climate enables the empowerment of Filipinas, who for many years have dominated the domestic service market in Hong Kong.[89] Indeed, the majority of the migrant labor organizations are "founded, staffed, catalysed or led by Filipinos."[90]

Singapore has a strong state and a weaker civil society, thus political organizing there is less vigorous than in Hong Kong. NGOs focus on service work rather than policy and "stay clear of human rights issues for fear that such advocacy work may be misconstrued as being 'political.'"[91] The government of the Philippines has intervened in labor relations, even temporarily banning Filipina domestic workers from going to Singapore in response to public outcry in the Philippines over the Flor Contemplacion case where a Filipina worker was executed in Singapore. Consequently, workers from Indonesia, where the government is less interventionist, have become more popular with Singapore job agencies and employers.[92] Indonesian domestic workers have fewer rest days and lower starting wages than Filipinas, but are now joining forces with Filipina-led NGOs in a growing show of transnational labor solidarity.[93] These encouraging developments suggest that in favorable labor-organizing climates, domestic workers can and will organize even across national lines to improve their situations.

Although better than the conditions in the Middle East, the situations in Singapore and Hong Kong compare unfavorably to the conditions in the European Union. For example, Leah Briones, who studies migration from the Philippines to Hong Kong and Europe, notes that Filipinas consider themselves better off working "illegally" in Paris than working legally in Hong Kong because Paris has a more liberal civil society.[94] Similarly, Sri Lankans now seek jobs in Italy, preferring them to jobs in the Gulf. Migrant women prefer jobs in Europe not only for the greater political freedoms but also for higher salaries. For example, Jacqueline Andall reports that live-in care work for the elderly pays between 500 and 900 euros a month in Italy.[95] Ecuadorian domestic workers in Madrid can make as much as 550 euros a month; lack of worker documents, along with the inclusion of food and lodging benefits, explains the lower wages in Spain.[96] Au pairs in Germany can make 205 euros a week.[97] In Germany, migrant domestic workers made between eight and ten euros an hour for cleaning and five to eight euros for child care; au pairs and live-ins earned less than live-out domestic workers with a larger circle of clients.[98] These wages compare favorably to the 100 to

125 dollars (65 to 80 euros) a month that Sri Lankan migrants report earning in the Gulf.

Wages and organizing conditions in various countries and regions correlate closely with migrants' valuations of jobs in these locations. Sri Lankan workers consider jobs in Singapore and Hong Kong much more desirable than jobs in the Middle East, and they value jobs in Europe most highly of all. They note, however, that agency fees for jobs rise in direct proportion to job desirability, with jobs in Europe (even illegal ones) unaffordable for most migrants, at least on their first journey abroad. Similarly, Filipina domestic workers often see Hong Kong as a steppingstone for moving on to Israel, Canada, and the EU.[99] These data suggest that workers value jobs in destinations that offer higher pay, greater labor protections, and more autonomy.

Assessing Activism: A Comparison between Sri Lanka and the Philippines

The evidence above suggests that the organizing climate in labor-receiving countries clearly influences the degree of guest worker labor activism. Asian and European destination countries provide more protection for migrant workers than do Middle Eastern countries.[100] Workers in Europe are more likely to organize than are those in Hong Kong and Singapore, with workers in the Middle East the least likely of all to organize. Does the degree of organization allowed in destination countries also correspond with organizing activity in the migrants' home countries?

Research suggests that in addition to shaping migrants' career trajectories, situations in host countries *do* influence behaviors at home. When worker initiatives (such as those organized by Filipinas and Indonesians in Hong Kong) and government activities (such as the Philippine intervention in Singapore) result in better working conditions, people are encouraged to organize and protest for their rights. In contrast, when the host government represses such initiatives (such as in the GCC), laborers face adversity by accommodating to difficult circumstances instead of seeking to challenge or change. In cases in which the larger social structures make protest difficult or fruitless, workers find it difficult and dangerous to organize; and labor unions, NGOs, and sending-country governments are also hampered in supporting migrants. In short, the larger structures in host countries constrain the changes people can envision making, either limiting or encouraging activities at home.

To illustrate this point, consider the relative paucity of organizing going on in Sri Lanka (discussed above) in light of the rich and energetic organizing done by Filipinas at home and even in some countries in which they work. In 1997, Maruja Asis observes, thirty-eight migrant worker organizations were operating in the Philippines.[101] In addition, Filipina domestic workers have organized a number of NGOs and labor unions in Hong Kong.[102] In Taiwan and Singapore they organize around churches.[103] Filipinas are thus active in a wide range of organizations in their home and host countries.

A number of unique factors have doubtless shaped the organizing trajectories of migrants from Sri Lanka and the Philippines. Significant among them, I hypothesize, are the political and personal freedoms that workers experience in the labor-receiving countries. The size, scale, and history of migration; degree of migrant education; and gender roles and norms are also influential.

To understand the effect of host country organizing climates on sending-country labor activism within the comparative framework proposed here, significant differences in the destination countries of Sri Lankan and Filipina transnational domestic workers must be noted. Nearly 90 percent of Sri Lanka's migrant women work in West Asia (particularly Saudi Arabia, Kuwait, the UAE, Qatar, Lebanon, and Jordan).[104] In contrast, Filipino women work in diverse locations around the globe, with only 30 percent going to the GCC (Saudi Arabia, UAE, and Kuwait), 60 percent going to countries in East and Southeast Asia (especially Hong Kong, Japan, Taiwan, and Singapore), and another 6 percent going to Europe (especially Italy and the United Kingdom).[105] Thus Filipinas predominantly work in states in East and Southeast Asia that give more chance for autonomous activities (socializing, moving around unsupervised) and are more conducive to labor organizing than the Middle East.[106]

The size and scale of the migrant flows from Sri Lanka and the Philippines also differ. In 2002, over twice as many migrant women left the Philippines (over 300,000) than left Sri Lanka (133,251).[107] With an estimated stock of 7.9 million overseas contract workers in 2003 and an estimated population of roughly 82.7 million, nearly 10 percent of the population of the Philippines worked abroad.[108] In contrast, in 2002 Sri Lanka's total of 1 million overseas workers and its population of roughly 19.3 million meant that a little over 5 percent of the population was employed abroad.[109]

Educational qualifications also make a difference. E.P. Thompson has decisively illustrated that the working class can generate leaders on its own without recourse to the bourgeois intellectuals that Marx assumed would spearhead the revolution.[110] Nevertheless, I include data on migrant education in hopes that the years people spend in school may be of practical use. The Philippines economy cannot absorb all its college graduates who enter the migrant labor market in search of jobs. Thirty-two percent of Filipina migrant domestic workers go to Hong Kong; of these, 62 percent had received some tertiary education, according to data gathered by Sim and Wee.[111] Similarly, a large majority of Filipinas entering Canada through the Live-in Caregiver Program had bachelor degrees or non-university diplomas.[112] One researcher noted that most of her Filipina interviewees had post-secondary training.[113] In contrast, a Sri Lankan survey found that less than 3 percent of Sri Lanka's housemaid returnees after the 1990 Gulf War had passed their A-level (end of high school) exams.[114] Most Sri Lankan migrant housemaids have only six to nine years of education.[115] Despite high numbers of unemployed female university graduates, educated Sri Lankan women continue to refuse to take on the low-status job of housemaids.[116] These significant educational differences between Filipina and Sri Lankan migrant women may in part account for the greater labor agitation among Filipinas.

The history of migration may also play a role in levels of labor activism. Filipino laborers have been migrating since the early twentieth century.[117] In contrast, Sri Lankan labor migration began in earnest more recently — in the mid

1970s. The longer the period of migration, the savvier and better organized the laborers. For example, Constable reports that Filipina migrant activists have become more visible and vocal in Hong Kong over the past ten years, and are now affiliating with newly arrived migrants from Indonesia.[118] Similarly, the second generation of Sri Lankan migrants seems poised to migrate in a new way: compared to the earlier generation of married Sri Lankan women working in the Middle East, among the current twenty-somethings, more unmarried migrants (male and female) are going abroad, and they seek better jobs in more liberal destination countries.[119] I argue that the levels of labor activism in the Philippines and Sri Lanka reflect the length of time that people from both countries have been migrating. It takes time for people to build networks of kin, acquaintances, co-ethnics, and other allies in destination countries to facilitate migration, share local knowledge, and provide security in case of difficulties. Future research could fruitfully explore whether Sri Lankan migration will transform as Philippine migration already has, with more educated, mobile migrants heading to "better" destination countries, where a politicized group of activists may voice sophisticated critiques of global capitalism.

To summarize this comparison, a greater proportion of the Philippines population works overseas, over twice as many women migrate from the Philippines as from Sri Lanka, Filipina domestic servants have higher educational qualifications than Sri Lankans do, and two thirds of them go to places where protest, though difficult, is more possible than in the Middle East. More (and more educated) Filipina migrants have worked longer in destination countries that offer more freedom, leading to more organizing activity. I argue that these factors in large part explain the greater NGO activity in the Philippines as compared to Sri Lanka.

Conclusion

In this article, I have argued that political freedoms in destination countries have a significant effect on organizing activities within host nations. Comparing the Sri Lankan and Philippine situations, I contend that the vibrant activism in the Philippines correlates with the liberal organizing climates in the EU and in East and Southeast Asia, while the paucity of organizing in Sri Lanka correlates with the strict repression of guest workers in the GCC.

Nevertheless, although the Philippines has greater government activity and the highest number of migrant NGOs among labor-sending countries in Asia, activists feel that the government and civil society efforts have still not sufficed to protect migrants adequately.[120] This raises the question of what factors hamper even the more proactive sending-country governments in their advocacy for migrant citizens. Economic evidence suggests that labor-sending countries are rarely in a strong position to influence guest worker labor conditions even in liberal, organization-friendly host countries. The institutions with the most power to protect Sri Lankan migrant workers are the governments in GCC countries — bodies that benefit from cheap, exploitable labor, and have no democratic obligations to these foreign nationals. This situation reflects the existing hierarchy among nations; it also reflects the expectation that a sovereign nation will regulate its own labor market and labor laws — an expectation that persists despite the increasingly transnational character of labor. Given the structures impeding civil and state representatives from interceding in favor of migrant laborers, the paucity of labor activism in Sri Lanka no longer seems so puzzling.

Since the inception of their discipline, anthropologists have argued about the relationship between the individual and society. Scholars ask how much agency actors have to resist and transform social structures.[121] The data presented here reveal the reasons that unions, NGOs, and politicians in Sri Lanka have not succeeded, despite the wholehearted efforts of well-meaning individuals, in their efforts to support migrant laborers. From whence, then, can change originate for Sri Lankan migrants, particularly given the strict political climate of the GCC? The weakness of labor-sending countries to protect their laborers highlights the need for two regulatory mechanisms: multilateral agreements between labor-sending countries about minimum contract elements and an international mechanism for enforcing standards and conditions. But states weigh the benefits of multilateral cooperation against the fear that by requesting improvements for their migrants they will lose their share of the guest worker market to other nations.

Having tried earnestly but inadequately to support and advocate for migrant laborers, migrant workers and activists alike point to the Sri Lankan government's responsibility to protect its citizens working abroad. But key consular staff members, such as Ruhunage, say that they do not have the powers to do their job adequately, shifting responsibility toward local officials in the GCC. I saw a certain irony in the fact that when I tracked down Ruhunage, the one person most Sri Lankans would hold responsible for bettering labor conditions in the UAE, he in turn suggested that change needed to spring from seminars, meetings, and academic research. Instead of merely reporting on and assessing labor activism, researchers are now called on to do the heavy lifting, providing a venue for voicing critiques related to neoliberal economic policies, labor issues, gender discrimination, and human rights. Repressive structures in the GCC, combined with a dearth of international regulatory devices and a disadvantageous division of international labor, leaves migrants, activists, government servants, and scholars alike facing an uphill battle to support and defend migrant workers.

ACKNOWLEDGMENTS: Research funding was provided by the American Institute for Sri Lankan Studies (AISLS), Portland State University, the Oregon Council for the Humanities, and the National Science Foundation. Special thanks are due to M.M. Deshapriya at the SLBFE for his help with statistical data. Prior versions of this paper were presented at the American Anthropological Association's annual meeting in 2005, the Social Science Research Council's International Conference on "Inter-Asian Connections" in Dubai, United Arab Emirates, in 2008, and at the conference "G.C.C. — Gender, Connectivity, and Change in the Gulf Arab States" at the University of California, Irvine, in 2008.

❑

5. Transcending the Border

Transnational Imperatives in Singapore's Migrant Worker Rights Movement

Lenore Lyons

THE FEMINIZATION OF TRANSNATIONAL MIGRATION has attracted the attention of numerous activists who have responded to the needs and interests of female migrant workers throughout the Asia-Pacific region. While the majority of these activists are affiliated with middle-class nongovernmental organizations (NGOs) that advocate in behalf of migrant workers, a growing number of grassroots organizations have also been formed by current and former migrant workers. Although a transnational dimension is emerging in the activities of these migrant worker organizations, as evidenced by the formation of regional NGOs and cross-border coalitions, scholars have focused little attention on the transnationalization of migrant labor activism in comparison with other social movements. Instead, the majority of studies of migrant worker NGOs in the Asia-Pacific region are individual country and/or organization studies.[1] Additionally, a few studies of trade union–NGO interactions have been produced,[2] along with several accounts of the roles regional advocacy networks have played.[3] What remains underexamined in this literature are the factors that promote or inhibit activist links between organizations based in different locations, as well as the challenges and contradictions confronting organizations that attempt to address the rights of female migrant workers within a transnational frame.

Attention to the connections between domestic workers and advocacy groups, as well as between groups working to address the rights of migrant workers, provides a means to trace the differences and similarities in the experiences of domestic workers and an opportunity to challenge taken-for-granted assumptions about the form and content of migrant labor organizing. Literature on global social movements tends to valorize activism that extends beyond the boundaries of the nation-state and to celebrate the role that activist groups and NGOs play in lobbying transnationally in behalf of both national and "global" citizens.[4] As a consequence, nationally based NGOs are being encouraged to "scale up" and regional/international NGOs and networks are increasingly seen as the key players in bringing about sustained improvements in the working conditions of migrant workers. In the rush to promote the transnationalization of migrant worker organizing, however, only a few critical voices have interrogated the motivations and implications of moving beyond the local and/or national scale to address the rights of migrant labor. Aihwa Ong is one scholar who has argued that NGO claims about building a "global public sphere" need to be regarded with skepticism. She states that because migrant worker NGOs are situated within "particular constellations of power and ethics; their interventions can actually generate new moral hierarchies" that can support national agendas and capitalist interests.[5] Writing about transnational feminist activism, Manisha Desai points to another problem with claims for scaling up, namely, that transnational social movements can engage with the forces of globalization at the level of discursive power and yet remain depoliticized at the level of policy-making.[6] In other words, criticizing globalization is one thing, but bringing about sustained improvements in the lives of women globally is an entirely different matter.

To further our understanding of these issues, this article examines the transnationalization of campaigns in support of foreign domestic workers through a case study of two advocacy-oriented NGOs in Singapore, Transient Workers Count Too (TWC2) and the Humanitarian Organisation for Migration Economics (HOME).[7] This study, which is based on an examination of over forty organizations working to address the rights of migrant workers in Singapore and Malaysia, combines in-depth interviews with key informants, documentary analysis of relevant print-based materials, newspapers, and internet sources. The organizational meetings and activities I participated in proved to be an important means to compare a group's official "presentation of self" (obtained through documents and interviews) against everyday practice. During the period of research, I also attended international meetings and conferences attended by a number of the organizations under study in order to examine the nature of their transnational and cross-border encounters.

Before discussing the specific case studies, I provide a brief discussion of the multiple meanings associated with the concept "transnational activism" as it is deployed in the literature on migrant worker organizing. Transnationalization processes, I argue, can best be understood when clear analytic categories are developed and applied to various types of organizing activities. I then provide an overview of the sociopolitical context in which civil society activists in Singapore operate. This synopsis outlines the key issues NGOs and other activists face as they work to address the rights of migrant women in Singapore. My analysis of TWC2 and HOME reveals that although a "transnational imperative" has begun to shape the activities of both NGOs, their motivations for engaging beyond the border are quite different. By revealing a diversity of forms and meanings associated with the processes of scaling up, this article contributes to the broader scholarly process of understanding the complex nature of transnational organizing and challenges previous studies that assert that transnational activism is a necessary and natural outcome of migrant worker organizing. Considering the factors that support or inhibit various kinds of transnational activist engagements by migrant worker organizations, allows us to measure the impact that migrant worker organizing is having on the lives of migrant workers.

Transnationalization of Migrant Worker Organizing

Most discussions of transnationalism in the context of migrant worker organizing are clouded by a lack of conceptual clarity about the meanings and usages of the term "transnational activism." One of the main ways in which the concept is used is to refer to instances of cross-border campaigning by nationally and regionally based organizations.[8] This usage is consistent with literature on global social movements that defines transnational activism as activism in which civil society organizations (CSOs) and individuals operate across state borders.[9] The most concrete forms of this type of activism are transnational advocacy networks (TANs), informal and shifting structures based on shared values through which NGOs, social movement activists, international agencies, and government officials exchange information and resources.[10] Several scholars have criticized this focus on TANs; they prefer instead to devote their attention to transnational social movements (TSMs), which they claim use more contentious methods of engagement than NGO-based networks.[11] Within the literature on migrant worker organizing, however, the distinction between TSMs and TANs is often blurred, such that any difference in the meanings and modalities of resistance between these forms of transnational activism is unclear.

Another understanding of transnational activism that emerges in the literature on migrant worker organizing is built around the concept of "transnational solidarity."[12] Here, the term "transnational activism" is extended to include national-level coalitions and alliances that are made up of individuals and/or organizations representing different national groups. These groups are said to be "transnational" in the sense that they transcend nationality as the basis for migrant worker organizing. To describe such coalitions as examples of transnational activism, however, is confusing and it potentially dilutes the analytic (and activist) potential of cross-border organizing efforts. For this reason, I prefer the term "trans-ethnic" advocacy or solidarity when describing the work of such groups. Trans-ethnic advocacy is an important means of ensuring that all migrant women benefit from the gains made by individual national groups and is especially important in situations where strong Filipino TANs have had the greatest success in improving the conditions of employment for Filipina domestic workers.[13]

In making a distinction between cross-border organizing and trans-ethnic solidarity I am not suggesting that trans-ethnic organizations or networks cannot cross national borders. For example, in discussing the example of the Asian Migrants' Coordinating Body (AMCB) in Hong Kong, Hsia points to the ways in which transnational solidarity can become the basis for linking the needs and concerns of one national group to the concerns of other groups at the global level.[14] She gives the example of the AMCB's involvement in antiglobalization campaigns in Hong Kong. In this instance, a nationally based coalition of migrant worker organizations participated in an events-based form of cross-border activism. The significance of this event was the promotion of a transnational (or global) frame of reference in understanding the role of globalization in shaping the particular circumstances facing migrant workers in Hong Kong, as well as the conditions facing the working poor in sending countries. Hsia describes this as a form of "transnationalism from below" that potentially links current and former migrant workers across national borders. Constable uses a similar understanding in her discussion of the participation of domestic workers in anti-WTO protests in Hong Kong in 2005.[15]

Widening our understanding of transnational activism to include how the transnational is constructed within the activist practices of migrant worker organizations (i.e., how local activists "frame" their work) provides a means to examine how ideas circulate between different scales and become translated into concrete practices within specific organizational contexts. To avoid replicating the conceptual sloppiness discussed above in relation to trans-ethnic solidarity, we must distinguish between cross-border organizing and adopting a transnational frame in local/national activism. While the latter may be an important factor determining the success of efforts to organize transnationally,[16] it is more accurately described as transnational framing (or the ability to "think transnationally") rather than transnational activism (which I use here in its narrowest sense to refer to cross-border organizing). Distinguishing between various forms of transnationalism (trans-ethnic solidarity, transnational framing, and cross-border organizing) allows for greater conceptual clarity when describing the work of activists engaged with transnational issues such as cross-border labor migration flows. As the following discussion will demonstrate, such distinctions are crucial if we are to evaluate the success of "transnational efforts" to address the problems faced by migrant workers.

State–Civil Society Relations

Migrant labor is an integral part of the Singapore economy and migrant women typically occupy positions in manufacturing, hospitality, and domestic work. Although it has been a major receiving country of foreign workers since the late 1970s, the Singapore government is reticent about releasing data on foreign worker numbers due to perceived public sensitivity about their presence. Figures from the 2007 edition of the *Manpower Yearbook* show that foreign workers constitute 27.5 percent of the total workforce (n=713,300).[17] About 550,000 of these workers are considered unskilled or low skilled, of which an estimated 150,000 are domestic workers, made up of a third each from the Philippines and Indonesia, and a significant minority from Sri Lanka.[18] This equates to approximately one foreign domestic worker to every seven households.[19]

Although Singapore is a major receiving country for female migrant labor in the region, migrant worker organizations are noticeably absent due to tight state control over the space of civil society and to the particular circumstances surrounding earlier attempts to advocate on behalf of migrant workers. The activities of NGOs in Singapore are curtailed by strict rules governing the formal registration of associations and societies, a strong interventionist stance by the state, restrictions placed on the activities of international NGOs and other agencies, and often-fraught diplomatic relations with the two major migrant-sending countries, Indonesia and the Philippines.[20] Opportunities for NGOs to advance their causes depend in large part on the extent to which their goals are congruent with the state's own ideology and interests. Moderation, consultation, and consensus are key modes of operation as NGOs negotiate the constraints of state–civil society relations.[21] When NGOs threaten the ruling party's political foundations, however, the state uses both legislation and other means to clamp down on activists. While the Constitution guarantees freedom of association (Article 14) in principle, organizations with more than ten members or committees with more than five members are required to register under the Societies Act or the Companies Act. Individuals who participate in groups that are not officially registered face the threat of arrest and imprisonment for participating in "illegal assemblies." Furthermore, all registered organizations are expressly prohibited from engaging in "political activity."

In relation to transnational connections, while activist groups mobilize around international support and standards, the anti-West/anti–U.S. position the Singaporean government often adopts (as evidenced in the rhetoric surrounding so-called Asian values) has made such connections more complex. Locally based NGOs are wary of receiving funding from overseas sources for fear that this may result in government suspicion about their activities.[22] Foreign-based NGOs find it difficult to become formally registered, and without registration cannot operate locally. In a 2004 statement explaining changes to the registration process for NGOs, the government stated that groups whose activities were related to religious, ethnic, civil, and political rights, or the governance of Singapore, needed to be carefully screened because they may potentially give rise to "law and order" problems and carry out activities that may be prejudicial to the national interest. In addition, these groups needed to be scrutinized closely to ensure that "foreign elements do not hijack [them] to serve a foreign agenda which is contrary to our national interests."[23] These restrictions have resulted in a very small international NGO presence and very few transnational linkages between local, regional, and global groups.

NGO workers and other activists working to support migrant workers have been subject to government surveillance and harassment. For many years issues facing female migrant workers have been off limits to civil society activists. Like many topics deemed "too sensitive" or "taboo" for activist intervention, the issue was never publicly identified by the state in its official statements as an area that was out-of-bounds. The governing elite refers to "out-of-bounds markers" (OB markers) as points that delimit acceptable civil engagement. Ho describes these as "issues that are too sensitive to be discussed in public for fear of destabilizing or jeopardizing public peace and order."[24] The ruling People's Action Party (PAP) government is responsible for determining the limits of the OB markers, a task that it largely performs retrospectively with the result that what actually constitutes "unacceptable political engagement" is unclear.[25] The association of migrant worker issues with the so-called Marxist Conspiracy has meant that few NGOs have been willing to address them. The Marxist Conspiracy is a term used to describe the arrest and detention of twenty-two people in

Lenore Lyons

T-shirts produced in 1007 for two foreign domestic workers campaigns in Singapore: the white shirt (left) was part of a TWC2–sponsored campaign and the dark shirt (right) was produced for the UnitedFDW's "Day Off" campaign.

May 1987 under the Internal Security Act (ISA)[26] for threatening the state and national interests.[27] Among those arrested were Catholic social workers and lay workers from the Geylang Catholic Centre for Foreign Workers. This group advocated for higher wages, social security benefits, job security, and fair employment conditions for all foreign workers.[28] At the time of their arrest, the government claimed that Catholic organizations were "a cover for political agitation" to "radicalise student and Christian activists."[29] Those arrested were detained without trial. Some later confessed and were rehabilitated with an agreement not to enter into "politics." The Geylang Center was subsequently closed.

The events surrounding the Marxist Conspiracy cast a shadow over advocacy efforts in support of foreign workers for the next decade because local NGOs were reticent to speak about migrant worker issues in case they were accused of posing a national security threat. This fear, combined with the relatively small civil society sector and an inherent conservatism amongst CSOs, meant that migrant workers lacked local supporters who could advocate in their behalf. Government restrictions on unionization of the migrant workforce also ensured that the traditional labor movement had a limited role to play in addressing the working conditions of low-skilled migrant workers. The exclusion of migrant domestic workers from the Employment Act further restricted opportunities to unionize foreign domestic workers (FDWs).[30] Tight state control over the registration of societies also meant that grassroots associations of migrant workers could not be established as formal civil society actors, although a number of informal social and self-help support networks were formed on an ad hoc basis by workers from different national groups.

Migrant worker issues only began to be publicly debated again in the late 1990s when instances of abuse and violence committed by or against FDWs were increasingly reported in the mainstream media. A number of high-profile cases attracted both local and international press attention, resulting in tense diplomatic relations between the Singapore government and the two major sending countries, the Philippines (over the Flor Contemplacion case[31]) and Indonesia (over the Muawanatul Chasanah case[32]). Public outrage over the latter case created a catalyst for NGOs, faith-based groups, CSOs, and members of the public to come together to demand better treatment of FDWs. As a consequence, since 2003 interest in issues migrant domestic workers face in Singapore has exploded. A number of new NGOs and networks have formed to address the needs and interests of this group of workers. The majority of these are faith-based groups attached to local churches that provide pastoral services, training courses, and leisure-time activities. Private enterprises and not-for-profit training and education centers catering primarily to migrant workers are also growing in number. Some migrant workers have established their own nationality-based support groups that function primarily as social clubs and sites for information sharing. In 2006 the local arts community also became involved with migrant workers, offering workshops for workers and staging public performances that highlight the issues faced by labor migrants. Only a limited number of groups engage in advocacy and research activities. Transient Workers Count Too (TWC2) and HOME (Humanitarian Organisation for Migration Economics) are the most active of these advocacy-oriented groups. To date, their activities have been focused mostly at the local level through their engagements with the Singaporean government, employment agencies, and employers. This orientation has recently begun to change, however, as they seek to develop transnational networks and support regional and international campaigns. In the next section I provide a detailed discussion of both groups, before turning to a discussion of transnationalism.

Transient Workers Count Too

Transient Workers Count Too was formed in 2004. In the previous year, a network of concerned individuals and representatives of NGOs and voluntary welfare organizations calling themselves "The Working Committee 2" (TWC2) met informally with the goal of addressing attitudes toward and treatment of domestic workers in Singapore.[33] After a successful yearlong public awareness campaign focused on the plight of foreign domestic workers, the group was formally registered under the Societies Act. Membership is open to all Singapore citizens, permanent residents, and work permit holders over the age of eighteen. There are currently fewer than one hundred members, the majority of whom are middle class and Chinese. Fewer than 20 percent of TWC2's members are foreign domestic workers. In accordance with the organization's constitution, foreigners who do not hold Singaporean permanent residency cannot join unless they hold a work permit (issued to lower-skilled migrant workers such as domestic workers), thus nonresidents and employment pass holders (skilled migrant workers) are excluded. The decision to restrict foreign membership in this way reflects the government's concern that groups such as TWC2 with an explicit focus on "non-Singaporeans" may be "hijacked" by outsiders.[34]

TWC2's stated objectives are: (1) To be a central resource center for foreign worker matters and a repository of information and material relevant to the position of foreign workers. (2) To be a coordinating and referral point for all stakeholders. (3) To work toward the professionalization of the foreign domestic worker industry and the development of a mutually satisfactory relationship between employers and foreign domestic workers; and (4) To encourage greater consideration for the requirements of foreign workers in general and to promote good employer-employee relations.[35] Although the original Working Committee 2 was focused exclusively on foreign domestic workers, its registration under the Societies Act TWC2 signaled a broadening of the organization's objectives beyond the needs and interests of FDWs to all "transient workers." While it claims that "Everyone is entitled to be treated with respect and dignity, with no discrimination of any kind, such as along lines of race, colour, gender, language, religion or class,"[36] TWC2 has been most active in relation to the issues facing FDWs and has had limited engagement with male workers, undocumented workers, and/or workers in the informal sectors such as migrant sex workers.

TWC2's work addresses extreme forms of abuse against domestic workers as well as ways to improve their working conditions. This includes the standardization and regulation of working hours and tasks, the equalization of wages, the incorporation of domestic workers into the Employment Act, and the implementation of the right of domestic workers to "live out." In December 2006, TWC2 launched a telephone help line that provides information and assistance to workers in need. Help line volunteers deal with a range of issues, including cases of abuse and nonpayment of wages. TWC2 manages a small amount of casework itself, and refers other migrant workers to the services of organizations such as HOME (which runs shelters for men and women) and the Ministry of Manpower.

TWC2 frames its work around the concept of "dignity" through its slogan "Dignity Overdue," which refers to the humane treatment of migrant workers in Singapore. TWC2's primary consideration has been putting the rights of all documented migrant workers in Singapore on the national stage and changing the mindsets and actions of Singaporean employers and policy-makers. In then vice president John Gee's words,

> What we want to do is to see that they get treated according to the standards that Singaporeans would want themselves.... We have to reach out to the public and try and bring about a change in attitudes so that the workers are treated more considerately.[37]

As Gee notes, TWC2 believes that the central problem facing FDWs in Singapore is a widely held view amongst employers that migrant workers do not deserve the same rights as local workers. Accordingly, Gee told me, a change in the situation facing FDWs will only occur when Singaporeans no longer treat migrant workers differently from the way they treat locals. The way to bring about an improvement in the lives of FDWs, TWC2 believes, is through structural reform (e.g., introduction of standardized contracts) and behavioral change by individual employers.

TWC2 has had limited contact with NGOs based overseas and until 2007 it was largely isolated from transnational activist networks. Prior to this date, its most visible form of cross-border engagement was participation in regional conferences and forums. Attendance at conferences is an important part of the knowledge production work that activists engage in within their own countries as well as transnationally. These interactions, however, did not translate into concrete cross-border collaborations or campaigns. Similarly, although TWC2 engages in frequent "dialogue" with non-Singaporean stakeholders such as diplomats in the embassies of sending countries, this too is not part of a strong cross-border focus. What this has meant at a practical level is that TWC2 has had little opportunity to observe and interact with NGOs that address the feminization of labor migration as an issue linked to globalization. Similarly, it has not been part of advocacy efforts that seek to develop regional (rather than national) responses to the problems FDWs face.

Recently this has begun to change. In 2007, TWC2 participated in the Asean Civil Society Conference (ACSC–3) hosted in Singapore and through that meeting was able to link up with the United for Foreign Domestic Worker Rights campaign.[38] As a member of this informal network, TWC2 shares its experiences and activities with other members via email and has had the opportunity to observe how other groups engage in regional policy-making processes. In 2007, TWC2 also became a member of Migrant Forum in Asia (MFA), a network of over 290 NGOs, associations, and trade unions of migrant workers, as well as individual advocates from both sending and receiving countries throughout Asia. MFA acts as a facilitator and regional communication point between member organizations and advocates, addressing discriminatory laws and policies, violence against women migrants, unjust living conditions, unemployment in the homeland, and other issues affecting migrant workers. The MFA's role extends beyond its lobbying efforts in relation to international regulatory regimes to solidarity actions and financial support for local NGOs, making it a very important component of the informal regime centered around migrant worker–related activism.[39] The decision to join MFA reflects a growing awareness within TWC2's executive committee that change at the local level may depend on regional pressure being placed on both sending and receiving countries to address the problems migrant workers face. The fact that MFA has twice hosted conferences in Singapore and invited TWC2 to participate is also significant.[40]

Humanitarian Organisation for Migration Economics

Like TWC2, the Humanitarian Organisation for Migration Economics (HOME) was also registered under the Societies Act in 2004. HOME was founded by Bridget Lew, a former coordinator of the Singapore Archdiocesan Commission for the Pastoral Care of Migrants and Itinerant People (ACMI), which is the Catholic Church's ministry for migrant workers in Singapore. Although HOME has a formal constitution and membership as required under the Societies Act, it does not solicit new members and its total membership is less than twenty indi-

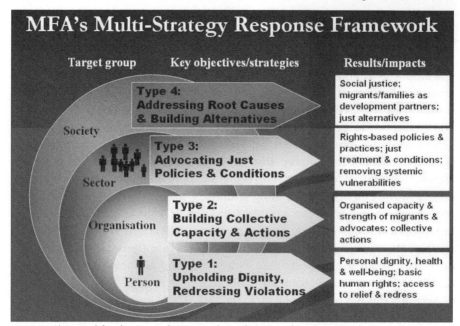

A poster designed for the Seventh Regional Conference of Migration, Jakarta, Indonesia, June 2001, illustrates the range and thrust of Migrant Forum in Asia's work.

viduals. Its members provide financial and moral support to HOME's activities rather than being a source of volunteer labor or campaign activism. HOME is linked to a for-profit sister organization — StarHome — a domestic worker employment agency. According to Lew, the majority of problems faced by workers can be attributed to poor practices by employment placement agencies. In founding StarHome, she wanted to establish an agency that would set an industry standard with regard to fees and contracts and the treatment of migrant workers. Lew also hoped that StarHome would provide an income stream to support HOME's welfare and advocacy services.

HOME runs two help desks and two hotlines — one specifically for female domestic workers and the other for "other migrant workers," with the latter functioning primarily as a support service for male migrant workers. HOME also runs two shelters — one each for men and women. While the majority of those in the shelter are documented migrant workers, HOME has also taken in a limited number of undocumented workers, including migrant sex workers. The shelters and help line services catering to migrant workers operate on sex-segregated terms, reflecting a division of HOME's activities between services primarily in support of migrant domestic workers (the largest group of migrant women seeking HOME's assistance) and services aimed at migrant men (primarily construction workers). HOME also operates two computer training centers (CyberHome) funded by a 2006 grant from Microsoft's Unlimited Potential Program to combat human trafficking in the region. The two centers provide basic IT education for migrant workers. In 2008, HOME was given a grant by Western Union to set up an English Language and Caregiver's training facility for migrant workers (LifeHome).

In addition to its welfare and training activities, HOME is engaged in the following advocacy and support efforts: (1) legal assistance for workers who have experienced abuse and injustice and highlighting these cases to the authorities (Ministry of Manpower/Police); (2) public education on issues affecting migrant workers; and (3) dialogue sessions with policy-makers, such as the Ministry of Manpower and other authorities and stakeholders.[41] Although HOME's advocacy activities are very similar to those performed by TWC2, the latter has developed a much more high-profile public awareness campaign in support of migrant domestic workers. Conversely, HOME has enjoyed better relations with the ruling party than TWC2, a fact that reflects the personalities and backgrounds of their respective executive committees and the nature of their advocacy efforts. TWC2 has adopted a more vocal lobbying and advocacy role, whereas HOME has taken a more low-key approach that focuses on service provision and "closed door" dialogue sessions with members of the bureaucracy. In many respects, HOME has been willing to let TWC2 take the more vocal position because TWC2 has less to lose in relation to possible government de-registration.[42]

HOME's philosophy is summed up in its "culture of welcome" in which "No man, woman or child is a stranger. We are family." HOME's slogan is "The Global Family" and its activities are aimed at promoting a "global image of a welcoming host country" that "welcomes guest workers to contribute to nation building."[43] HOME's name reflects the organization's underlying philosophy, as formulated in this statement of Lew's:

The underlying reasons for migration are basically, at this moment, economic reasons. There are pull and the push factors. Overseas workers, they come here [because] they are pulled by the better economy in Singapore and they are pushed out by the poor economy in their own country.... We are not political, we are humanitarian. And our concern is something to do with economics because our government always talks about economics, so practical and pragmatic. So when I chose the name, I decided [on] a name that does not scare the authorities or scare society. And also the acronym is "home."[44]

Lew's emphasis on the organization's humanitarian role is reflected in HOME's focus on welfare service provision. Although Lew believes that advocacy efforts are important to bring about long-term systemic changes, she feels personally compelled to address the physical and emotional abuse suffered by many migrant workers whom she describes as "victims." With few other shelter options available to migrant workers in Singapore, HOME provides an important service to migrant workers waiting to have their cases dealt with by the Ministry of Manpower, the Immigration and Checkpoints Authority, or the courts.

In comparison to TWC2, HOME has been much less tentative about engaging transnationally. Although HOME is a secular organization, Lew has been able to form connections with a range of faith-based groups in the region through her involvement in the Catholic Church. In 2006, Lew met with the Scalabrini Sisters based in Manila with the aim of establishing a Scalabrini lay center to assist migrant workers in Singapore. Amid ongoing concerns about the risks of establishing a Catholic-based migrant worker organization in Singapore, Lew decided to establish a shelter to assist foreign domestic workers in Indonesia. In May 2007, Solidaritas Migran Scalabrini Indonesia (SMS Indonesia) was registered in Batam, an Indonesian island a short distance by ferry from Singapore. SMS is a secular organization whose members are or were women migrant domestic workers. Its stated objectives are

> [to] provide pre-departure human rights based education for women migrant workers; provide social and advocacy services for women and children victims of human trafficking; develop and implements [*sic*] reintegration livelihood projects for victims and their families; and collaborate strategically with global and local government and non-government agencies to uphold the dignity and rights of women migrant workers.[45]

SMS Indonesia runs a shelter catering to the needs of FDWs from HOME who are transiting in Batam on their way back to their villages in Indonesia. A similar shelter has also been established in Manila (SMS Philippines).

HOME joined Migrant Forum in Asia in 2006, and through its affiliation became involved with the Asian Domestic Worker Assembly (ADWA) held in Manila in 2007.[46] ADWA, which is co-organized by MFA, the Coalition for Migrants Rights (CMR), Asian Migrant Centre (AMC), Alliance of Progressive Labor (APL), and Human Rights Watch (HRW), is an assembly of FDW grassroots organizations that provides a forum for migrant workers to discuss common issues and concerns.[47] HOME participated in the first and second assembly meetings as an NGO supporter. HOME representatives also attended the MFA conferences held in Singapore in 2006 and 2007, and the executive director, Jolovan Wham, was on the ACSC–3 organizing committee. Wham is also a member of the Singapore Working Group for an Asean Human Rights Mechanism, and in this role has continued to promote migrant worker issues at both a regional and local level. His involvement in the ACSC–3 ensured that migrant worker issues were placed at the forefront of matters Asean civil society groups debated throughout the conference. Lew and the SMS Indonesia coordinator also participated in the UnitedFDW meeting held during the conference and, together with TWC2, signed the UnitedFDW Statement presented to Asean member governments.

There was some rivalry between the HOME and TWC2 in the first few years of their establishment, but more recently they have begun to work together. In December 2007, together with Unifem Singapore, they launched a "Day Off" campaign. These collaborative efforts, however, are still in their infancy as both organizations seek to find their specific niche in relation to migrant worker issues. Given the limited amount of funding available to support civil society activism in relation to migrant labor, and the costs associated with running service activities, some rationalization and/or specialization of activities may occur as the two groups mature.

Transnational Imperatives

In order to understand the nature of transnational organizing in behalf of FDWs in Singapore it is important to recognize that HOME and TWC2 have both emerged out of Singapore's predominantly middle-class civil society sector.

Thus, unlike the majority of organizations that are the focus of scholarly interest in FDW activism in Hong Kong, TWC2 and HOME are not formally linked to social movements in migrant labor sending countries. This significantly alters the nature and form of their transnationalism. HOME and TWC2 have always been "trans-ethnic" in the sense that their membership is open to Singapore citizens and permanent residents and FDWs of all nationalities. Domestic workers (or former FDWs) have taken on a range of roles in both organizations, primarily as volunteer event organizers, trainers, and counselors. Due to state-imposed restrictions on the registration of NGOs, however, the executive structure of both groups is limited to Singapore citizens and permanent residents. Trans-ethnic solidarity is thus inhibited by state policies regulating the operation of CSOs, and consequently migrant women have a limited voice in shaping the activities of both groups.

Despite these limitations, trans-ethnic solidarity is evident in the decisions both NGOs have made to address the needs of migrant domestic workers of all nationalities rather than specific national groups. In an environment where employment agents actively market "maids" on the basis of national characteristics (e.g., Filipinas are good with children, Indonesians are better at manual labor) and where market differentiation has real consequences in relation to conditions of work (particularly wages and rest days), focusing on the similarities in working conditions women migrant workers face serves an important political purpose. It has positive benefits in moving attention away from the national stereotypes that circulate within employment agencies and amongst the wider public. An unintended consequence of focusing on FDWs as a group, however, is that the particular experiences of women as national subjects are rarely enunciated. Instead, TWC2 and HOME address the common experiences of all migrant workers once they arrive in Singapore rather than the circumstances that led them to travel abroad for work or the ways that nationality and ethnicity shape their experiences of labor migration.

This form of trans-ethnic advocacy has implications for the emergence of transnational solidarity between members of both organizations and between members and the wider FDW community. Genuine transnational solidarity would require both organizations to pay greater attention to their own location within the global economy. It would involve moving beyond issues surrounding conditions of work at the local level to an understanding of how the global division of labor operates. This in turn would require a more reflexive stance about their members' own class location within the global capitalist system and recognition that middle-class Singaporeans are consumers of other (poorer) women's transnational labor. This form of transnational solidarity would require a simultaneous framing of migrant labor issues at both the global and local levels and a critical interrogation of Singapore's economic dependence on foreign workers in order to move beyond statements about the need to treat workers "better" in order to ensure continued levels of household (and by association, national) productivity. Instead, both TWC2 and HOME frame their activism as supportive of the state and the capitalist system and ultimately as supportive of employers. TWC2's website, for example, declares that its aim is "promoting good employer-employee relations,"[48] and HOME takes an active role in recruiting and deploying workers through its employment agency. Their support for the rights of employers marks a significant point of difference with many grassroots migrant worker organizations in other receiving countries.

This positive framing of employer and employee rights is based on an argument in support of migrant women's "right to work" (as opposed to their "labor rights"). This notion of rights is frequently deployed by middle-class employers who emphasize the inevitability (due to poverty, corruption, and the lack of economic development in sending countries) of poor women's need to work abroad in order to support their families. Claims about women's "right to work" are linked to similar statements made by Singapore's middle-class women's movement about Singaporean women's right to work outside the home. In the face of state-sponsored pro-natalist policies, equal employment opportunities for female citizens are dependent on the importation of cheap foreign domestic labor.[49] The foreign domestic worker scheme guarantees poor (foreign) women's right to work — a gesture that middle-class Singaporean families can bestow (at below market wages) but which sending governments seemingly cannot. In my fieldwork I have observed many faith-based NGOs, embassies, and nationality-based support groups embrace this "rights-based approach" by organizing training activities that encourage FDWs to become "better cooks" and "better carers." In her study of Indonesia, Aihwa Ong observes a similar phenomenon amongst NGOs that support migrant women's role as economic agents by marketing and training them for overseas work.[50] Ong's analysis unfortunately lacks any empirical discussion of specific organizations, so it is difficult to know which NGOs her study refers to.[51] In the case of Singapore, the example of HOME provides a clear example of an advocacy-oriented NGO that also actively recruits and markets women for the domestic service industry.

In supporting poor migrant women's right to work, I have observed some faith-based NGOs encourage middle-class families to treat FDWs as family members and not as employees. Ong notes a similar deployment of migrant women's "biowelfare" as the basis for moral claims against the host society in her discussion of migrant worker NGOs in Southeast Asia. She argues that NGOs negotiate with various governments for a "transnational sense of moral responsibility" to migrant workers by mapping "political systems that are neither state nor market, but that articulate with both."[52] While rejecting the idea of FDWs as "family members," HOME and TWC2 nonetheless tap into these ideas and invoke compassion and dignity as the key ingredients of their separate campaigns to improve FDW conditions of work. Rather than invoking human rights as the basis for addressing conditions of work, they call for the humane treatment of workers while they are in Singapore. While Ong sees this approach as an important site of "neoliberal exception" and as the basis for undoing the "conceptual separation between rights and ethics,"[53] I am less positive than she is about the actual benefits that accrue to migrant women by using this strategy. Such a stance serves to entrench the gendered positioning of women as vulnerable subjects by invoking their status as daughters and mothers who deserve protection from violence. It also serves to cement the hegemonic position of an authoritarian state that promotes the role of "voluntary welfare organizations" (VWOs) as care units in a developmentalist model of economic growth.[54] VWOs are increasingly being encouraged to take on welfare services (such as shelters and health-care programs) that remove the state's responsibility to both citizens and others. HOME's provision of a dedicated migrant worker shelter thus removes the onus on the state to address the needs of workers (and women) in distress. In this case the blurring between the right to work and an ethics of care masks the vulnerable position of FDWs who are located inside the private space of the home and outside of the space of formally regulated labor laws.

In the context of a middle-class NGO sector that is at times skeptical of and at other times reliant on the academy, Ong's account also risks becoming the source of NGO wisdom on the way to deal with the complexities of national, regional, and global rights claims. This danger is not merely hypothetical. At a regional sociology conference in 2008, a member of the TWC2 used Ong's thesis to argue that reformulating labor rights into "productivity" and "health" concerns, which are palatable to the host society at large, is a strategic adaptation of humanitarian aims into the dominant discourse and it therefore does not equate to co-option by the state.[55] The significance of conference and meeting attendance as nascent forms of cross-border organizing should therefore not be underestimated. Conference attendance is part of a process of activist "knowledge-creation"[56] in which ideas are circulated between different scales. This example clearly demonstrates the role of conferences as sites for the re-articulation and re-inscription of a range of transnational discourses, including those that we might regard as progressive (e.g., universal human rights) and those that entrench the status quo (e.g., "Asian values"). In this instance, the process of transnational framing that occurs as a result of engaging with ideas that circulate at a supra-national scale serves to restrict (rather than open up) the choices available to NGO activists and migrant women.

Conferences are not only crucial in shaping the ways that migrant worker issues are understood at the national level, but they are also a way of ensuring that locally specific understandings of conditions on the ground are filtered back up into transnational campaigns. In the case of TWC2 and HOME, this process is most evident in the ways in which both organizations employ the term "workers" instead of "maids" in their campaigns in support of migrant worker rights and in their claims that housework is "work." By replacing the value-laden term "maid" with "foreign domestic worker," they move away from class- and gender-based ideas about the implied servility of migrant domestic workers. Migrant worker NGOs elsewhere have employed this strategy, one that draws on international labor rights and women's rights campaigns. In suggesting that TWC2 and HOME frame their discussion of the problems facing FDWs using terms that are shared by other migrant worker groups outside of Singapore I am not suggesting that they have simply taken these concepts from the international arena and transported them into the local context. Their use reflects an organic process of engagement with transnational ideas and their application and reinterpretation at the local level. They also draw on Singapore's own indigenous labor rights and women rights movements.

Both TWC2 and HOME are beginning to take steps beyond transnational framing toward more concrete forms of cross-border organizing. HOME's involvement in the establishment of SMS in Batam and Manila, and Lew's participation in ADWA, represent attempts to move beyond the boundaries of the Singapore nation-state. A number of factors explain the relatively recent engagement in regional activities by both organizations. In their early years they were primarily focused at the local level because this was where they perceived the greatest need and where they saw the most efficient use of their limited resources. Members of TWC2's executive committee have consistently told me that their priority is "dealing with local issues first" before embarking on transnational connections. As TWC2's membership and volunteer base has grown and as greater financial and organizational stability has been achieved, more time and energy can now be devoted to engaging in regional efforts. While HOME has also been primarily focused on introducing services at the local level, it has a longer history of regional connections to the Catholic Church through Lew's former position as ACMI's chairperson. Lew's decision to create SMS reflects her awareness of the significant role that the Catholic Church plays in providing assistance to migrants globally. The church is potentially an important regional ally and Lew recognizes the moral benefits that accrue to the organization through her association with it.[57]

The nature of state–civil society interactions is another significant factor moderating the regional activities of both organizations. The Singapore state's recent tacit support for Migrant Forum in Asia (through its collaborations with the National Trade Union Congress [NTUC]) has provided a means for both organizations to become more involved in regional advocacy campaigns. TWC2's lack of engagement in cross-border activities between 2003 and 2007 can partly be interpreted as a strategy designed to avoid state scrutiny. During this period, TWC2 consistently stated that its underpinning objective was to address issues facing female migrant workers at the national level. This focus became clear in its early campaigns when members of the public accused TWC2 of damaging Singapore's international reputation by publicizing instances of violence by Singaporean employers. In justifying its antiviolence campaign, TWC2 claimed that its focus has always been internal (i.e., the national level) and that it had never initiated contact with non-Singaporean journalists.[58] TWC2 asserted that although foreign journalists reported on their work, advocating beyond the borders was not part of its mission. This stance has recently begun to change, with TWC2 issuing press statements via email that get taken up by regional and global listservs and networks.

In comparison to TWC2, HOME has enjoyed a much more positive relationship with the Singapore state. Despite her strong connections with different regional arms of the Catholic Church, Lew has consistently maintained a strong secular stance in her presentation of HOME's activities. This has helped to avoid any remnants of a negative concern that the state may harbor about the link between the Church and migrant worker activism. She has also worked to develop a productive relationship with various government ministries, and the success of this strategy was demonstrated in her appointment as founding director of the government-sponsored skills training program FAST (Foreign Domestic Worker Association for Skills Training). Lew asserts that she has a positive relationship with the state because

I am useful to them. Our government is so pragmatic. As long as I don't embarrass them, and not do things that are without basis, they keep me on because I am useful, because they can tell the world that they work closely with NGOs; it's good for the world to know that they are also working with independent groups.[59]

HOME's positive relationship with the state is also reflected in the organization's active efforts to obtain funding from foreign sources to support its welfare and training services. In contrast, TWC2's executive has said that they are wary of accepting funds from international bodies lest their actions antagonize the Singapore government. In this regard, TWC2's practices of self-regulation are consistent with a number of other Singaporean advocacy-oriented NGOs.[60] It is important, however, not to overplay the role of the state in determining NGO activities. As I have argued elsewhere, such a view is not only premised on the idea of a unitary Singaporean state (i.e., a state that acts consistently in its dealings with all civil society actors) but also underplays the role of class, ideology, and NGO histories in shaping organizational goals and objectives.[61]

Conclusion

This discussion of migrant worker organizing in Singapore reveals the complex issues facing nationally based NGOs as they attempt to scale up their advocacy efforts in response to the needs of foreign domestic workers. My analysis reveals that TWC2 and HOME have primarily responded to the problems facing FDWs as "local" issues to be solved at the national level. Thus, although they deal with a transnational phenomenon, their ability to engage transnationally by organizing across borders is limited. This focus on the national arena is the product of two interrelated factors — the relatively short period of time in which they have been operating (i.e., as young organizations their efforts have been focused on consolidating their work at the local level) and an inherent conservatism that reflects the nature of civil-society/state interactions in Singapore. In addition, the forms of trans-ethnic solidarity observed in other receiving countries such as Hong Kong have not been witnessed in Singapore, perhaps partly reflecting the limited presence of grassroots migrant worker organizations. In the cases of both TWC2 and HOME, trans-ethnic solidarity is most commonly expressed in a membership made up of Singaporean citizens, permanent residents, and FDW members from a range of different national backgrounds, as well as in the decision by both groups to address the needs of all FDWs regardless of nationality.

In distinguishing between cross-border organizing, transnational framing, and trans-ethnic solidarity, I have suggested that a transnational response to the issues faced by female migrant workers does not necessarily require a cross-border campaign, although this might be one element of a successful transnational advocacy effort. Rather, it implies that problems that are observed at the national level require solutions that take the global as their reference point. Such an approach involves understanding how the conditions facing migrant workers at the national level are connected to the global division of labor that provides the conditions for middle-class families to appropriate the labor of poor women from developing countries throughout the Asia-Pacific. Thinking transnationally about the feminization of labor migration therefore requires activists to interrogate the reasons why different nation-states respond to foreign domestic workers in similar ways. The presence of a shared language built around concepts such as "domestic work is work" reflects this type of transnational framing in the activities of both TWC2 and HOME. At the same time, it is important to note that the ability to "think transnationally" is not necessarily a prerequisite for engaging with activists on the other side of the border. The examples of TWC2 and HOME show that nationally based NGOs may belong to formal or informal regional networks that allow them to share ideas and garner support for national campaigns, without framing their responses in transnational terms. Instead, both organizations argue that the problems facing migrant workers require local-level solutions.

By advocating at the local level, HOME and TWC2 position themselves as partners in national development; their work ensures that Singapore's reputation as a global city-state that abides by the rule of law is upheld in the international arena. In appealing for the humane treatment of FDWs, they call for the protection of vulnerable mothers/daughters and invoke an ethics of care that resonates with state-sponsored campaigns aimed at producing a volunteering middle class. In fact, it could be argued that in a context where the state takes a negative view of the role performed by some international NGOs and transnational networks, failing to forge transnational linkages may constitute a more effective strategy of dealing with the problems FDWs face. For this reason, we should be careful not to overstate the benefits that accrue from belonging to transnational networks. Although transnational links are an important source of moral support and can provide access to resources not readily available at the national level, in the context of Singapore they appear to provide few tangible means to combat an authoritarian state that has little interest in regulating the labor market or improving the conditions of work faced by migrant workers. If the links between Singaporean NGOs and regional and international migrant worker groups continue to expand, this situation may change. At present, however, research shows that transnational networks offer few substantive benefits to local organizations.

ACKNOWLEDGMENTS: The research on which this article is based is supported by a four-year grant from the Australian Research Council titled "Transnational Activism: Organizing for Domestic Worker Rights in Southeast Asia" (DP0557370).

❏

6. The Making of a Transnational Grassroots Migrant Movement

A Case Study of Hong Kong's Asian Migrants' Coordinating Body

Hsiao-Chuan Hsia

INTERNATIONAL LABOR MIGRATION has regained significance in academic writings as capitalist globalization has intensified in recent years. Studies have shown how globalization has increased the extent of labor migration and how it has greatly affected the lives of migrant workers There is little documentation, however, of how migrant workers have made collective efforts to resist capitalist globalization.

Among the few scholars paying attention to activism relating to migrant workers, the focus has been primarily on the efforts of nongovernmental organizations (NGOs). Ford examines the emergence and operation of both migrant labor NGOs and migrant labor associations and argues that NGO-sponsored foreign domestic worker organizations are an important new form of labor movement organizations both in host and home countries and stresses that migrant labor NGOs' organizing function is the most incontrovertible indicator that migrant labor NGOs are part of the labor movement.[1] Sim celebrates the significance of NGOs in advocating migrant issues and argues that NGO activism has made visible arenas of potentiality and has yielded insights into the contested political spaces in transnational migration.[2]

Acknowledging the contribution of NGOs in advocating for migrants' rights is indeed important, but we should not neglect criticisms of NGOs for being elitist and nonrepresentative and consciously or unconsciously serving as the support mechanism of imperialism.[3] Government-organized NGOs ("Gongos") and mafia-operated NGOs ("Mongos") are not uncommon, and thus we should not assume that all NGOs lead to genuine protection of migrants' rights and welfare.

While many migrant NGOs claim their goals are to "empower" migrants and protect migrants' rights, it is not uncommon for NGOs to "speak on behalf of" migrants and the so-called "empowerment" can thus be more rhetorical than

Glossary of Organizations

AMCB	Asian Migrants' Coordinating Body
APMM	Asian Pacific Mission for Migrants
APMMF	Asia Pacific Mission for Migrants Filipinos (see APMM)
ASL	Association of Sri Lankans in Hong Kong
ATKI	Association of Indonesian Migrant Workers in Hong Kong
BH	Bethune House
CTU	See HKCTU
Feona	Far East Overseas Nepalese Association
FMWU	Filipino Migrant Workers Union
FOT	Friends of Thai
Gammi	Indonesian Migrant Muslim Alliance
HKCTU	Hong Kong Confederation of Trade Unions
HKPA	Hong Kong Peoples Alliance [on WTO]
IMA	International Migrant Alliance
IMC	International Migration Conference
KMP	Peasant Movement of the Philippines
MFMW	Mission for Filipino Migrant Workers
Panap	Pesticide Action Network – Asia Pacific
Pilar	United Indonesians against Overcharging
TRA	Thai Regional Alliance
TWA	Thai Women Association
Unifil-Migrante-HK	United Filipinos in Hong Kong

practical. Many studies do not distinguish NGOs from *grassroots* migrant organizations and often conflate the efforts and achievements of grassroots organizations with those of NGOs.[4] Studies such as these risk overlooking how migrants have organized themselves and developed their own migrant movements at the grassroots level. Although NGOs can play a catalytic role in the development of grassroots migrant movements, as we will see below, not all NGOs share the values of grassroots movement building. It is thus crucial to analyze how migrant NGOs position themselves in handling migrant issues. Does the NGO act as the "agent" who speaks on behalf of migrants? Or does the NGO clearly define itself as the "supporter" of migrants and gear its efforts to developing grassroots migrant organizations?

Activism on migrant issues always has elements of "transnationalism." As Parreñas points out, despite differences in "contexts of reception," migrant Filipina domestic workers share experiences of dislocation, leading them to establish cross-national alliances on the basis of this shared experience.[5] Most studies of migrants' transnationalism focus on transnational movements of one nationality that organizes across national borders. That is, "transnational" in these studies means "cross-border organizing" rather than "trans-ethnic solidarity," activism by migrants of different nationalities.[6]

Studies suggest that as a result of competition among different nation-states and various labor brokers, migrants of different nationalities are often divided rather than united.[7] Thus, in order to protect the rights of migrant workers, some scholars call for transnational solidarity among migrants.[8] Few studies, however, address the critical question of how migrants of different nationalities overcome the divide and rule tactics of brokers and states and form transnational solidarity.

As Evans argues, analysis and theory have not caught up to practice when it comes to progressive action at the global level.[9] According to Evans, the global rules and networks currently being constructed around the interests of transnational corporations are "hegemonic" and therefore "globalization from below" is "counter-hegemonic," allowing ordinary citizens to build lives that would not be possible in a more traditional world of bounded nation-states.

"Globalization from below" has received much attention, especially since late 1999, when tens of thousands of protesters brought the Seattle meeting of the World Trade Organization (WTO) to a halt.[10] However, most studies focus on big events such as protests against WTO, G8 Summit, and Asia-Pacific Economic Cooperation (APEC) and typically conclude that transnational activism as such is unplanned, spontaneous, nonorganizational, anarchistic, or postmodern, with the participating networks described as fluid and loose. The daily and regular organizational efforts of grassroots organizations trying to organize across nation-state boundaries have been neglected. Unlike resource-rich NGOs and advocacy groups, most grassroots organizations do not have the wherewithal to make themselves globally visible. Furthermore, grassroots organizations need to do a lot of groundwork, including conscientization,[11] empowerment, and mobilization, because their members often lack confidence, access to information, and resources.

With regard to transnational social movements, Porta and Tarrow identify three important processes in the transnationalization of social movements, namely, diffusion, domestication, and externalization.[12] They also separate nation-bound domestic activism from global activism, though they recognize interactions between the two levels of activism. Similarly, Evans separates local from transnational struggles: "Building transnational networks gives local organizing new prospects of success, and local mobilization is an essential element of counter-hegemonic globalization."[13]

Smith suggests, however, that the types of grassroots political practice that have emerged among transnational migrants and refugees do not fit well into the restrictive boundaries of local politics conventionally used in connecting the local to the global.[14] Grassroots migrants' struggles must simultaneously encounter the states of their origins, the states of their workplace and settlement, and supranational institutions, the "politics of simultaneity" or a politics that brings together multiple actors from multiple places. Similarly, Law argues that it is not enough to localize the transnational advocacy of migrant NGOs in Hong Kong, contextualizing it as a contemporary form of local politics.[15] Rather, she explains, Hong Kong is one "site" of transnational activism within a broader "social space" where new alliances between migrant, feminist, and workers' organizations take place.

Hong Kong as a "site of transnational activism" for migrant issues has been well researched,[16] but, as we have noted, earlier studies have overlooked the unique importance of *grassroots* migrant organizations or have conflated them with migrant NGOs. The Asian Migrants' Coordinating Body (AMCB) is particularly interesting and important not only because it is the first coalition of migrants from several Asian countries, but also because it is a coalition of grassroots migrant organizations of different nationalities.[17] AMCB's grassroots transnationalism crosses not only geographical borders but those of nationalities as well.

Some studies have documented the importance of the AMCB,[18] but none has investigated the AMCB's origins. Law argues that the AMCB's formation was motivated by the Asian financial crisis and its aftermath.[19] Yet even before the 1997 Asian financial crisis, efforts were being made to form a coalition of migrants from different nationalities. The financial crisis itself did not automatically trigger the successful formation of the AMCB; the continuous efforts of migrants themselves were required.

The primary concern of this article is what I call the "methodology of activism." By studying the AMCB in detail, I ask how migrant workers from several Asian countries were able to work together across nation-state, racial, and gender boundaries; what they achieved; what made this transnationalism of grassroots migrants possible; and what lessons are to be learned from the AMCB's grassroots transnationalism. In addition to printed and on-line documents, this study draws from interviews with five leaders and five active members of the AMCB's member organizations, two organizers of NGOs that helped the AMCB develop, and three leaders of local social movement organizations in Hong Kong.[20]

Migrants Divided in Capitalist Globalization

Migrant domestic workers (MDWs)[21] comprise the majority of migrant workers in Hong Kong. In 2005, there were 223,200 MDWs in Hong Kong, a significant and visible number among Hong Kong's total population of 6.9 million.[22] Almost 98 percent of these MDWs are women.

MDWs in Hong Kong were once predominantly Filipino women. In 1997, Filipinas accounted for more than 80 percent of all MDWs in Hong Kong. Beginning in the late 1990s, however, Indonesian domestics began to arrive in increasingly large numbers. By the midpoint of the following decade, the proportion of Indonesian MDWs had risen to 43.4 percent (2005), while the number of Filipinas had decreased from 66.7 percent of the total in 2001 to 52.9 percent in 2005.[23] Besides the Philippines and Indonesia, other major countries that supply MDWs to Hong Kong are Thailand, Nepal, Sri Lanka, and India.

Although migrant workers in Hong Kong all work under conditions regulated by the Hong Kong government, they do not automatically share a sense of "community" or solidarity across national lines. On the contrary, many migrants have stereotypes and prejudices against migrants from other nationalities, as the following observations make clear:

> Filipino migrants consider Filipinos good and educated and migrants from other nationalities are not educated so they can be exploited. Especially the images of Indonesians are from poor families and countryside, not ready to work, just here for playing, because of their young age and low educational levels. (Chairperson, Unifil).

Thai migrants don't like Indonesians because they have been replaced for their lower wages. Thai used to be the second largest and now the third. They feel Indonesians are not educated and willing to take very low wage. They thought Filipino migrants are sexually abused because they are too open and forward. (Chairperson, Thai Regional Alliance [TRA]).

Indonesian migrants are afraid of Filipinos because Filipinos can speak English, and they know how to fight, so they deserve higher wages. (Chairperson, Association of Indonesian Migrant Workers in Hong Kong [ATKI])

These negative impressions of migrants of other nationalities are constructed in the context of capitalist globalization where developing countries compete with one another to expand labor export markets. To become more competitive in the global labor markets, labor-sending states often need to demonstrate their comparative advantages, that is, how workers from their countries are "better" than others. For the Philippines, whose labor export policy has a long history and is more systematic, the competitive niche of its workers is their "skills," including their English-speaking abilities. For governments that are latecomers in formalizing labor export policies, their marketing niche is workers who are cheaper and more docile. To ensure the steady export of labor, the governments of sending countries are often unwilling to protect the welfare and rights of migrants; some are even actively engaged in creating conditions that are detrimental to migrants. Taking Indonesian MDWs for example, during one pre-departure group briefing, an Indonesian labor department official is reported to have said that it is "normal" for Indonesian migrants to have lower wages than migrants from different nationalities.[24] Thus, comparative advantages for the state can be comparative *disadvantages* for migrants.[25] When Indonesian migrants have encountered problems, the Indonesian Consulate in Hong Kong has discouraged them from taking legal action against employers.[26]

Recruiting agencies in Indonesia also play a crucial role not only in making Indonesian migrants more "docile," but also in perpetuating negative images of migrants of other nationalities.[27]

All Indonesians are told many times by agency: don't befriend Filipinos. Ordinary Indonesian migrants feel that it's OK to have lower wages because Filipinos speak English, they know how to fight, so only they deserve higher wages. (Chairperson, ATKI)

Antagonism among migrants of different nationalities is thus a barrier that needs to be overcome when building solidarity. As we will show below, the AMCB has successfully overcome divisions and prejudices between different nationalities of workers.

Development of the AMCB

The AMCB was established in 1996 as a coalition of grassroots migrant organizations of several nationalities in Hong Kong. Member organizations of the AMCB now include the Far East Overseas Nepalese Association (Feona), Association of Sri Lankans in Hong Kong (ASL), Association of Indonesian Migrant Workers in Hong Kong (ATKI), Thai Regional Alliance (TRA), Friends of Thai (FOT), and

United Filipinos in Hong Kong (Unifil-Migrante-HK), and Filipino Migrant Workers Union (FMWU).

Although formally established in 1996, the AMCB's origins go back to the multinational network of organizations that formed around the first Asian Cultural Festival held in Hong Kong on 23 October 1994. This festival gave more than 1,500 migrant workers from India, Indonesia, Thailand, Nepal, and the Philippines a venue in which to meet and begin working together as they shared traditional cultural dances and songs in a spirit of international solidarity.[28] Organizations present at the festival were the Thai Women Association (TWA), Feona (Nepal), and Unifil-HK (Philippines). Two months after the cultural festival, the organization representing migrant workers from Sri Lanka, ASL, joined the other groups in organizing the International Human Rights Day celebration on 10 December. (India and Indonesia had no formal groups representing their migrant workers in 1994.)

In 1996, a committee of representatives from Unifil, Feona, and the Mission for Filipino Migrant Workers (MFMW) was formed to draft a declaration of unity, which was later presented and discussed by representatives of migrants of several nationalities. After a series of meetings, the declaration was approved and the AMCB was launched on 10 December 1996 during the Third Asian Migrants Festival in observance of International Human Rights Day.[29]

The AMCB's work includes advocacy and organizing, networking and cooperation, and educational activities. Every member organization functions independently and the AMCB's coordinating committee is composed of executive committee members from each member organization. They meet regularly and plan actions and activities. Celebrations of International Labor Day, Women's Day, and International Human Rights Day are key times when the AMCB mobilizes its members as part of its educational activities and cultural exchanges.

The AMCB networks and consults with migrant groups that are not yet part of the AMCB. On 25 November 2007, the AMCB organized the First Asian Migrant Workers Summit in Hong Kong to strengthen solidarity work with other migrant organizations. The AMCB also works in partnership with regional and local institutions, advocating for the rights and welfare of migrants, and has established working relationships with major trade unions and women's and community-based organizations. To enhance the understanding of its members and their respective countries, educational activities are held to share experiences and struggles, to provide leadership training and opportunities for discussing crucial issues.

The AMCB's Achievements

The AMCB's signal achievement has been the creation of a grassroots migrant movement in Hong Kong. Before the AMCB was established, many migrant organizations were active, but each group typically represented just one nationality of workers. With the establishment of the AMCB, migrant worker issues were no longer confined to individual nationalities or racial or gender groups because the AMCB brings together migrants across national lines and includes men as well as women. A pertinent example is the case of Nepali male construc-

AMCB demonstration, Hong Kong, 2006. "The common basis of unity in the AMCB is the struggle against issues affecting migrants, which is why member organizations identify themselves as part of a migrant movement, rather than simply organizations established for the welfare of their fellow compatriots." — Hsiao-Chuan Hsia

tion workers who felt discriminated against because they had not been given the safety equipment that their local counterparts had been given. The AMCB joined rallies in behalf of the Nepalese workers and the ensuing dialogue with the Hong Kong government resulted in promises to change the occupational safety conditions for the construction workers.

The common basis of unity in the AMCB is the struggle against issues affecting migrants, which is why member organizations identify themselves as part of a migrant *movement*, rather than simply organizations established for the welfare of their fellow compatriots. Moreover, their unity is based on a common understanding of the root causes of forced migration, as Unifil's chairperson explains:

> The basic understanding within the AMCB is that all migrant workers from different nationalities are victims of poverty back home. From this basic understanding, we link to the locals, national movements, and global movement. From this understanding of root causes, migrants easily understand why we address issues to Hong Kong government and governments of our home countries. (Chairperson, Unifil)

This unity is translated into growing numbers of migrants who participate in street protest and marches, ranging from five thousand up to the peak of twelve thousand in demonstrations against cuts in wages.[30] The AMCB's ability to mobilize significant mass mobilizations has led the Hong Kong government to recognize it as a legitimate representative of migrant workers and has resulted in changes in the government's migrant-related policies, as the following examples show.

— Since its establishment, the AMCB has organized campaigns against government proposals to cut wages.[31] In August 1998, a provisional councilor had proposed a 20 percent cut in the Minimum Allowable Wage (MAW) for MDWs; at the same time, the Employers Association of Foreign Domestic Helpers called for an even deeper cut of 35 percent. The AMCB responded by organizing a march with an estimated two thousand migrant worker participants during the celebration of International Human Rights Day.[32] In January 1999, the Hong Kong government agreed to reduce the wage cut to a token 5 percent.

— In 1999, the Hong Kong government proposed a ban on driving duties for MDWs and abolished maternity protection and "live-out" arrangements for the workers. Meetings were held among the AMCB members and between MDWs and employers and a petition opposing the ban on driving drew thousands of signatures. In 2000, the government shelved the three proposals.

— In July 2001, the Labor Department proposed a HK$400 levy on employers who hired MDWs. The money was supposed to be used for retraining programs for locals who wished to work as domestic helpers. The AMCB immediately opposed this initiative and the Labor Department withdrew its levy proposal. Later in November, the Hong Kong government proposed "measures to raise revenues," including a 15 to 20 percent wage cut for MDWs. The AMCB held a press conference to register its opposition to the proposed measure and, on 2 December 2001, it organized a protest march from Victoria Park to the Central Government Office. More than three thousand migrants participated. Five days later, the Education Manpower Bureau was forced to call for a dialogue with the AMCB about the issue.

— Following a 5,000–strong mobilization on 13 January 2002 against government-proposed wage cuts, the government agreed to freeze rather than cut the MAW. A month later, on 23 February, a series of protests and signature campaigns culminated in a march of 12,000 migrant workers.

The MAW remains a concern, however. As Constable has explained in detail, the MAW rose steadily from 2005 through 2007, but the high it reached in June 2007 (HK$3,480) was still below the minimum wage in March 2003, HK$3,670.[33] The MAW is reviewed every year and the AMCB organizes protests around wage issues whenever needed.

A related issue of concern to the AMCB is the HK$400 levy the government imposed on employers of foreign domestic workers in 2003. The authorities explained that the money would be used to support retraining program for local (as distinct from foreign) workers. Just months before this action, the government had imposed a HK$400 wage cut on foreign domestic workers arguing that employers needed relief. The AMCB has consistently called for abolition of the levy and an increase in wages for MDWs, explaining that the levy benefits the government, does not help the employers (who pay HK$400 less in wages but HK$400 more for the levy), and comes at the expense of the MDWs.[34]

Though there is no simple causal relationship between the AMCB's struggles and changes in the government's migrant-related policies, and acknowledging that the AMCB is not the only group to advocate and protest against these issues, still even the leading local labor organizations consider the AMCB's ability to promote mass mobilization to be crucial. The chief executive of the Hong Kong Confederation of Trade Unions (HKCTU) noted that the HKCTU's secretary general, who is also a legislator, had himself brought the migrant issue before parliament. But, she acknowledged, "the mass mobilization of migrants puts more pressure on the government."

The productive relationships the AMCB has forged with trade unions and women's and community-based local organizations in Hong Kong have helped make its campaigns successful. To strengthen its ties with local organizations, the AMCB supports solidarity actions that relate to issues and problems these other local organizations face. For example, the AMCB's campaign against the government's proposed abolition of maternity protection — which stipulates that pregnancy is not cause for termination of employment — enlisted support from local women's groups because all the groups saw the proposed abolition as an infringement of the rights of migrants not only as workers but as women as well.[35]

As migrants of different nationalities are pitted against each other, locals also express prejudice and discrimination against migrants. As a result of working in the AMCB, migrants have realized that they need to overcome barriers in order to unite with local organizations. As ATKI's chairperson observes, "The only solution is to be active in local activities…. To show we are here to support."

Leaders of other workers unions in Hong Kong expressed in interviews how much they valued the support of migrant workers in their campaigns. The joint struggles against the WTO's Sixth Ministerial Meeting in Hong Kong in 2005, for example, demonstrate the strength of the links between migrant workers and these other labor groups. The AMCB, along with six other member organizations, joined the Hong Kong Peoples Alliance on WTO (HKPA), the organizers of the anti-WTO "People's Action Week" actions, and it mobilized hundreds of migrants to join the anti-WTO demonstrations as marshals. Speaking after the WTO events, HKCTU's chief executive, who was also a member of HKPA's decision-making body, described how impressed other social movement organizations in Hong Kong were with the AMCB's work in the campaign:

> The local organizations were very impressed by AMCB's capacities of organizing and mobilizing. AMCB also helped "open the eyes" of the locals by their deep understanding of the impacts of WTO on ordinary people's lives, which Hong Kong people did not know much about. Our union leaders say that we should be more like the migrants. We should learn from the way they organize and express themselves. Their rallies are very dynamic and creative.

Being able to mobilize more than five thousand migrants at the centralized march on the opening day of the anti-WTO demonstration illustrates the strength of the migrant movement the AMCB leads[36] and also shows how well it links with a wider global movement. The wider connections are the result of deliberate efforts to establish and enrich AMCB's international alliances. Attending conferences is one method that has been successful in this regard. Participating in the World Conference against Racism and Discrimination (in Durban, South Africa, 30 August to 5 September 2001), for example, gave the AMCB an opportunity to establish many international contacts. The AMCB was represented in this event through the Asia Pacific Mission for Migrants (APMM) and Unifil. AMCB representatives also attended the International Migrant Conference (IMC) held in November 2001 in Manila. This conference passed a resolution establishing the International Migrant Alliance (IMA). Most of the AMCB representatives were part of the International Initiative Committee responsible for the formation of the IMA. A third conference AMCB representatives attended was a tripartite conference in 2001 on "Trade Union, Migrants Organization and Women's Organizations" organized by the Asia Pacific Women Law and Development and Migrante-International.[37]

In mid June 2008, the IMA, the first global alliance of grassroots migrant organizations, held its founding assembly in Hong Kong. The significance of the IMA's foundation is captured in these words from a film shown at the assembly: "For a long time, others spoke on our behalf. Now we speak for ourselves." Eni Lestari, the chairperson of ATKI and an AMCB representative in the assembly, was elected the first chairperson of the IMA in recognition of the AMCB's achievements.[38] The HKCTU's chief executive later told me that seeing the AMCB in action during the People's Action Week convinced her that AMCB members have a "deep critical insight about the problems" that were their common concern. "Most local organizations," she explained, "did not know what the WTO was all about, so we had to do a lot of education work during the anti-WTO campaign. In that process, many local organizations realized that the AMCB understood the WTO very well. For example, they knew how the WTO affected the livelihood of people in Indonesia and the Philippines and caused them to have to look for jobs overseas."

The AMCB's knowledge of the WTO was the result of countless educational activities. For more than a year, the AMCB worked with the APMM and other institutions to illustrate the negative impact that the WTO had on migrant workers. In September 2004, for instance, it sponsored an educational forum on the WTO and migration in conjunction with the People's Caravan for Food Sovereignty of the Pesticide Action Network – Asia Pacific (Panap).[39] Through its organizing and educational work in the weeks leading up to People's Action Week —an effort called the "Migrants' 10-Week Countdown"[40] — the AMCB countered the argument that grassroots migrants don't have the time and resources to understand "big" issues such as the WTO. At the same time it demonstrated that mobilization demanded continuous mass education work; mobilizations were not just "spontaneous," as some studies of anti-globalization have assumed.

The AMCB's transformation from a cultural sharing network (in 1994), to an alliance for migrant sectoral movement, and then to an actor in the anticapitalist globalization movement has inspired migrant organizations in other countries: in South Korea, for instance, efforts have been made to establish a similar formation as the AMCB; in Japan an annual cultural festival of migrants from different nationalities has been organized. In turn, this recognition by migrant organizations in other countries further encourages the AMCB.

Transformation of Migrant Workers within the AMCB

Working in the AMCB is a transformational process, according to the many members of the AMCB with whom I spoke. The united strength of migrants from different nationalities has shown workers that they can make change happen. The chairperson of ATKI expressed her feelings of empowerment poetically: "I see victims become heroes for themselves!" She described to me her personal change after being involved in the migrant movement:

> Before, I could not imagine a movement. But now I know we are part of the migrant movement.... When I was working underpaid, I thought that I could only be like that, even I didn't like it. I only could try to learn how to be a "good," meaning obedient, DH [domestic helper]. But deep in [my] heart, I felt I deserve fair treatment. I ran away and triggered everything that has happened..... From this experience, I have learnt that change should come from the migrant workers themselves.... The major impact of the AMCB on me is politicizing, realizing that the only way to protect ourselves is to fight.

For Filipino migrants who are already experienced in organizing, working in the AMCB can also be empowering:

> I used to be a student activist. But organizing migrants is much more complex. Especially, when I became leader of migrant organizations, I need to think more about what I say, especially when talking to the press. I have learnt a lot and felt that I have become a more comprehensive organizer. I need to study how to work with different persons, especially people from different nationalities. (Chairperson, Unifil, 14 March 2007)

By being involved in the AMCB, stereotypes and prejudices against migrants of other nationalities have been transformed, as TRA's chairperson and others explain:

> Before, many Thai migrants felt negative about Indonesian migrants. But because of the AMCB, now Thai migrants know why and know the situations of Indonesian workers. Thai migrants now even went to help Indonesians. (Chairperson, TRA, 14 March 2007)

> I only found out at Bethune House [a domestic worker shelter] that the reason why Filipinos are more advanced and brave is because they have a strong movement, which is led by migrant workers themselves. Now many ordinary Indonesian migrants still think what I used to think about Filipinos. But we try to organize them, give them confidence, for them to realize that the issues are not between Filipinos and Indonesians. The issue is that we are commodities. They think that we Indonesians are obedient. But why are we obedient? It's because we are afraid of losing jobs. (Chairperson, ATKI, 13 March 2007)

> Because of the decrease of Filipinos and the increase of Indonesians, ordinary Filipino migrant workers think it's a problem of Indonesian migrants accepting lower wages.... But now since the AMCB, Filipinos are even inspired by Indonesians because they are young and energetic. Indonesians are always active in rallies, marches, and are very creative! Now the

Filipino migrants even say, "We should be more like Indonesians!" (Chairperson, Unifil, March 14, 2007)

Interview materials suggest that members of the AMCB value the importance
of transnationalism:

> We are determined to learn from each other [across nationalities] and
> develop a culture of giving in the AMCB. (Chairperson, Unifil, 12 March
> 2007)

> With the AMCB, we can get more chances and more powerful to protect
> rights of migrants. If small group, we can't do much. If working together,
> we can get it more easily. (Leaders, ASL, 11 March 2007)

> We are part of the migrant workers movement.... We can't do move-
> ment individually or nationally, though we also recognize national dynam-
> ics.... All ATKI members feel strong solidarity with the AMCB. We become
> more encouraged when seeing other nationalities support. (Chairperson,
> ATKI, 12 March 2007)

> Members of Unifil are very proud of the AMCB, because now migrant
> workers are more organized. They are happy to see other nationalities are
> also organizing themselves. Some non-Unifil Filipino organizations also
> want to join the AMCB. (Chairperson, Unifil, 14 March 2007)

This sense of transnationalism is felt not only among leaders but also among
grassroots members of AMCB affiliated organizations, as one ATKI member explained to me: "I like working with the AMCB, because we can learn so much
from each other. Like we Indonesians learnt a lot from the Filipinos how to fight
for our rights. We also learnt a lot how to educate our own people and how to
organize them."

Context of Reception in Hong Kong

Two factors have contributed to the AMCB's success: Hong Kong's openness
and the influence of Filipino migrant organizations. As Constable explains,[41] key
to understanding the Hong Kong government's permissive stance toward migrant protests is the uniqueness of the post-1997, postcolonial Hong Kong SAR,
with its claims to maintaining its status as a global city and its historical development as a "space of neoliberal exception."[42] This is not only a post-1997 phenomenon, however. Even during the colonial years, the British colonial government favored more liberal governance in order to project a picture of Hong
Kong as a "modern city" with social and political stability, especially after the riot
in 1967.[43]

This historical projection of Hong Kong as a "modern" colony and "global"
city explains why the government gives migrants more room for organizing
work. First of all, unlike in Taiwan, for example, where a maximum length of
stay is imposed on migrants, migrant workers can stay in Hong Kong on a series
of two-year visas and work contracts. Even though MDWs are not eligible to apply for permanent residency, the practically limitless time they may work in
Hong Kong makes it easier to maintain and consolidate organizing work, where
leaders of migrants can be gradually developed and become organizers without
much fear of deportation.

Second, Hong Kong's labor-related laws do not separate foreign workers from the locals, allowing migrants to form and join unions and associations.[44]

Third, to ensure that local workers would not complain when MDWs began to arrive, the Hong Kong government made the hiring of MDWs appear to be a "privilege," meaning that employers had to be rich enough to provide airfare, private accommodation, minimum wage, and a full day off each week, all conditions spelled out in a standard contract. This regular 24-hour day off is crucial for organizing work, because MDWs can then congregate on Sundays and avail themselves of opportunities to become conscientized and organized. Fourth, both the British colonial government and the post-1997 Chinese government are relatively tolerant of protests. The director of MFMW notes that before the transfer of sovereignty in 1997, the police did not intervene as long as the protest was not against the HK government. Even after 1987 when the two-week rule was imposed, the migrant protests against the Hong Kong government did not trigger much reaction from the police, as long their actions were peaceful.[45]

Aside from the projection of Hong Kong as a modern and global city, the actual need for migrant workers in Hong Kong's economy, especially the need for MDWs to serve the interests of expatriates, makes the Hong Kong government more lenient to migrants' demands.

No matter how liberal the context of reception, however, conditions for migrants would not have changed without pressure from a strong social movement. Social action by local Hong Kong people contributed little in the past to migrant activism, especially before the mid 1990s. When Filipino workers first came to Hong Kong in 1981, they were able to establish the MFMW with support from some Church institutions and individuals. But local organizations gave them very little other help.

The chief executive of the HKCTU recalls that in the beginning, the local trade unions opposed migrants, and in 1987 they voted against allowing migrant organizations to join the forum of unions.[46] The HKCTU eventually accepted migrant workers unions in 1995, in part because the union leaders saw that migrants had already organized themselves and so the HKCTU had no right to deny them membership.

Studies have shown that the opening up of the political structure in the 1980s and the growing involvement of local leaders in electoral politics have contributed to a decline in social movements in Hong Kong. As a consequence, connections have weakened between pressure groups and community movements.[47] The development of a significant migrant movement in Hong Kong — particularly the pioneering Filipino migrant movement — has to be seen therefore as the result, in part, of persistent work by migrant organizations themselves, coupled with the Hong Kong government's more liberal environment.

The Influence of the Filipino Migrant Movement

Leaders of MDWs of various nationalities pointed out to me that they were inspired and helped by Filipino organizations. Filipino leaders and organizers highlighted the importance of international solidarity, as the chairperson of Unifil explains:

We know Filipino organizations are far advanced than other nationalities, but we do not take it as advantage. We don't see other nationalities as competition. We formed the AMCB to show to our community that we should not fight against each other, but we should help each other.

Filipino organizers with whom I spoke saw clearly that divide and conquer is a tactic of the rulers:

Not only Filipinos are exploited. Other states also export people, so we need to share experiences of organizing migrant workers in Hong Kong, where there are migrants from many different nationalities. To protect migrants' rights and welfare, we need to deal with both sending and receiving countries. That is, we need to deal with Hong Kong government and other states. It is much better to come together with different nationalities, so we can be more powerful. (Managing director, APMM, 15 May 2007)

Filipino organizers consciously make efforts to show Filipino migrant workers the importance of international solidarity:

We don't want Filipinos to be divided from other nationalities as the governments intended. Instead of competition, we need to show Filipino migrants that we need solidarity with other nationalities. We explain to the Filipino migrants, at the same time reach out to other nationalities. (Managing director, APMM, 15 May 2007)

Not without difficulty, Filipino organizers take many approaches in helping Filipino migrants realize the importance of collaborating with migrants of other nationalities:

When we explained to ordinary Filipino migrants, some accepted our views, but some were suspicious. So we tried to educate them about solidarity through informal and formal discussion. For example, when we were invited to attend other's activity, we explained to them why it's necessary to attend this activity and what should be our attitudes. Now, some Filipino migrants even realized that other nationalities are even more exploited than Filipinos and they have more empathy with them and even try to help them. They appreciate it when Filipinos have issues, other nationalities help us, so they want to help others as well. (Managing director, APMM, 15 May 2007)

Filipino organizers have found creative ways of realizing international solidarity, starting with cultural sharing, and gradually developing a transnational network for migrant issues:

We started with cultural exchanges...because many migrants were interested in showing their own cultures and learning from others. When Filipino organizations had their cultural presentations, they incorporated issues in their presentations. Other nationalities found this type of presentation interesting, so they also learned how to do it. Then we began to have discussions about issues, before and after cultural events, aside from preparing for the cultural event. During the discussions, we tried to raise some issues to other nationalities and see how they react to those issues. They got interested and later on, ask more questions about issues. When discussing these issues, such as wage cuts, we asked them how we could stop it. Then they decide that it is better to organize ourselves and fight together. (Managing director, APMM, 15 May 2007)

These creative ways of reaching out to migrants of other nationalities lowered linguistic and cultural barriers, as one active member of ATKI explained:

Filipinos expressed their problems through the theater presentation, so we can easily understand even though our languages are different. From their performance we also found that our situations are similar. And we also learnt how to express our issues through cultural presentation.

Supporting Mechanism to Nourish Migrant Organizations of Other Nationalities

In addition to developing the AMCB, Filipino organizations have contributed to the strengthening of other nationalities' grassroots migrant organizations. The story of Eni, the chairperson of ATKI, best illustrates how Filipino organizations have helped not only her but also the ATKI organization:

I was underpaid.... I endured the work for about six and a half months, so I could pay back the agency fees. Then I felt I could not take it any more. I was finally referred and accommodated in Bethune House. In this shelter, we learn a lot of things and they taught us how to handle my own case.... The way they handle cases in Bethune House was very empowering. Bethune House helped me by education and exposure to ways of handling different cases. Mission [MFMW] provided education and helped me see the importance of organizing migrant workers. APMM also helped with various trainings. Bethune House is the second home for many Indonesians. It's also for empowerment. I was sheltered at Bethune House for four to five months. From the shelter, I learnt from the Philippine movement. I attended their forum and activities, and I was so impressed by Filipino migrant organizations. They are also migrant workers, but it did not prevent them from fighting and organizing themselves. I see how the victims become heroes for themselves! So we Indonesians also felt the need to form an organization for fellow Indonesians.

Four Filipino organizations collaborated in the development of ATKI: MFMW, the Bethune House Migrant Women's Refuge, APMM, and Unifil. The aim of the first three, which are all NGOs, is to help migrants form their own organizations. After the organizations are established, the three NGOs respect the independence of the new organizations and offer help only when requested. Unifil, one outcome of the work of the "triangle supporting network" (the three NGOs), later became part of the supporting mechanism for migrants from other nationalities.

Launched in 1981, MFMW was the first NGO established in Hong Kong to benefit migrant workers. The ecumenical organization started mainly to assist Filipina domestic workers; later it began assisting other nationalities. Among the MFMW's achievements was the setting up of a shelter, the Bethune House, which today is a full-fledged charitable institution that provides accommodation, counseling, and legal and mediation services to distressed foreign women workers. Since 1981 MFMW has handled over 23,000 cases. Of the workers helped, 8 to 10 percent later became active in various grassroots migrant organizations.

In addition to providing individual counseling, the Mission also helps migrants understand the causes of the problems they face and how to solve them collectively. Rather than simply offering conventional problem-solving counseling services, MFMW helps migrants make their own decisions. In this way the workers learn to take responsibility for the consequences of their actions. While waiting for their cases to be resolved, migrants are encouraged to volunteer at other migrant organizations and participate in campaigns for migrants' rights.

Most clients leave MFMW after their cases have been settled. But at Bethune House, much more can be done to empower migrant workers because they typically live at the shelter for a long period of time. ATKI's chairperson points out the benefits of this extended contact: "When ATKI was formally established on October 1, 2000, there were twenty-four members, and half of them were former clients from Bethune House." APMM provides training for the migrants in the shelter, with topics including leadership, organizing, writings (for newsletters, statements, etc.), advocacy, and alliance work. When ATKI's founders lived at the shelter, APMM provided weekly training for three to four months. As ATKI was newly established, APMM continued to provide regular training until ATKI members were more experienced. ATKI now operates independently and consults APMM only when they need advice or assistance.

When migrants of other nationalities seek help from MFMW and Bethune House, the Filipino organizers often invite them to attend activities organized by Unifil and other Filipino organizations. There, they help those with problems identify causes and decide what they think can be done to solve these problems. MFMW's executive director explains how crucial this problem-posing method is:[48]

> We do not know much of their situations, especially in their countries, so encourage them to find out the problems for themselves and later on find out what they can do to solve these problems. It is empowering for them to find out the causes of the problems. Later on, they are more empowered by making the decision to do something to stop the problems. (Executive director, MFMW)

The Unifil alliance of grassroots Filipino migrant organizations has a membership of more than five thousand domestic workers; more than 95 percent are women. Unifil was formed in May 1985 by organizations that had campaigned in Hong Kong against the Marcos government's policy of "Forced Remittance," which compelled overseas contract workers to remit 50 to 70 percent of their total earnings to the Philippines.[49] At present, Unifil is composed of twenty-five organizations, including religious, cultural, and socio-civic organizations. Inspired by Unifil, ATKI also links with other Indonesian migrant organizations and has established two alliances: Pilar (United Indonesians against Overcharging) and Gammi (Indonesian Migrant Muslim Alliance), which have mobilized Indonesian migrants in Hong Kong and pressured the Indonesian government to meet their demands. Filipino organizers advise and physically accompany members of ATKI and other groups in situations of difficulty — sup-

port that is especially important for migrants who have no experience of organizing and campaigning. ATKI's chairperson recalled how a Filipino organizer
helped them to solve their problems when ATKI was newly established:

> When we started to organize, I realized how many Indonesian migrants
> were afraid. For them, being leaders meant death! When we just began in
> 2000 and 2001, it's not safe to even go to Victoria Park, because agents and
> Indonesia Consulate staff monitored, checked on migrants. So we de-
> cided to move to Star Ferry at Kowloon side, but it did not work. Because
> how could we organize Indonesian migrants when we could not even en-
> ter the park where most Indonesian migrants congregate?! In 2001, after
> consulting with Filipino organizers, we launched a survey about condi-
> tions of Indonesian migrants. It's an entry point for organizing. The first
> protest action was at the consulate; to expose issues and break fear, we
> even had to wear black masks so migrants would not be identified by
> agents of the government. This protest was on a weekday and so only
> about one hundred were able to attend. But the action was still significant
> and it made the news. So we gained confidence. We continued to stay at
> Victoria Park. Edwina from Bethune House accompanied us every week
> for a month, because we did not know how to deal with harassment and
> intimidation. She helped us and we learnt how to deal with it. Later on, we
> could handle things by ourselves, so she did not have to accompany us
> anymore. (Chairperson, ATKI, 13 March 2007)

Criticism of NGOism and Stress on Grassroots Organizing

As its declaration of unity makes clear, the AMCB believes that a strong mass
movement is the only solution to the plight of migrants:

> We share the belief that only through step-by-step organizing and educat-
> ing our ranks, engaging ourselves in worthwhile mass actions, shall we ad-
> dress our homesickness and ensure the protection of our rights, welfare,
> and dignity.

The step-by-step organizing the Filipino organizations favor became the key to
the AMCB's success in mass mobilization. This style of organizing "begins with
initial social investigation to building contacts, organizing groups, a committee
of organizing groups, and the formation of a formal mass organization that will
genuinely uphold the interest of migrant Filipinos and the Filipino people."[50]
This time-consuming and painstaking process of organizing reflects the principles and beliefs of Filipino organizations that the prime mover for social change
should be the exploited masses. This approach debunks the anarchist and
postmodernist views of social movements as spontaneous or nonorganizational.

   This emphasis on solid grassroots organizing is a result of many years of experience in the Philippines — especially learnings gleaned from negative experiences such as attempts to undermine the development of grassroots organizing. A historical review and critique of NGOs in the Philippines by the Peasant
Movement of the Philippines (KMP) highlights the lessons drawn from the Philippine people's movement with regard to the danger of "NGOism."[51] The study

criticized what it called NGOism for fostering greater loyalty to funding agencies than to the people's movement; socioeconomic work that fails to take class struggle and structural change into account; bureaucratism; corruption of the NGO service orientation; professionalism; adoption of corporate practices and standards; and "turfism." By reflecting on the development and problems of NGOism, Filipino progressive organizations affirm their belief that the exploited masses — and not NGOs — should be the prime movers of genuine social transformation. NGOs *are* important to the people's movement, but they should define themselves as a supporting force for the mass organizations, rather than impose themselves as "representing" the masses.

To help the masses gain the knowledge and skills necessary for organizing work, in 2000 Asia Pacific Mission for Migrants Filipinos (APMMF, later became APMM) produced an educational manual for organizing migrants. Summing up the experiences of Filipino organizers and migrant leaders in Asia and the Middle East,[52] the manual served not only as a general reference guide for organizing migrant Filipinos but also provided guidance to non-Filipino migrant organizations in the AMCB.

In its work APMM tries to transfer organizing knowledge and skills to migrants with no prior organizing experience. Its training sessions, for instance, help inexperienced migrants become organizers and develop creative ways of organizing. ATKI's more than one hundred active members join other Indonesian migrants in the parks on weekends. There, ATKI organizers offer "mobile counseling" services since many Indonesians do not enjoy a regular day off. ATKI's chairperson explains:

> We used mobile counseling. We have trained twenty to twenty-five counselors and we divide our tasks to make sure that we call our members regularly to know their needs and counsel them what to do if they have problems…. Since we have more active members now, we also want to train them to be experienced organizers. We decided to divide ourselves to four groups and each group goes to different areas of the parks on weekends, to integrate with Indonesian workers and discuss issues with them.

Another ATKI member adds:

> I am now in charge of the area called "under the bridge," one of the gathering places in Victoria Park of Indonesian migrants. I and my other partners responsible for this area go there every Sunday, asking how they are doing, discussing their problems and issues, and we mobilize them when there are campaigns.

* * *

Guided by the principles illustrated above, the MFMW, Bethune House, the APMM, and other NGOs instrumental in developing cross-national migrant organizations support the efforts or desires of migrants to organize themselves, rather than impose themselves as the saviors or spokespersons on behalf of the migrants. Despite these noble aims, however, one can argue that NGOs still substantially control the daily operational machine, since they have more resources, such as full-time professional staff, representational skills, funding and educational resources, office space, and transnational connections. To bridge the gaps between NGOs and grassroots organizations, the "triangle" association of MFMW–BH–APMM has taken the following steps. First, grassroots migrant organizations have been given access to NGO resources, such as office space and equipment. Second, the three NGOs provide systematic training so the grassroots migrant organizations can develop presentation skills, writing (for fund raising, public statements, etc.), and other organizational management skills. Third, the NGOs give financial and other support to organizers from other countries to come and work in Hong Kong in order to help local migrant organizations. This not only helps develop grassroots migrant organizations but also strengthens links with movements in the home countries. Fourth, to ensure that the grassroots migrants' concerns are highlighted, the NGOs make sure that representatives from grassroots migrant organizations are part of the decision-making body of the NGOs. The chairpersons of Unifil and Migrante-International (an alliance of Filipino migrant organizations) are both on APMM's board of directors, and one representative of Unifil serves on MFMW's board of directors.

Linked to Movements in Home Countries

Although the Hong Kong government is often the target of protest actions, the AMCB helps migrants understand that problems in their home countries are a root cause of forced migration and therefore they invest energy to develop and strengthen people's struggles in their home countries.

The strength of Filipino migrant organizations can only be fully understood if situated in the broader context of the Filipino mass movement. The four Filipino organizations that helped establish the AMCB are all part of the progressive mass movement in the Philippines. Unifil is linked to many Filipino grassroots migrant organizations that form Migrante-International, which was formed in 1996 as a member organization of Bayan, a multi-sectoral national alliance of mass organizations.[53] Migrante-International represents the migrant sector within Bayan, convinced as it is that the solution to the migration of Filipinos abroad lies in resolving the basic problems of the Filipino people and that cross-sectoral work is therefore necessary.[54]

Filipino migrants often come to Hong Kong with some organizing experience — experience that contributes to the formation of the migrant movement overseas. For example, the chairperson of Unifil was a student activist in the Philippines. After working as a domestic worker for nine months she began to participate actively in Filipino migrant organizations; her experiences in the Philippines help her organizing in Hong Kong, since she already understands the fundamental problems in the Philippines and how to organize other Filipinos to deal with them.

Filipino organizations encourage and inspire migrants of other nationalities to seek the root causes of their forced migration and to link themselves to the organizations and movement back home. Links to the home country not only help migrant organizations broaden their perspectives on their struggles, but also helps organizations in their home countries better understand migrant issues. The chairperson of Thai Regional Alliance declared with pride: "Our organization is the first overseas labor organization in Thailand!"

The link between migrant organizations and activism or the movement in home countries is developed through exchanges such as when Thai union members and labor NGOs come to Hong Kong for trainings or as speakers with Thai migrant organizations. TRA also uses newsletters and radio programs (available via the internet) for migrants and people in Thailand to better understand migrant-related and other issues in their home countries. ATKI collaborates with organizations in Indonesia in sponsoring organizing and training initiatives in Hong Kong and training ATKI officers who return home for visits. From my interviews, I learned that ATKI officers who return to Indonesia make an effort to raise awareness about migrants' concerns in Hong Kong and other countries. This experience is especially unique for Indonesian migrants, most of whom are young and have no prior organizing experience. Thus, ATKI officers are not only involved in the Hong Kong migrant movement, but also in the movement back home. As their perspectives are broadened, they can see the importance of building a stronger movement in Hong Kong, Indonesia, and in other countries. (ATKI officers have helped organize Indonesian migrants in Macau, for example.) Some ATKI members have returned to Indonesia as activists, joining such campaigns as that against oil price hikes. When protestors against oil price hikes were arrested by the police in Jakarta, ATKI-HK also mobilized protest actions in front of the Indonesian Consulate in Hong Kong, demanding the release of activists back home.

In an article on transnational activism, Law argues that the AMCB's transnational activism constitutes a new domestic worker subject, one that loses the specificity of national debates.[55] The AMCB, she believes, has shifted the debate for Filipino activists: the Filipino feminist-nationalist movement can no longer construct the female migrant worker subject as dependent upon neocolonial government policies. Global social movements can help bolster the national agendas of Filipino organizations, Law contends, but the stability of the AMCB might be jeopardized because of the importance of national politics in labor migration." Based on my analysis, I believe that Law's analysis and prediction may not be accurate. First, the AMCB has not lost the specificity of national debates: migrant organizations and their members continue to link wider migrant issues to national concerns. Second, the bolstering of Filipinos' national agendas has not jeopardized the stability of the AMCB. On the contrary, the AMCB has expanded as Filipino organizations have encouraged other nationalities to link to their home country struggles.

Organizing Style of Filipino Organizers

The low-key organizing style of Filipino organizers in the AMCB is a crucial factor in the AMCB's work with other nationalities. As MFMW's director observes, "the key to organize other nationalities is to learn from them about their cultures and histories." Thus, when engaged in joint activities, Filipino organizers deliberately downplay their roles in order to encourage more active participation from other nationalities.

Filipinos are often treated as "experts," but we always try to explain thoroughly so other nationalities can fully understand the issues and we can have more involved discussion…. In rallies and marches, Thai and Indonesian organizations are usually in the front. Their cultures are more impressive and they are very creative. Filipinos are often at the back. (Chairperson, Unifil, 14 March 2007)

Other migrants voice an appreciation for this low-key approach:

Filipinos don't take advantage even though they are much advanced. Indonesians appreciate Filipinos very much. At marches, Filipino walk in the back, so Indonesians and other nationalities can walk in the front. Simple things like that make Indonesians appreciate Filipinos. (Chairperson, ATKI, 13 March 2007)

The election of an Indonesian — the chairperson of ATKI — as the first chairperson of the IMA is an example of how Filipino organizers decline to push themselves forward into power positions. Filipinos were the prime movers in IMA's foundation, and thus it would have been appropriate for the chairperson of Migrante-International or Unifil to fill this leadership role. However, in order to encourage other nationalities, Filipino organizers deferred to ATKI.

Lessons from the AMCB's Grassroots Transnationalism

Leaders and organizers of the AMCB recognize the challenges they face: language barriers, limited time and resources, varying levels of politicization and organizing experience among members, and the need for expanding and consolidating organizing work, among others. Nevertheless, the AMCB continues to provide an inspirational example of "transnationalism from below."

The transformation of migrant workers within the AMCB can be looked at in the context of Alain Touraine's concept of the shift from personal subject to historical subject.[56] Writing in 1988, Touraine introduced the concept of "societal movement" in which "historicity" and "subject" are two key elements. Elsewhere, I argue that in addition to "personal subject" and "historical subject" there is a "communal subject" (developed through a sense of collectivity) who must be created in the subjectivation process. That is, "subjects" do not exist automatically. A long process of development and transformation is required, one that involves continuous and painstaking efforts. Thus, we conclude, migrants can become historical subjects, the movers of histories, but their subjectivity does not arise spontaneously.[57]

The problem-posing methods that MFMW and Bethune House use help migrants develop a sense of personal subjectivity as they come to understand that their conditions are not due to fate or luck, but are instead the result of forced migration and that they can do something to improve their own lives. By linking with other migrants, first with compatriots and then with members of other nationalities, migrants develop a sense of communal subjectivity that enables them to see the collective strength of migrants. I argue that linking the migrant movement to movements in their home countries and then to the global movement against capitalist globalization, migrants within the AMCB have developed historical subjectivity and they are making their marks on history by remaking the social relations and the cultural model that define their identity.

The development of the AMCB offers many lessons about transnationalism:

First, it shows that migrants at the grassroots level are able to defeat the divide-and-conquer rule of domination by working collectively with other nationalities.

Second, contrary to what anarchist and postmodernist theorists and activists maintain, this grassroots transnationalism does not happen spontaneously or automatically. It involves the continuous and painstaking efforts of step-by-step organizing.

Third, while NGOs can assist the development of grassroots migrant organizations they must be willing to shift from a representative role to a supportive role. This shift in roles involves bridging the gap between grassroots organizations and more resourceful NGOs; providing opportunities for systematic training; sponsoring organizers from the home countries to work in Hong Kong with migrant organizations; and ensuring that the representatives of grassroots migrant organizations are part of the decision-making body of NGOs.

Fourth, organizing work with migrants of respective nationalities is useful in the development of solid grassroots transnationalism because it helps to overcome linguistic and cultural differences and the lack of sufficient knowledge of contexts in other countries. Moreover, as the managing director of APMM points out, "without solid lessons from organizing migrants of our own nationalities [Filipinos], we cannot share with migrants of different nationalities the methods of organizing that have been proven useful in practice."

Fifth, linking to struggles in their home countries strengthens migrant organizations because this effort helps them identify and address the root causes of forced migration. At the same time, this is a risky course of action and organizers must be careful not to put leaders and active members of grassroots migrant organizations at risk of deportation by carelessly encouraging action against host governments.

Finally, finding a common ground for collaboration enables grassroots migrant organizations to forge a basis of unity, a sharing of cultures, experiences, and common concerns across national barriers. The necessary basis of unity for migrants of different nationalities is, as we have shown, issues of mutual interest in the host countries.

In her keynote speech at IMA's founding assembly, Dr. Irene Fernandez, a prominent advocate of migrant rights, declared that in the context of modern-day imperialist globalization migrants must carry out dual struggles: one in their home countries and the other in their countries of reception. The AMCB has shown in practice that these dual struggles are essential to protect migrants and to develop genuine transnational grassroots migrant movement against capitalist globalization.

❑

7. Migrant Workers and the Many States of Protest in Hong Kong

Nicole Constable

THIS ARTICLE TAKES MIGRANT DOMESTIC WORKERS' anti-World Trade Organization (WTO) protests as an entrée through which to ask what it is about Hong Kong and the structural position of women migrant workers there that permits such public protests and shapes their form and content. Such protests, I argue, are shaped by domestic worker subjectivities, including their flexible noncitizenship, by the dynamics of inter-ethnic worker affiliations, and by the socio-historical context of Hong Kong as a postcolonial "global city"[1] and a "neoliberal space of exception."[2]

The Consulate Hopping Protest

The Consulate Hopping Protest and the presentation of Hall of Shame Awards took place on Thursday, 15 December 2005, a warm Hong Kong winter's morning. One of many events that took place during the People's Action Week against the WTO (10–18 December 2005), the protest began with a small but boisterous gathering of two to three dozen people, including Filipina, Indonesian, and Thai foreign domestic workers, Nepali migrant workers who were active in Hong Kong's grassroots worker organizations, a few friends and supporters, and several members of the local media. The group congregated first outside of the Nepalese Consulate, in the shadows of the shiny high-rise buildings of Tsim Sha Tsui East. Behind a metal police barricade, protestors passed out fliers, made speeches, and presented the first Hall of Shame Award. A migrant worker/activist (carrying a cardboard gun and wearing a crown) served as a stand-in for Nepal's king, Gyanendra. The "king" was ceremoniously presented with a paper award reading "King of Tyrants" by the vice chairman of Feona (Far Eastern Overseas Nepali Organization) for his dictatorial rule and curtailing of democratic rights. He was then unceremoniously beaten to the ground by the jeering protestors, with appropriate sound effects (see fig. 1).

Some of the protestors next crowded into a large bus that had been hired for the event, while others rushed to the subway. They all headed to the Indonesian Consulate across the harbor, in Causeway Bay, where a costumed domestic worker representing Indonesian President Susilo Bambang ("Bangbang") Yudhoyono — balancing large burlap sacks filled with money on the backs of two domestic workers — was presented with the "Rookie of the Year" award by the chairperson of the Association of Indonesian Migrant Workers (ATKI–HK) for Indonesia's success and expertise as a "rookie exporter of labor" — second only to the Philippines as "biggest exporter of cheap labor in Asia" (see fig. 2).

Fig. 1. At the Nepalese Consulate, the first stop for the Consulate Hopping Protest, a migrant worker dressed as King Gyanendra was presented with the "King of Tyrants" award and then knocked to the ground. 15 December 2005. (Credit: Peter C. Alter)

Fig. 2. A domestic worker disguised as Indonesian President Yudhoyono was presented with the "Rookie Labor Exporter of the Year" award as he balanced two large bags of Hong Kong dollars on the backs of domestic workers. 15 December 2005.

The next stop was the Malaysian Consulate where Mahathir bin Mohamad, former prime minister of Malaysia (whose term lasted twenty-two years) — represented by a domestic worker dressed in black leather carrying a whip and maintaining a very stoic appearance — received the "Sultan of Crackdown" award for the massive arrests, harsh treatment, and deportation of migrant workers in Malaysia. The award was presented following a speech by Connie Bragas-Regalado, a Filipina former domestic worker who had served as chairperson of Unifil (United Filipinos in Hong Kong), a Hong Kong grassroots domestic worker organization, and who had returned to the Philippines to become the chairperson of Migrante International, an international alliance of migrant organizations based in Quezon City.

The Philippine Consulate was the next stop. The Filipina domestic worker who was the current chairperson of Unifil presented representatives of President Gloria Macapagal-Arroyo with the "Milkmaid Award" for "milking the maids" — figuratively sucking them dry and threatening the subsistence of their dependents — by charging excessive fees and relying on them to support the country economically. Milking the maids is a particularly evocative gendered symbol of political and economic exploitation (see fig. 3). A group of about ten Filipino protestors, including two domestic workers wearing flowered maid's aprons and symbolizing the government's greed by waving U.S., Philippine, and Hong Kong currency at the onlookers, then entered the office building and delivered the statement to a Philippine consular official.

At the next stop Thaksin Shinawatra, the twenty-third prime minister of Thailand at that time, was presented with the "absentee government award" by the vice chairperson of the Thai Regional Alliance, for neglecting migrant workers from Thailand and for the lack of services the Thaksin government offered its citizen migrants.

The Hong Kong Government Offices in Hong Kong's Central District were next. There, a young man representing Chief Executive Donald Tsang was presented with the "Edward Scissorhands Award" by a domestic worker who was Unifil's vice chairperson. The award was presented — along with giant cardboard scissors that cut

Fig. 3. The "Milkmaid Award (Milking of the Maids)" was presented to President Macapagal-Arroyo at the Philippine Consulate on 14 December 2005. In the picture, President Arroyo is bathing in the liquid from a bottle labeled "State Extraction of OFW Remittances."

Peter C. Alter

Fig. 4. Hong Kong's chief executive Donald Tsang was presented with the "Edward Scissorhands Award" as giant scissors cut though "wages" and "social services." Other signs read "abolish the levy" and "bring back HK$3670."

through the words "wages" and "social services" — for cutting wages, slashing benefits, and for imposing a monthly levy of HK$400 (US$51) on employers of foreign domestic workers to support a training program for local domestic workers[3] (see fig. 4).

Nicole Constable

Fig. 5. A migrant worker serves as a stand-in for President George W. Bush, who is presented with the "Terror Award."

The final stop was up the hill (near the Peak Tram stop) outside of the gates of the U.S. Consulate. Many more people had joined the protest by then, as had more members of the media, and the spirit and noise intensified. After several speeches by worker activists, including Carol Pagaduan-Araullo, chairperson of Bayan (New Patriotic Alliance) and vice chair of ILPS (International League of Peoples' Struggle), a stand-in for George W. Bush, was given the "Terror Award" amidst chants of "U.S. imperialist, number 1 terrorist"; "Down with George Bush; Down with WTO"; and "Junk, junk WTO" (see fig. 5). Finally, some of the protestors returned to Victoria Park to join the Korean farmers and the other protestors in Causeway Bay. Others returned to work.

Before unpacking this rich symbolic expression of migrant domestic worker political perspectives, and the workers' critical commentary on their position in Hong Kong and within the wider global economy, some methodological and contextual background is necessary. In the following section, I briefly describe the wider context of the protest and of my research methodology. This is followed first by a discussion of the specific meanings of this protest and then of the wider significance of migrant worker protest within the context of contemporary Hong Kong, a self-described postcolonial global city and a space of neoliberal exception.

Background and Context

For several months in 2005 and 2006, I returned to Hong Kong to conduct ethnographic follow-up field research among Filipina domestic workers, after a hiatus of almost ten years, during which time Hong Kong had become a Special Administrative Region (SAR) of the People's Republic of China. My main focus was on changes that had taken place in the decade since my earlier research on worker protests. I observed numerous protests firsthand and interviewed participants, observers, and organizers. Although much remained the same in postcolonial Hong Kong, I was immediately struck by three significant changes relating to domestic workers. Primary among them was the phenomenal increase in the number of Indonesian domestic workers; the proliferation of nongovernmental organizations (NGOs), unions, and grassroots associations focused on migrant worker issues; and the wider scope of domestic worker's political protests that were now defined mainly in terms of broader human rights, in contrast to the more narrowly defined labor issues that were the main concerns of the early and mid 1990s.[4]

Shifting demographics are among the most obvious and significant changes visible over the past decade. Intensified by the Asian financial crisis of the late 1990s, and propelled by political-economic crisis and change in Indonesia that prompted the government to promote the exportation of female labor, the number of Indonesian domestic workers in Hong Kong and other parts of Asia and the Middle East has increased dramatically. Filipinas still constitute the majority of foreign domestic workers in Hong Kong, as they have since the 1980s and throughout the 1990s (numbering 124,000 in 2005), but the number of Indonesian domestic workers in Hong Kong rose from just over 6,000 in 1993 to more than 90,000 in 2005, outnumbering all nationalities of domestic workers except Filipinas.[5] The business of recruiting and training Indonesian domestic workers to work abroad has become big business and a major source of foreign currency remittances and income for the Indonesian government, following the example set by the Philippines.[6]

Before the Asian financial crisis, as historian Susan Blackburn has observed, Indonesian Embassy officials denigrated women who took "lowly positions as servants," and the wider Indonesian population expressed "repugnance at Indonesians working overseas in what were regarded as menial capacities."[7] Indonesian women's activist groups protested in Indonesia in the 1990s against the maltreatment of Indonesian domestic workers in the Middle East,[8] but the main reason behind their calls for a halt to such labor exportation was a desire not to "lower the dignity and status of Indonesian women." Only a few Indonesian organizations in those days focused on the human rights of migrant workers.[9]

By the mid 1990s, however, the Indonesian government began to actively promote overseas contract work in Asia and employment agencies and obligatory "training camps" for prospective domestic workers sprang up to meet the demand. In the camps, Indonesian women recall being warned to avoid troublemaking Filipina domestic workers in Hong Kong who might cause them to lose their jobs. As Indonesian domestic workers grew in number, bolstered in large part by employers and recruitment agencies that considered Indonesians "better" than Filipina workers (less savvy, more passive, and appropriately submissive), they also gradually became more aware of their rights.[10] On the subject of Hong Kong protests involving Indonesian migrant domestic workers, Blackburn notes with surprise, "remarkably, some Indonesian maidservants in Hong Kong succeeded in organising themselves into an Association of Indonesian Migrant Workers [ATKI], which in 2001 staged a protest rally against exploitation by employers, recruitment agencies and the Indonesian government — something which has never happened in Indonesia itself."[11] Indeed, in 2006 one Indonesian domestic worker laughed as she showed me photographs of the ATKI protest in which women's faces were completely covered with black masks. They had worn the masks, she recalled, out of fear of recognition and reprisal by their government. Today, she noted, they openly express their concerns, waving at television cameras and drawing attention to themselves. As another Indonesian activist domestic worker explained to me in 2005, Indonesians have become emboldened in the more democratic post-Suharto period; they are aware of workers' rights and of the legality of labor organizing in Hong Kong.

The post-1997 policies and rules governing the rights and obligations of foreign domestic workers (FDWs) in Hong Kong remain fundamentally unchanged from a decade earlier. Migrants still come to Hong Kong as temporary workers with a two-year employment contract and temporary visa, and they are required to "live in" and work for one employer.[12] Domestic workers are the only Hong Kong workers with a minimum wage stipulated in their employment contracts.[13] On the level of domestic worker activism, however, much has changed. Concerns about wages and work conditions are still commonly voiced, but they are increasingly framed in relation to discourses of global justice and human rights. This shift is linked in part to the growth of NGOs and grassroots activist organizations in Hong Kong and to an ever more extensive and complex framework of domestic worker organizations and labor unions.

Although it was small and did not attract much media attention, the Consulate Hopping Protest in 2005 involved a lively and diverse group of migrant workers and reflected the key demographic changes among domestic workers, the proliferation of organizations and NGOs affiliated with migrant workers, and the wider global and transnational framing of their "antiglobalization" message that might best be seen as a "pro social justice position" focusing on migrant rights as human rights.[14]

The protest and award presentation was sponsored by the HKPA (Hong Kong People's Alliance) on the WTO, an umbrella organization that included hundreds of local and international NGOs and grassroots organizations that had not received approval to take part or observe the actual WTO Ministerial Conference meetings that took place inside the Hong Kong Convention Center in Wanchai. Elizabeth Tang, chief executive of the Hong Kong Confederation of Trade Unions (HKCTU), served as HKPA's chairperson. Planning and educational outreach for the protest events began almost a year earlier. The Consulate Hopping Protest was listed in the HKPA calendar of events that took place during People's Action Week, one of dozens if not hundreds of planned activities and demonstrations that took place under the umbrella of the HKPA, some involving thousands of people in marches and rallies in Causeway Bay and Wanchai and others involving much smaller groups in events scheduled throughout the nine days in various Hong Kong locations and culminating on International Migrants Day, December 18 (see fig. 6).[15]

The protest organizers had expected the Consulate Hopping Protest to be small, since it was held on a Thursday, when most domestic workers had to work. The choice of day was nonetheless intentional because the organizers did not want to compete with the larger weekend events that they planned to attend and hoped would draw the largest crowds. At any one time the Consulate Hopping Protest had about thirty-five to forty-five protestors plus a dozen mem-

Fig. 6. Waving flags of the Asian Migrant Coordinating Body (AMCB), the Thai Regional Alliance, the International League of People's Struggle (ILPS), the Asia Pacific Mission for Migrants, Migrante International, and others, migrant domestic workers join the anti-WTO march on 11 December 2005.

Nicole Constable

bers of the press. Some domestic workers attended only part of the 4.5–hour event and then went back to work; dozens of other domestic workers had helped prepare for the protest (creating props and contributing ideas) even though they could not attend.

The largest numbers of participants were Filipina and Indonesian domestic workers; a few were former domestic workers who were no longer based in Hong Kong. Many of the participants in the Consulate Hopping Protest were unemployed migrant domestic workers who were temporarily living in domestic shelters as they awaited their hearings. Such shelters are no doubt the single most important avenue through which domestic workers of various nationalities, but especially Filipinas and Indonesians, are exposed to political and labor activism. In the early to mid 1990s, such shelters, established by NGOs and Filipino migrant worker activist groups and staffed largely by Filipina domestic worker volunteers, housed mainly Filipina workers who had been abused, laid off, or underpaid, and were awaiting hearings with the labor tribunal. Among these workers were some who later returned to the shelter, with their consciousness raised, to work as volunteers or to participate in related grassroots organizations. By the late 1990s, as the number of Indonesian workers grew, and as the rates of abuse of Filipinos declined, the abuse suffered by Indonesian workers increased and they became the main residents of Filipino-run shelters. Both IMWU (Indonesian Migrant Workers Union) and ATKI trace their origins to Indonesian women's encounters with Filipino domestic worker activists and labor organizers in domestic worker shelters.[16] Within these "safe," gendered spaces, formerly abused and displaced maids share eye-opening and politically transforming experiences.[17]

Despite the small turnout at the mid December event, much larger constituencies and collaborative efforts of multiethnic migrant domestic workers were behind the Consulate Hopping Protest and the criticisms voiced during the demonstration. The protest and award presentation was planned, coordinated, and organized over the course of several months by migrant worker groups in Hong Kong and in the Philippines under the umbrella of the Asian Migrants' Coordinating Body (AMCB)[18] and the demonstration successfully incorporated several nationalities of workers and activists: Filipino, Thai, Malaysian, Indonesian, and Nepali, among others. The Consulate Hopping Protest and its participants vividly and literally mapped the transnational, multiethnic, and multi-issue dimensions of migrant workers' concerns. It raised important questions about the position of domestic workers in Hong Kong, relationships between different nationalities of workers, and the rights and concerns of workers. It also mapped wider geopolitics and networks of activist affiliation. Several well-known international activists joined in the later stage of the protest, giving speeches and showering the protestors with praise and support. These included officials from Bayan, a Philippine alliance of grassroots worker and peasant organizations founded in 1985, and representatives of ILPS, an anti-imperialist democratic international alliance with hundreds of member organizations in over forty countries worldwide.

Comparative Disadvantage

As indicated above, the social organization of the protest and the wider network of grassroots activist organizations within which it is situated are significant. Another important dimension is its performed meaning. Unlike other more militant aspects of protests during Peoples Action Week, the Consulate Hopping Protest and the Hall of Shame Awards had a playful, clever, and creative dimension to it. Each segment can be seen as a Bakhtinian carnivalesque street theater that produces an encapsulated critique of neoliberal globalization and its inherent inequalities.[19] The protestors produced a skillful parody of neoliberal notions of "comparative advantage" in the global arena of free trade.[20] Contemporary free trade interpretations of David Ricardo's nineteenth century notion of comparative advantage posit that every nation stands to gain by exporting what it produces at relatively low cost. In many regions of Asia, migrant workers — mainly women — are the low-cost specialized product, but their performances creatively beg the question of comparative advantages. To whose advantage is it when workers are marketed as commodities or resources, exploited by recruitment agencies, employers, and their home governments? Protestors, most of whom were women migrant workers, literally embodied in their protest actions the comparative *dis*advantages for the workers themselves (as women who are "milked" for profit) and the advantages for the leaders, officials, and class elites of various countries.

In the Consulate Hopping Protest, Nepal is not depicted as a tourist's mountain paradise, but as a kingly autocracy that specializes in and benefits from repression and political violence. Indonesian officials are shown to be increasingly skilled at profiteering from the growing exportation of female migrant labor and Malaysia's officials are portrayed as engaging in antidemocratic crackdowns and violent expulsion of illegal immigrants. In other depictions, Philippine officials "milk" migrant women workers and profit from the export of their sweated labor; Thai officials neglect their migrant workers; Hong Kong authorities cut migrant worker's wages and benefits in order to subsidize local interests; and U.S. government officials are patriarchal exporters of violence and the greatest beneficiary of the overall comparative advantages of world trade.

Through such creative and humorous protests migrant workers and other protestors aptly articulate that comparative advantage is relative to one's class position. An advantage to some is revealed to be no such thing from the grassroots perspective of exploited workers. Protestors point to a variety of factors that reveal the underlying power structures that perpetuate a cycle of exploitation and exportation of workers. WTO-supported agricultural policies that put small-scale local farmers out of business, for example, fuel dissent, increase poverty, lead to the growth of urban slums, and result in women's migration as one of few alternatives to unemployment. The seemingly endless supply of low-cost workers for export depends on maintaining a pattern of underemployment, unemployment, and military repression of protests back home that could threaten the valuable image of the ideal worker-for-export. In their repression of protests, local governments often receive U.S. support, previously under the guise of "fighting communism" and more recently under the guise of "fighting terrorism" — caricatured by President George W. Bush receiving the "Terror Award" during the Consulate Hopping Protest. Such theatrical public criticisms of comparative advantage point out that what is promoted as an ideal and profitable solution from the perspective of local governments and class elites in both the sending and receiving countries depends on the perpetuation of structural violence and economic inequality.

Hong Kong: Asia's World City

In the context of a strategic space such as the global city, the types of disadvantaged people...are not simply marginal; they acquire presence in a broader political process that escapes the boundaries of the formal polity. This presence signals the possibility of a politics. What this politics will be will depend on the specific projects and practices of various communities. Insofar as the sense of membership of these communities is not subsumed under the national, it may well signal the possibility of a transnational politics centred in concrete localities. — Saskia Sassen 2001

Hong Kong is a global capitalist city, self-proclaimed to be "Asia's World City" and a "poster child for world trade."[21] As Saskia Sassen has observed, a global city involves not only the movement of capital, but also the movement of a transnational workforce, "both rich, i.e. the new transnational professional workforce, and poor, i.e. most migrant workers; and it is a space for the transmigration of cultural forms, for the reterritorialization of 'local' subcultures."[22] Within this context, corporations and governments valorize global capitalism even as they produce new inequalities. An important question Sassen raises is whether the global city "is also a space for a new politics."

Aihwa Ong, by contrast, posits a notion of spaces of neoliberal exception in which categories of people such as migrant domestic workers are excluded from the benefits of citizenship and denied human rights or where the privileged citizens and skilled or professional migrant workers receive special benefits.[23] As Ong argues, the Special Administrative Region of Hong Kong is a neoliberal space of exception. "The SAR framework allows for experimentation with different degrees of civil rights in a vibrant capitalist setting, a milieu that acts as a laboratory for China's future." Within this SAR context, even more than within China's Special Economic Zones (SEZs) "pockets of agitation for civil rights" are accommodated and do not threaten economic, national, and collective security.[24]

Bearing in mind Sassen's ideas about global cities in which new politics emerge and Ong's ideas about neoliberal spaces of exception, I ask what it is specifically about Hong Kong and about the position of women migrant workers — whose mobility and voice is both a product and a symptom of globalization — that quite literally *permits* these protests and shapes their form and content at this particular historical point in time? What is it about Hong Kong — beyond generalities about global cities — that both empowers political protest and at the same time defines its limits?

Unlike post–World War II migrant workers in Europe[25] — who were initially allowed entry as temporary "guest workers" in response to labor shortages and were soon granted legal permanent residency, citizenship, or citizenship-like rights — Hong Kong's migrant women domestic workers protest in a place where they remain highly vulnerable as guest workers and temporary migrants, remaining in Hong Kong on precarious two-year visas and denied the opportunity of becoming citizens or permanent residents. Their family members are not permitted to live in Hong Kong, unless they come with their own temporary work visas, and they do not receive the medical and educational benefits that citizens, permanent residents, and more privileged immigrants receive. By contrast with the "flexible citizenship" of Hong Kong's elite multiple passport holders (and their parachute families),[26] migrant workers can be said to have a particular type of flexibility associated with their *noncitizenship*. "Citizenship" here refers not only to the legal membership and voting rights in a particular nation-state (e.g., Indonesia or the Philippines), but also to the more contested claims to recognition or belonging to specific sociocultural communities or territories — including gendered ones — and the sense of political responsibility this claim entails.[27]

These flexible noncitizens, who are *trans*national in the sense of both *trans*forming and *trans*cending the borders of nation-states, work in a space of exception that simultaneously permits their protests (within limits) and denies them the rights of citizens and citizenship.[28] As oppressed and exploited workers who have been "sold out" by their own governments and by neoliberal global capitalist forces, migrant domestic workers contribute labor that privileges the upper and middle classes of the Hong Kong SAR. Indeed, President Macapagal-Arroyo's promise in 2006 to establish training programs to produce more Filipina "super maids" to send abroad was vehemently criticized by migrant workers and their families as yet another form of government extortion and of milking the maids, since prospective workers would be required to foot the bill for the newly required (and dubiously beneficial) training programs. Ironically, within the SAR's neoliberal space of exception, foreign domestic workers are permitted to express public criticism.

Yet Hong Kong does not offer the same opportunity for protest and mobilization of transnational interests to all migrants. As Nicole Newendorp points out, the "right of abode" protests of Mainland Chinese wives of Hong Kong citizens — who wait many years to become residents of Hong Kong, but in so doing lose their rights to residency in the mainland and do not gain the rights of Hong Kong citizenship — have been largely ignored.[29] Prospective mainland immigrant wives, by virtue of their claims to the benefits of nationality and citizenship, present a threat that foreign domestic workers do not. This underscores the significance of the racial/ethnic national otherness and the flexible noncitizenship of migrant workers, their claims to human rights and proper treatment as global workers (as opposed to citizenship), as well as the essential work they perform for Hong Kong's privileged citizens within the global economy.

As noted earlier, temporary migrant domestic workers typically do not take part in public protests, and such protests are virtually unheard of among

Nicole Constable

Fig. 7. As the anti-WTO protests intensified, more police were seen in full riot gear. 18 December 2005.

Filipina and Indonesian domestic workers in Singapore, Taiwan, and Malaysia, even less imaginable in the Middle East or Gulf States. Hong Kong allows protests that might take on a very different tenor and become violent or dangerous if they took place in other cities such as Singapore, Manila, Beijing, Taipei, or Jakarta. The Hong Kong police force — linked as it is to Hong Kong's image of peaceful and subtle forms of modern governmentality and to the social stability needed for economic prosperity — is a key factor. The Hong Kong police compare favorably to more violent and militaristic police and governments elsewhere: Nepal's military police; the Korean police; the Philippine army and police violence against labor organizers and members of the media; and the violent crackdowns and repression by Malaysian, Indonesian, and Mainland Chinese police and military forces. The fear of deportation and arrest and the outright banning of specific nationalities of workers clearly inhibit potential activism among foreign domestic workers in other Asian and Middle Eastern locations.

In the summer of 2005 a rumor spread among HKPA participants that mainland Chinese police might be brought to Hong Kong during the WTO conference. In the end that did not — and perhaps could not — come about alongside the Hong Kong government's claim to being Asia's world city and a premier center for global trade. I was told in summer 2005 and early during People's Action Week that in comparison to police in Mainland China the Hong Kong police were more sympathetic to protestors. As People's Action Week continued, however, and the protests escalated and the police became more visible — wearing riot gear and masks in rows lined up five officers deep — they were taunted as naïve, inexperienced, and incompetent at dealing with protestors (see fig. 7). I was told that in the Philippines, for example, confiscating a police shield is a badge of honor. During the first march, the protestors managed to take a several shields in a very short period of time then voluntarily returned them to the police, implying that they posed far too little challenge for it to be any fun. Hong Kong police reportedly looked fearful and were ill prepared for what was child's play compared to protests in Korea or the Philippines. What began as praise of police restraint or gentle mocking of their inexperience at the beginning of the week was debated by week's end, especially following the arrest of hundreds of protestors as police used pepper spray, tear gas, and hoses to hold back protestors.[30] But despite criticism of the police for their inexperience, overreaction, and lack of restraint, they were still described as relatively peaceful.

Migrant workers interpreted the trials in 2006 of two Korean anti-WTO protestors and the eventual dismissal of charges against all of the arrested anti-WTO protestors as further evidence that Hong Kong was not like their own (or Mainland Chinese) repressive states. The concern over police violence — should it go too far — risked incurring criticism from local Hong Kong citizens and professional expatriates, sullying Hong Kong's reputation for peaceful governmentality, weakening its ability to rule in more subtle and less overtly repressive ways, and undercutting its claim to being a modern, global Asian city.

The Consulate Hopping Protest thus reveals the multiethnic and international composition of the participants, the central role of domestic workers, but the inclusion of other types of migrant workers as well. The breadth of their concerns was expressed at two significant sites: Hong Kong's government offices, where local concerns were voiced, and the U.S. Consulate, where anti-WTO and anti–U.S. imperialist (including anti–Iraq War) sentiments were voiced alongside issues involving immigrant workers in U.S. sweatshops and the like. Representatives from organizations such as AMCB, Unifil, HKCTU, Migrante, Bayan, and ILPS reflected the shifting roles and subjectivities of domestic workers. I was struck by the number of domestic workers who had used their activist experience in Hong Kong as a stepping-stone to other NGO or activist work and politics back in the Philippines. The clear patterns of networking between and through Unifil and Migrante — in relation to the new migrant political party in the Philippines and the recently acquired vote for Filipino overseas workers — points to the political and activist education of women domestic workers and the way in which such experience is linked to newly forming political parties and pressure groups in the Philippines as has been the case elsewhere.[31] Indonesian domestic workers are not far behind: several activist Indonesians involved with ATKI and IMWU described their political awakening in Hong Kong and their plans to continue their activism upon return to Indonesia.

The Consulate Hopping Protest and the role of migrant domestic workers in the wider anti-WTO protest illustrate the increasingly global and transnational issues that domestic workers have taken on. No longer do their organizations focus solely or primarily on local issues such as the minimum wage, the levy, and the government's "two-week rule" (which dictates that domestic workers whose contracts have ended or been terminated must return home within two weeks if they have not signed a new contract), although these are clearly still im-

portant, but many organi-
zations have become
transnational in the sense
of taking on a much
broader array of human
rights issues and express-
ing critiques that are targeted not only at the Philippine and Hong Kong
governments and their
policies, but also at a number of other governments
and at neoliberal global-
ization in general.[32] Such
protests teach migrant
worker observers about
the ways in which their
personal experiences and
the difficulties they experience as migrant workers
are embedded in a wider
global context. They learn
the language of human

Nicole Constable

Fig. 8. Domestic workers wearing boxes marked "for
export" and T-shirts reading "Junk WTO" were among
the thousands of members of the Hong Kong People's
Alliance (HKPA) who marched against the WTO on 18
December 2005.

and global rights, as well
as the critique of
neoliberalism, by observ-
ing and listening to pro-
test organizers and activists and other worker participants.

These protests are not devoid of conflict and competition. There is, for example, competition between Filipino groups for influence over and affiliation with
other nationalities of workers, and also competition between Indonesian
groups, each claiming authority to speak for the interests of Indonesian workers
as a whole. Two different migrant worker coalitions, for example, sponsored
consulate or embassy protests: one was the Consulate Hopping Protest described above, the other was a march that seemed to attract a larger proportion
of international protestors from abroad. The AMCB was closely affiliated with
the HKPA and depended on the official HKPA stage and speaker system that was
set up in the soccer field of Victoria Park while the Asian Migrant Centre (AMC),
another Filipino-led organization, set up its own stage and audio system on the
other side of Victoria Park and became more closely allied with some of the international protestors — the highly visible Korean Peasants League (KPL) and La
Via Campesina (an international peasant/small farmer advocacy organization)
— which put them more squarely in the media and the public eye. Domestic
workers often learn after the fact that affiliating with one activist organization or
network can also alienate them from others. Some of the divides that exist

among migrant workers (Indonesians as well as Filipinos) seem to structurally replicate left-wing political fissures in the Philippines.

Choosing whether or not to join the protests is also significant. Some Indonesian domestic workers who regularly spend their Sunday holiday in Victoria Park in Causeway Bay expressed sympathy for the anti-WTO platform, but most avoided the scene on the advice of employers or recruiters. They were reluctant to participate in the protests for reasons that ranged from a lack of interest to fear of violence. Workers voiced concerns about job security should their employers who had warned them to stay away from the protests see them on the evening news. They also spoke of their vulnerability, as temporary migrant workers at risk for deportation, and of family members who would lose an essential source of income if they were arrested. Yet despite such concerns, other domestic workers chose to actively participate (see fig. 8). Some left the protest area only when so-called "street battles" erupted between police and protestors — the point at which they perceived a serious risk of injury or arrest. Most domestic workers (some with deep ambivalence) left the scene before the arrests began.

No Filipinos — neither domestic workers nor activists from abroad — were among the nine hundred or so protestors who were arrested at the end of the week of anti-WTO protests. Those arrested were predominantly male Korean protestors. Some Filipinos, men and women, expressed their sense of "shame" that although Filipino groups were among the most numerous participants in the protests, and despite their glorious reputation for protest, no Filipinos, not even the famous revolutionaries and radical labor activists who had come to Hong Kong specifically for the protests, had been arrested. Their Korean com-

Fig. 9. In one anti-WTO protest march on 15 December 2008, Korean farmers (whose jackets read "WTO kills farmers") processed from Causeway Bay to Wanchai by walking three steps then bowing their heads to the ground. This kowtowing, an ancient Buddhist rite, moved some local observers to tears.

rades had not only made a powerful statement and a more coordinated stand in the protest (visually and dramatically), winning over many local observers, but they had also taken the brunt of the violence and the arrests.[33] The Korean protestors groups included some women, but overall they were male dominated, militaristic, and hierarchically organized in appearance and style, with drums, chants, and shrill whistles leading military-styled marches (see fig. 9 above).

Organizers and domestic worker activists (as well as HKPA organizers) were publicly committed to peaceful protest. Domestic workers and their supporters did not want to risk being arrested, endangering their visas and their livelihood, and leaders of migrant worker organizations feared placing members at risk. Nor did they want to damage the hard-won and valuable alliances that they had formed with the HKPA organizers, including leaders of the HKCTU and the legislators who organized or supported the anti-WTO protests. Interestingly, after People's Action Week was over, several foreign domestic worker organizations hosted Korean protestors as they awaited the release of their compatriots. They welcomed them to their shelters and meeting places, provided them with mattresses, blankets, and food, and organized protests and vigils for the detainees, even after their compatriots had to return home, thus extending their gendered transnational domestic work to another political realm.

Conclusion

On Sunday, 2 July 2006, just hours after returning from a conference in Europe, Elizabeth Tang, chairperson of the HKPA and chief executive of the HKCTU, addressed a cheering crowd of four hundred domestic workers from eighty organizations at the first Filipino Migrant Workers Summit held in a large lecture hall at the University of Hong Kong. She said, "The people of Hong Kong are very impressed with what you [foreign domestic workers] did at the WTO meetings. Korean protestors set the standard, but you persisted until the end of the week. You are number two [after the Koreans]!" She praised the foreign domestic workers' participation in a recent May Day rally as well. Whereas locals "ran away" to shop, picnic, and escape the heat, "migrant workers stayed until the end and did not run away!" To a roar of applause, she proclaimed that the HKCTU executive committee members all agreed that Hong Kong locals could and should "learn from the migrant workers."

The vast majority of overseas domestic workers are women. The gendered aspects of their work and family roles (their gendered labor within private domestic spaces of a global workplace; the commodification of care work that allows women in one location to become the managers or do more highly valued labor outside of the home; their negotiation of gendered familial expectations across transnational space) have received much scholarly attention.[34] Scholars have also focused on the formation of NGOs and migrant worker political organizations.[35] An examination of the global context of paid household work forces a shift in the scale and reach of what is defined as "domestic." Domestic workers perform intimate household and family labor across the divides of nation-states. They participate in transnational labor and contribute to public discourse and debate about human rights and globalization. This adds a new twist to the by now classic feminist critique of domestic/public, private/political dichotomies (in which women were once assumed to occupy a feminized private and domestic sphere), demonstrating that the domestic *transcends* and *transforms* the public, political, transnational, and global.[36]

The messages conveyed in domestic worker protests are born in part of their realization that their personal and individual troubles and difficulties (and those of other domestic workers) are not just private and personal (local and domestic), but are linked to larger political issues and deeper global economic inequalities. Their political activities and concerns do indeed involve "home country local and national politics";[37] they are also increasingly framed within a transnational and global context; they are "deterritorialized" in certain ways, extending beyond the binary national boundaries of nation-states, involving issues of human rights and a critique of neoliberalism more generally.[38]

The majority of foreign domestic workers in Hong Kong are not politically active, but those who are, are highly visible, vocal, and influential. Their expressions of protest — aimed in multiple directions and at various levels of power — contribute to a rethinking of the ways in which feminized labor and migration are both a symptom of specific patterns of globalization and also create and redefine it.[39] Women domestic workers are very much entwined (increasingly so) in a critique of the global. As such they develop new political subjectivities and come to see themselves, in the course of their experiences and their encounters with others in shelters, public spaces, and at work, as global laborers whose voices belong and deserve to be heard in public spaces that reach far beyond their household workplaces.

Since the 1990s, the scope and significance of domestic worker activism in and beyond Hong Kong has increased. Filipino overseas workers, for example, have gained the right to vote in Philippine national elections and have established their own political party. Filipino domestic workers are widely considered to be shrewd and politically savvy activists whose "negative" influence is rubbing off on formerly less assertive Indonesian workers. Different sorts of protests — the massive public protests involving locals and migrants on the 1 July anniversaries of Hong Kong's reunification with China; Filipino and Indonesian domestic worker protests criticizing local abuses and exploitative state practices; and migrant worker involvement in international protests such as the anti-WTO protest in 2005 — illustrate the development of new transnational affiliations and oppositions and reflect protestors' performances and reformulations of their own gendered noncitizenship and migrant worker subjectivities.[40]

Such migrant domestic worker protests — criticizing the local Hong Kong government, their own and other Asian governments, the United States, and symbols of economic globalization such as the WTO — are highly unusual and do not take place in Singapore, Malaysia, or Taiwan, much less Saudi Arabia or the United Arab Emirates. Why are such protests tolerated in Hong Kong? A major factor is the uniqueness of the post-1997, postcolonial Hong Kong SAR, with its claims to maintaining its status as a global city and its historical development as a space of neoliberal exception. Also relevant is the fact that migrant domestic workers are women who are not demanding citizenship or permanent residence (in contrast to Mainland Chinese right of abode protestors). They advocate for worker's rights and human rights; their flexible noncitizenship provides assurance that they cannot remain there permanently. Like migrant domestic workers elsewhere, they play a critical role in the global economy. Yet their interests increasingly resonate with the concerns, fears, and growing commitments of Hong Kong citizens and more privileged expatriates to protect their right of assembly and freedom of expression — especially against the backdrop of mainland China's increasing crackdowns and the perceived threats to Hong Kong's self rule.[41] Hong Kong's leaders, moreover, even those aligned with the Chinese government, have a vested interest in promoting postcolonial Hong Kong as a well-governed, democratic, and thriving world city, a center for world trade and globalization. They tolerate protests that are peaceful and support or do not threaten the wider economic interests of Hong Kong and its proper citizens. Unlike mainland protestors in Hong Kong, whose demands for right of abode threaten the well-being of Hong Kong citizens, domestic workers pose little threat to the interests of Hong Kong's privileged locals. Their labor is essential to and their protests are defining of the Hong Kong SAR's particular brand of postcolonial neoliberalism.

ACKNOWLEDGMENTS: With admiration and appreciation, I gratefully acknowledge Cynthia Abdon-Tellez, Corazon Amaya Cañete, Rodolfo (Jun) Cañete, Eni Lestari, Dolores Balladares, Eman Villanueva, Norman Carnay, Ramon Bultron, Christina DeFalco, and many others in Hong Kong for the assistance they provided in the course of my research and for their commitment to social justice for migrant workers. My thanks to those who offered comments on earlier drafts of this paper at the Association for Asian Studies meetings, Stanford University, the Fairbank Center at Harvard University, the University of Michigan, and the Social Movements Forum at the University of Pittsburgh. In particular, I thank Nancy Abelmann, Joseph Alter, Kathleen Blee, Suzanne Brenner, Melissa Brown, Lisa Brush, Vanessa Fong, Michele Gamburd, Deborah Gould, Ching Kwan Lee, Haiyan Lee, John Markoff, Kevin Ming, Nicole Newendorp, and Donald Nonini for their probing questions and excellent suggestions. Funding for this research was provided by the School of Arts and Sciences at the University of Pittsburgh.

❏

8. Undocumented Indonesian Workers in Macau

The Human Outcome of Colluding Interests

Amy Sim and Vivienne Wee

ACCORDING TO THE UNITED NATIONS, the twenty-first century is to be one of Asian urbanization[1] with twelve out of the world's twenty-two mega-cities[2] in 2020 (that is, cities with more than 10 million people) located in Asia, accounting for more than half of the world's urban population of 2.66 billion out of a global urban population of 4.94 billion.[3] Current discourses on Asia's megacities tend to celebrate their capital accumulation, infrastructural development, and geographical spread. Ong and Roy,[4] for example, applaud "the role of Asian cities as 'worlding' nodes: those that create global connections and global regimes of value…whereby urban elites borrow, copy, and articulate city-making across national borders."

Celebratory discourses underpinned by developments in international regimes of governance[5] remain ahistorical[6] and conservative, however, focusing on power and structural reproductions, wealth, and accumulation by a narrow elite and offering glimpses of privileged realities. Such tropes neglect the importance of labor as key in the making of these megacities — particularly blue-collar, migrant, informal workers and invisible domestics — dwelling instead on urban elites in tertiary sectors and sidestepping the real issues of power distribution, social inequalities, and those on whom cities depend.

The labor required to build these sites is usually migrant labor imported not only because of local shortages, but more importantly because migrant labor has a cost-lowering effect that enables a higher return on investment, thereby creating, at least in part, the so-called regimes of value.[7] Elsewhere we have analyzed how migration lowers labor costs through the articulation of spatially separated capitalist and noncapitalist modes of production, such that capital accumulation is subsidized by labor imports from noncapitalist economies.[8] In Macau, for example, Choi has noted that unskilled migrant labor has been present since at least the mid nineteenth century.[9] The cost-lowering effect of such labor has persisted from then until present. Macau government statistics for

2000 to 2003 indicate that migrant workers are paid from 20 percent to 35 percent less than local workers for comparable jobs. The presence of these migrant workers is "greeted with hostility by locals who accuse them of depressing wages, and taking away their job opportunities."[10] Some economists back the Macanese government's approach of allowing entry of unskilled migrant workers *precisely because* labor import reduces wage pressures and helps to maintain Macau's competitiveness.[11]

Projections of declining migrant flows have not been borne out.[12] From 1995 to 2003, the number of registered migrant workers in Macau did decline from 35,286 to 23,221, or from 16.4 percent to 11.5 percent of the employed population (approximately 200,000). In 2004, however, nonresident workers increased from 27,736 to 39,411 in 2005, to 64,673 in 2006, and to 85,207 in 2007. Moreover, quarterly increases of nonresidents in 2007 over 2006 registered year-on-year increases of up to an astounding 41 percent.[13]

In this article we argue further that the cost-lowering effect of migrant labor is magnified by *undocumented* migration, which feeds a black labor market of even more exploitable workers. The Macau government's apparent tolerance of growing numbers of undocumented workers may indicate its positive valuation of this type of labor in the development of Macau as a "wannabe global city."[14] It was only the structural limitations of social services that motivated a policy change in 1988 to regulate migration inflows.[15] Macau's position as a capitalist state with a pro-business approach means, however, that business interests in cheap labor is "given much heavier weight inside the government."[16] At the same time, the hostility of local workers to migrant labor has led the Macau government to adopt an unofficial "don't ask, don't tell" stance, allowing the presence of undocumented migrant labor, without having to report their numbers.

Analyses of disparate sites of accumulation have tended to ignore their historical interconnection. For example, Hong Kong's rise in the 1840s eclipsed Macau's, draining Macau of wealth and population.[17] This historical connection remains salient today with Macau now serving as a willing dumping ground for migrant labor from Hong Kong. This interconnectedness exemplifies clustered urbanization on a global landscape, including many of the places where our Indonesian respondents have worked: Hong Kong, Macau, Singapore, Taiwan, Malaysia, and the Middle East. Knowingly or unknowingly, they have become members of a cross-border labor pool, accessible to multiple sites of urbanization.

This article shows how labor export policies in Indonesia and immigration policies in Hong Kong are key factors in the creation of a pool of undocumented Indonesian overstayers in Macau. It shows how oppressive practices in labor export and discriminatory exclusions lead Indonesian women workers to "try their luck" in Macau where, instead of opportunity, they often unwittingly become entrapped in a cycle of poverty and irregular status, with decreasing options available to them. Their options are either to return to Hong Kong or to return home to Indonesia. Visions of an urbanizing Asia built by low-skilled migrant workers are premised on their disposability and exclusion. The human costs of such exclusion are borne by the workers themselves, and thereby externalized by the urban economy (in the case of Hong Kong) or even regarded as beneficial to the formal economy (in the case of Macau).

Lastly, this article criticizes nonfeminist theorizing in "globalization" literature, in which the role of states in the construction of gendered work and mobility is treated unproblematically, as if irrelevant in the perpetuation of "gender-class."[18] It argues that even as women migrate to find ways to live independent lives, their agency comes to be seamlessly integrated into patriarchal class relations between men and women.[19] This article provides firsthand empirical evidence of how women who are undocumented migrant workers are subordinated through "control of...access to the means of their livelihood," how this is "the essence of patriarchy, its universal function and effect,"[20] and how state agendas are complicit by limiting women's access to secure employment.

Male migrants are subjected to domination by class, "race,"[21] ethnicity, and national identity, but they are often protected by the minimum standards found in employment codes in the formal sphere in which they are employed. Men do not, as a rule, work in isolation in the domestic sphere and are hence not at as much risk of invisible physical and sexual abuse as are the women migrants. Indonesian male migrants to other destinations share many of the problems that female labor migrants from Indonesia to Hong Kong and Macau confront, especially the high fees that recruitment agencies require. Both male and female migrants are thus motivated to attempt to avoid formal systems of recruitment, resulting, for example, in large undocumented groups of Indonesians in Malaysia. But among all migrants, including those documented and undocumented, women migrants comprise nearly 80 percent of Indonesia's annual labor export, thereby becoming the most lucrative source of revenue for labor brokers. Furthermore, the Indonesian government justifies the maintenance of a system of women's labor export, legitimizing their exploitation in terms of a gendered ideology of "protecting" women.[22]

Undocumented Indonesian Migrant Labor as a Growing Phenomenon in East Asia

The role of the state remains highly contested in discourses on international migration, while push-pull theories, which account for migratory flows with seeming inevitability (without considering state or business agendas) are increasingly untenable.[23] To Sassen, it is the penetration of capitalist agendas that uproots people from their traditional sources of livelihoods and the unevenness of global development that sets up core countries as magnets for "surplus labour."[24] Her argument challenges claims of substitution effects between capital and labor, which argue that export-oriented industries can ameliorate push-pull effects by providing employment in the developing world to prevent the dispossessed from migrating overseas.

Choi testifies to the role of a pro-business state in Macau in ensuring flexible and cheap sources of labor fueling the economy.[25] The state's construction of cheap labor is based on its ability to control entry into the territory, to confine migrant labor through labor segmentation in order to prevent it from commanding market prices, and to manipulate the labor market through policies,

Amy Sim

Indonesian migrant domestic workers enjoying a day off in Macau's central plaza, San Ma Lo.

laws, and practices. According to Parreñas, "migration...is a state-manipulated process of citizenship diminishment and re-assignment."[26] Choi agrees that migrants are accorded economic "citizenship" in order to work, but are denied social and political rights to be treated equally as citizens. Rosewarne goes further to say that the existence of "undocumented workers is a deliberate state creation intended to deliver to the private sector a group of workers it is free to abuse [as] their presence in the economy gives the state more flexibility in the manipulation of the labour market."[27] Indonesian migrants in Macau who "overstay" beyond the terms of their work visas are hence a state-engineered outcome of calibrations of labor supply, not just in Macau but also in Indonesia and Hong Kong.

Nearly 80 percent of the estimated half a million Indonesian migrants annually are women. Sixty-five percent head for Asian destinations and 35 percent to the Middle East.[28] Among migrant workers in East Asia, Indonesian labor migrants generate the highest rates of overstayers. For example, in Japan, one in four Indonesian female migrants in Japan was undocumented in 2002. The number increased by 1,450 percent between 1990 and 2003.[29] In South Korea, in 2002, 3,117 Indonesian women workers were undocumented, compared to 1,646 with valid documents — that is, 189.3 percent more undocumented than documented.[30] From 1999 to 2002, the number of male and female Indonesian overstayers soared 807 percent, from 1,865 to 15,054.[31] In Taiwan, the number of undocumented Indonesian women workers jumped from 477 in 1993 to 3,809 in 2002, an increase of nearly 800 percent.[32] The rate of runaways among Indonesian migrant workers also rose: from 156 in 1992 to 3,809 in 2000 (a 2,400 percent increase), with women outnumbering men by four to one, or 1,633 to 449.[33]

Chiu confirms that the number of undocumented migrants in Hong Kong is unknown, while Skeldon estimates about 20,000.[34] The number of prosecutions of undocumented workers for overstaying in Hong Kong dropped from 17,681 in 1998[35] to 1,981 in 2002, and 2,757 in 2003.[36] Hong Kong's Statistics and Immigration departments were unable to provide a breakdown of these figures by nationality or occupation. The Indonesian Consulate in Hong Kong could not give any estimates of overstaying Indonesian migrants. Without matching arrival and departure cards, it is impossible to determine therefore whether the reduction in numbers of prosecutions in Hong Kong is due to a real decrease in overstaying, to official leniency, to the ingenuity of these immigrants in avoiding the police, or to the possibility that they move on to Macau as a last resort.

Statistics for undocumented migrants in Macau are even less available as we have found that migrants who overstay and are apprehended are often not prosecuted but are instructed to leave the territory by their own means — i.e., by purchasing their own air tickets. Those without sufficient funds are told to acquire enough money to buy their air tickets, even though they are not given work permits to earn money and have to report to Macau immigration authorities on a weekly basis. Given the opacity of these arrangements, the number of undocumented migrants who have been "deported" this way is unknown. This lends credence to the argument that the state manipulates this reserved labor pool as a calibrating device for managing labor supply without the need for politically unpopular policies.

Investigative Research on Undocumented Indonesian Migrant Workers in Macau

While statistics are not available for verifying the numbers of undocumented migrants in Macau, our investigative research uncovers at least a partial view of this hitherto hidden reality. As the data obtained in this study have legal ramifications for our respondents, the research was conducted with particular emphasis on confidentiality and by ten Indonesian women who were employed on a regular status as foreign domestic workers in Macau. The women belonged to an Indonesian migrant workers' organization in Macau. The organization was selected on the basis of its experience in assisting migrant workers in need. The ten members of this organization were selected for their ability to conduct interviews and were provided guidance for interviewing undocumented migrant workers. The interviews were conducted in Indonesian and Javanese.

The field research from August 2006 to March 2007 was based on a set of semi-structured questions in the interviews. Semi-structured questions were chosen to address two concerns: (1) Because of the sensitivity of the research topic, the interviews had to be carried out by Indonesian migrant workers, with a need to ensure consistency in the questions asked. (2) The questions had to be open-ended because so little is known of the undocumented migrants that there was no way of predicting which questions would be more relevant to them.

The questions were structured to explore this uncharted terrain and the selection of respondents was based on introductions, as trust was key to their willingness to be interviewed. Given that open-ended questions were asked, it was striking that many of the answers were so similar. This indicates the existence of regular patterns in the experiences of undocumented migrants.

One issue that all interviewers repeatedly encountered was the respondents' appeal for assistance. This was expected as this study focused on women in extreme states of vulnerability. The interviewers were briefed not to intervene but to refer the respondents to sources for assistance. Privacy was guaranteed to the respondents as a condition for their participation, with no personal information or phone numbers recorded in our database. While this assured their anonymity, it makes it impossible to check back afterwards with those interviewed. Our desire to protect the respondents from official harassment made this condition inevitable.

Documenting Undocumented
Indonesian Migrant Workers in Macau

Sixty-six undocumented Indonesian migrant workers were interviewed in Macau. These represent a small percentage of the yet unknown numbers in this community, but their responses nevertheless reveal recurrent patterns and structural processes. Of these sixty-six respondents, sixty-five originated from Hong Kong, entering Macau legally. The flow of Indonesian women, former domestics in Hong Kong, to Macau, stems from a Hong Kong Immigration Department policy issued in 1987 known as the "new conditions of stay" or the "two-week rule." This policy requires foreign domestic workers in Hong Kong to leave no later than two weeks after the completion of their employment contracts or after their contracts have been terminated, either by themselves or their employers.[37] Those who are able to find new employment before the end of two weeks are obligated to exit the territory and wait for the six weeks needed to process a new employment visa. Indonesian migrants who are unable to secure new employment within two weeks must return home to begin the process of finding an employer from there. This means that they are subjected again to an indefinite period of virtual incarceration in training centers while they wait for new employers to be found.[38] And once again they fall into debt bondage due to the high recruitment fees they must pay. The only exceptions that allow migrant workers in Hong Kong to transfer directly to a new employer without first going home are cases in which the worker can provide certifiable evidence of maltreatment or of the former employers' emigration, demise, or bankruptcy.

Officially, Hong Kong's two-week policy was instituted to stop foreign domestic workers from job hopping.[39] The use of the term "job hopping" implies that foreign domestics are at liberty to hop from job to job. In fact, besides being bound by the two-week rule, foreign domestic workers have very limited occupational mobility, meaning they are prohibited from moving from sector to sector in search of types of work. Furthermore, they are required to "live-in" with their employers. Because all potential employers of foreign domestic workers have to be vetted by the Labour Department, it is very easy for the government to prevent changes of employers.

The two-week rule compounds the vulnerability of foreign domestic workers because their employers can fire them for any reason and at any time. Foreign domestics in Hong Kong are mostly women. They are allowed to enter to replace local women's traditional domestic roles in the household. The two-week rule thus targets foreign domestics on the basis of their gendered work as women, that is, gender discrimination of women as a class. Male foreign domestics in Hong Kong, who constitute less than 5 percent of the total number of foreign domestic workers, are similarly penalized for their participation in what is deemed to be "women's work." The forced repatriation of unemployed workers after two weeks has been a focus for labor organizing and protest since 1987. Migrant domestics demand that they be given the same rights as foreign professionals and, like them, be allowed to stay until the end of the visa-contracted period in order to find new employment. But this does not appear to be likely. In 2003, a Hong Kong Immigration Department official told us that foreign domestic workers who are unable to find new employers within two weeks would not do so if given more time. This policy doubly penalizes workers who have been unjustly terminated. Early terminations of contracts and subsequent enforced departures within two weeks may befall indebted workers who have not worked long enough before termination to cover their recruitment fees and who thus fall deeper into debt.

One unforeseen consequence of the two-week rule is the emergence of increasing numbers of undocumented migrants, who stay on in Hong Kong when they are unable to find new employers in two weeks because they are unwilling to return to Indonesia in debt and with no prospects of leaving again to work overseas soon.[40] The number of "overstayers" in Hong Kong increased by 14 percent in one year alone — from 15,554 to 17,681 between 1997 and 1998.[41] As a sending country, the Philippines estimates that there are more undocumented (5.3 million) than documented (4.7 million) Filipino workers overseas.[42] Evidence of the growing numbers of undocumented migrant workers in Hong Kong, who are trying to evade the two-week rule, indicates that this policy might, in the end, compromise the welfare of a society where migrants, who have lost their jobs and cannot find new employment in two weeks, disappear into the underground economy.

The emergence of a pool of undocumented Indonesian workers in Macau is very likely a spillover of the increasing population of undocumented migrant workers in Hong Kong. Our focus here is on what happens to the migrants who go to Macau to escape the consequences of the two-week rule, which would have rendered them as overstayers in Hong Kong. This move to Macau is perceived as a last chance to stay on legally in order to find legitimate employment before all their options run out and they have to return to Indonesia.

When Indonesian workers in Hong Kong have their contracts terminated and they go to Macau, they find themselves in the following situation. Upon arrival in Macau, they are given a thirty-day visitor's visa. If they cannot find an employer in Macau within thirty days, they go across the land border to southern

Table 1. Age

	Ages 21–29	Ages 30–37	No answer
No. of respondents	59	6	1
	(mostly 24 to 26)		

Table 2. Religion

	Muslim	Protestant	Catholic	No answer
No. of respondents	60	3	2	1

Table 3. Marital status

	Single	Married	Widowed	Divorced
No. of respondents	51	8	4	3

Table 4. Place of origin

	Java	Sumatra	Sulawesi	Nusa Tenggara Barat
No. of respondents	58*	4	3	1

* East Java = 33 Central Java = 19 West Java = 6

China. On their reentry into Macau, they are permitted to stay for another twenty days. This process may be repeated only once more, with returnees given a final ten-day extension. It is only after they have exhausted these visa extensions that they become undocumented, when the final visa expires after a total of sixty days.

At the same time, once they leave Hong Kong, they are not allowed to reenter Hong Kong from Macau unless they show that they possess a valid Hong Kong work visa, evidence of employment in Macau, or an air ticket that shows that they will be leaving for Indonesia via Hong Kong's airport. Therefore, once women migrant workers leave for Macau, their options become very limited.

The scenario described above is the general pattern that emerges from our analysis of the experiences recounted by sixty-five respondents who had gone to Macau from Hong Kong. (Only one of the sixty-six women had gone there directly from Indonesia.) All had gone to Macau by ferry to find work. Most had either come to the end of their contracts in Hong Kong or had been prematurely terminated. The rest had completed their legal claims against their Hong Kong employers and were required to leave Hong Kong immediately.

Their average length of stay in Macau at the time of the interviews was 10.6 months. As explained above, the women became overstayers in Macau when their visitor visas ran out and they had no possibility for further extensions or when they were unable to go to Mainland China for a second time to extend their stay in Macau. It should be noted that sixty-three out of sixty-six respondents wanted to return to Indonesia at the time of this study and the predominant reason for not leaving Macau was their lack of funds to buy an air ticket. One (respondent no. 66) did not respond to this question; another (respondent no. 55) did not want to return to Indonesia; and a third (respondent no.

57) wished to return, but replied "not yet" because she wanted to save money to bring home with her.

The general profile of the sixty-six respondents is given in Tables 1 to 4 above.

Table 5 indicates that among the sixty-six respondents, thirty-one had been instructed to go to Macau by their labor agencies in Hong Kong, but were required to pay for their own ferry fare. Some agencies made arrangements for them to stay with their associate firms in Macau. However, they were evicted from these temporary lodgings once their Macau visas expired. In a few cases, the agencies held on to the workers' passports until their Macau visas had expired and it was too late for them to do anything except become undocumented overstayers. One respondent who had overstayed since May 2006 said, "Every time I had an interview with a possible employer, I was always considered unsuitable by the employer, until my visa expired." In other words, some employers may prefer to hire undocumented workers. The one undocumented overstayer who had been sent by her agency in Indonesia directly to Macau, had no job or work permit arranged for her when she arrived and soon became undocumented.

Table 5 shows that the overwhelming majority of the sixty-six respondents had gone to Macau to look for jobs as domestic workers, but as overstayers they generally take up any activity that generates income, including the hawking of food that they cook themselves. Those who went with the encouragement of their agencies in Hong Kong expected that their agencies would assist them in finding jobs. As our interviews elicited open-ended answers, those respondents who said that they are "waiting for Hong Kong visas" were also depending on their agencies. It should be noted that among those who had been encouraged by their agencies to go to Macau, two had been waiting seven to nine months for Hong Kong visas.

Conditions of Sixty-Six Undocumented Workers

Table 5a. Who told her to go to Macau?

Agency in Hong Kong/Indonesia	31/1
Friend	17
Self	15
Employer's sister	1
No information	1

Table 5b. Reason for going to Macau

To look for a job	51
Waiting for Hong Kong visa	4
Terminated by Hong Kong employer	5
Hong Kong visa expired	2
Trying out a new environment	1
Resigned from Hong Kong job	1
To look for a job, did not want to return to Indonesia*	1

* Two reasons given

Table 5c (see next page)

Table 5d. Future plans

Wishes to go back to Indonesia	63
(Purchased air ticket already	3)
Not yet ready to return to Indonesia	2
No information was given	1
Total	66

Table 5e. Reason for staying on in Macau

No money to buy air ticket	60
To earn more money*	1
No information	3

* She had a ticket to return (2 more with air tickets are not included here).

Table 5c. Length of time in Macau					
First year		Second year		Third year	
Months	Numbers	Months	Numbers	Months	Numbers
1	1	13	2	25	-
2	1	14	-	26	1
3	3*	15	-		
4	10	16	2		
5	4	17	1		
6	5	18	1		
7	2	19	-		
8	8	20	-		
9	3	21	-		
10	3	22	-		
11	2	23	1		
12	8	24	6		

One respondent said that she had not intended to overstay but did so in July 2006 because of the agencies' reputation for duplicity. She said, "I overstayed because I saw that many Indonesians' jobs are terminated after they finish paying the agency fees." She had gone to Macau through her agency and was committed to paying the agency HK$2,000 per month for five months, but because she had witnessed the regularity with which her compatriots became jobless once their agency fees were paid, she decided to cancel the arrangements with her agency. She added, "We only work for the agency's profits."

If we can extrapolate from these sixty-six cases, Macau evidently serves as a port of convenience for agencies in Hong Kong, giving them a flexible labor pool, at hardly any cost to themselves. They can draw on this labor pool as and when demand rises either in Hong Kong or Macau. The total duration of sixty days for which the workers can get legal visas in Macau seems to be the time limit of the usefulness of this flexible labor pool to the Hong Kong agencies. As soon as the workers' visas in Macau expire, with no hope for extension or renewal, their usefulness as potential workers ceases for Hong Kong agencies. The workers are then evicted from agency lodgings and their passports and expired visas are returned to them.[43] Respondent number 64 said of her agency, "They are not good. When my contract was terminated, I was abandoned. They did not even attempt to assist me to get further employment."

The other respondents who had gone to Macau on their own also had hopes of finding jobs there. In one case, the respondent said that her previous employer in Hong Kong had given her an air ticket from Hong Kong to Indonesia. She had decided not to use this ticket, however, choosing instead to go to Macau. Had she returned to Indonesia, she thought she would have difficulties trying to leave again for another overseas job. She, like many others, wanted to avoid the Indonesian government's "One-Door Exit Policy" for those seeking overseas employment, which subjects potential migrant workers to long periods of incarceration as labor stock, saddling them with hefty recruitment fees that they are obliged to repay during employment. In Hong Kong, these fees lead on average to a seven-month deduction of almost all their wages. In Macau, these fees cost migrant workers ten months wages, with no guarantee of a job once these fees are paid.

The Indonesian government justifies the system of incorporating private-sector recruitment agencies into national deployment policies supposedly to protect Indonesian women migrant workers from being trafficked. In reality, it would seem that this is the Indonesian government's way of outsourcing the management of mass labor export that has very little to do with the protection of migrant women overseas. Going to Macau from Hong Kong often represents the Indonesian women's last hope of avoiding the formal systems instituted by the Indonesian government that result in debt bondage and agency control.

As we have shown elsewhere, many employment agencies in Indonesia treat applicants for overseas work as domestic workers in a very coercive and restrictive manner.[44] Apart from the wage deduction for seven months, potential Indonesian migrant workers are confined, prior to their departure, for indefinite periods in labor camps, which are euphemistically called "training centers." From our research, Indonesian workers in Hong Kong are held by their agencies in these pre-departure labor camps for an average of six to eight months. The fact that even seasoned migrant workers, who have completed years of work overseas, are still detained for months makes it clear that the motive of agencies is to warehouse labor stock, even when they have no ready jobs for the applicants. Because of coercive practices endorsed by Indonesian laws, Indonesian workers in Hong Kong and elsewhere try to avoid returning to Indonesia after the end of their contracts, if they wish to pursue further overseas employment.

This was a key motivation for at least fifty-one out of sixty-six respondents, who had gone to Macau to look for jobs. The fear of having to return to Indonesia led at least one respondent to give up her air ticket from Hong Kong to Indonesia just to gamble on getting a job in Macau. Thus, even without any encouragement from labor agencies, more than half of our sixty-six respondents had gone to Macau in the hope of getting jobs there, based merely on information supplied by friends. Another motivation stems from their commonly shared view that there are no jobs for them in Indonesia.[45]

The reality in Macau, however, is that as undocumented overstayers they are only able to get temporary jobs as irregular domestic workers, as food sellers in markets, or even, as one respondent admitted, as sex workers.[46] Although they had originally gone to Macau to find work, they ended up in dire straits, with almost all respondents saying that they wished to go home because they were unemployed, broke, and insecure. Only one respondent said that she did not want to go home, because there was no money at home. But those who wished to go home did not have the money to buy air tickets. Among the sixty-six respondents, only three had managed to accumulate enough money to buy air tickets, mostly paid for by their boyfriends.

Table 6. Intimate Relationships: Number and nationality

Partners of respondents	Heterosexual		Homosexual	
	In Macau	Outside Macau	In Macau	Outside Macau
Nationalities/No.	*10*	*9*	*16*	*1*
Canada	0	1		
Indonesia	2*	7	16	1
India	1	0		
Macau	1	0		
Malaysia	0	1		
Nepal	4*	0		
Pakistan	1	0		
Sri Lanka	1	0		
United Kingdom	2*	0		

* 1 respondent with partners from Nepal, Indonesia, and the UK.

Hardly any of the respondents obtained assistance from nongovernmental organizations (NGOs) in Macau. Most felt that they could not get any help from the police or the Indonesian government. Many were afraid of being arrested or blacklisted and prohibited from being migrant workers again. Most are aware, however, that they can approach the Macau authorities if they have accumulated enough money to buy a ticket home. When asked if they had ever approached the Macanese authorities, most had not. The most common expectations of any official response include: "They will keep our passports; ask us to go get money to buy our own air tickets home; or ask us to report back regularly" or "They will put us in prison, blacklist us, never help us, and surely only get angry at us." Their greatest wish is to earn enough money for a ticket home to Indonesia. The most common plea registered by all field researchers is, "Please help me to buy an air ticket to go back to Indonesia."

Most of the respondents had no stable places of residence. They stay with their friends, sometimes with as many as seven to ten other workers. Given the economic hardships faced by the undocumented migrants, friends and partners can become an important source of assistance, and arguably, those with partners in Macau have a certain degree of social capital.

This preliminary study, which aims to give an overview of the lives of undocumented Indonesian migrants in Macau (comprised totally of women) would be incomplete without relating their work situations to their social and personal relations, which are shaped by the conditions of their insecure existence. Ten of the women had boyfriends in Macau; nine, outside of Macau; and among women in same-sex relationships, sixteen had female partners in Macau while one had a female partner outside of Macau. The breakdown of nationalities of their partners is given in Table 6 above, but the notable difference is that all same-sex relationships were between Indonesian women. This is indicative, as

Sim has pointed out, of women's emotional and physical needs during migration and as a defense against male predation.[47]

For those with female Indonesian partners in Macau, the response is typically, "I am supported by my girlfriend who is working in Macau and stays with me," meaning that she lives with her partner and not with her employers. The degree to which undocumented migrants benefit from such social capital is debatable, however, as some of their partners may also be undocumented workers. In some cases, dependence results in abusive relationships. One respondent, who had worked in Singapore, Hong Kong, and Macau, said that her worst experience was in Macau because, "I became an overstayer with no money and I am always getting physically assaulted by my boyfriend." Of the nineteen women in heterosexual relationships, most were single women, followed by married women with husbands in Indonesia and by one divorcee. In their precarious situation, however, some of these relationships may have a commercial or economic aspect, as the one respondent who performs sex work claims that her client is her "boyfriend."

Civic Actions, Policy Implications, and Counter-Geographies

The vulnerability of undocumented migrants is exacerbated by the fact that there is no Indonesian Consulate in Macau. The Indonesian government does not recognize Macau as a destination for Indonesian labor export and hence does not provide any assistance to undocumented Indonesian workers stranded there. The Indonesian Embassy in Beijing is too remote, reportedly does not understand the issue, and sees Macau as falling outside its jurisdiction.

Informal reports from the field indicate a struggle for turf between the Indonesian Embassy in Beijing and the Indonesian Consulate in Hong Kong for the management of approved "job orders," an industry term for Indonesian government-approved contracts for migrant labor export. As these generate income from the private agencies that bid for these job orders, the management of these orders can be equated with the acquisition of state concessions. On 23 February 2007, it was announced that four job orders with four agencies in Macau had come through the Indonesian Embassy in Beijing, for the deployment of 270 Indonesian migrant workers annually per job order, or a total of more than one thousand workers annually.[48]

In other words, anticipating that Macau might soon become an approved destination for Indonesian labor, the overseas representative offices in Beijing and Hong Kong were, according to field reports, jostling for control of the licensing of agencies that will oversee Indonesian labor export to Macau. This is evidently the most profitable area of consular/embassy services, involving the disciplining of errant agencies at the local level. The management and discipline of licensed employment agencies by consular officials in places like Hong Kong are generally nontransparent and unaccountable to migrant workers. Determining whether recalcitrant agencies are punished and how is at the discretion of local consular personnel. By and large, Indonesian laws pertaining to recruitment agencies do not criminalize private-sector abuses of migrant workers. Instead, the government relies on a system of suspensions, with civil and administrative "measures" to discipline this sector — processes that are highly prone to rent seeking and corruption.

Despite generally negative perceptions by its migrant workers, considerable weight is still attached to the role of the Indonesian government. For some workers it remains a beacon of some hope in their despair. Some respondents' views of what the Indonesian government can do for them are:

"I hope the Indonesian government will pay attention to the welfare of Indonesian migrant workers abroad."

"Overstaying Indonesians are looked down upon and treated like rubbish by our friends. It is very difficult to find work. So I think we should not stay longer but what can we do? Therefore I hope for help from the Indonesian government."

"When will Susilo Bambang Yudhonyono [the Indonesian president] act and provide concrete assistance to us?"

"As migrant workers, we must assert our rights fully. The [Indonesian] government just creates bad policies, which we are forced to obey. I do not know when the overstaying migrant workers can go back to Indonesia if the Indonesian government just ignores us and falls asleep on their own dreams. Can't they hear a little of our demands?"

Few civil society groups in the region provide assistance to undocumented migrants. One of these is the Hong Kong-based Association of Indonesian Migrant Workers (ATKI).[49] In 2004, ATKI set up a branch in Macau, which provides paralegal advice and counseling. (Providing shelter to overstayers is a punishable offense in Macau.) Another organization in Macau providing assistance is Matim. With the sponsorship of Dompet Duafa, an Islamic charity, in Hong Kong,[50] Matim assists overstayers by donating half the cost of a limited number of air tickets to return home.

In the absence of a consulate in Macau, the Indonesian Consulate in Hong Kong had, until mid 2007, offered Indonesian migrant workers working in Macau a one-day application and collection process for the renewal of their passports in Hong Kong, to minimize disruptions to those with regular employment, saving them the costs of multiple trips to Hong Kong. In mid 2007, however, this service was suddenly withdrawn. So Pilar, an alliance of twenty-two Indonesian migrant organizations in Hong Kong, commenced a series of demonstrations and rallies for the resumption of this service and for consular services to be made available in Macau.[51] Although the Indonesian Consulate in Hong Kong agreed to resume the one-day service, to date it has not done so.

Civic actions, undertaken in behalf of Indonesian migrant workers in Macau by their counterparts in Hong Kong, are rooted in their shared experience as migrant workers.[52] In addition, awareness is growing of their position and potential as "global" subjects in a "migrant corridor," to borrow a term from Ong and Roy.[53] Such "global subjectivity" operates in a meta-state context that is not constrained by state boundaries, but rather, utilizes discrepancies across state boundaries to fulfill meta-state agendas.

Sassen makes a distinction between globalizing circuits that are typically represented as connected to globalization versus those that she has termed "counter-geographies of globalization."[54] She identifies the former with "some of the major dynamics that compose globalization: the formation of global markets, the intensification of transnational and trans-local networks and the development of communication technologies, which easily escape conventional surveillance practices," while "counter-geographies…are part of the shadow economy, but they also use some of the institutional infrastructure of the formal economy." Furthermore, she sees these as often operating "outside and in violation of laws and treaties, yet are not exclusively embedded in criminal operations."[55]

We argue that the irregular migration of undocumented Indonesian overstayers in Macau exemplifies one of these "counter-geographies of globalization." Undocumented Indonesian overstayers are part of the shadow economy even as they rely on and are a product of the institutional infrastructure of the formal economy. Strikingly, their status as undocumented overstayers derives from the ease of migration to Macau, as a result of the territory's extremely laissez-faire immigration policies, enabling the workers to get up to sixty days of legal stay without having to show an air ticket or proof of adequate financial resources. This ease of acquiring a legal stay for sixty days attracts many Indonesian workers to come to Macau after their contracts and visas in Hong Kong have expired. Furthermore, if these workers remain in Macau after their visas expire, thereby becoming undocumented overstayers, they will apparently not be arrested, jailed, or deported if they are apprehended by Macanese authorities, unlike in Hong Kong where such actions would follow automatically. Instead, they will be released to earn the money necessary to buy air tickets, which can take a long time, given the irregular and low wages of overstayers. Significantly, these authorities do not question how overstayers earn such money, given that they do not have employment visas. There is thus unstated official tolerance of "illegal" work done by overstayers, based on the excuse that they need transportation money. Although Macau's laissez-faire approach is rooted in its colonial history, when the then Portuguese-ruled territory sought to attract trade in competition with then British-ruled Hong Kong, these structural patterns have not changed. Present-day Macau still needs to attract trade, in competition not only with Hong Kong, as before, but also with the Pearl Delta Region of southern China, especially Zhuhai, which Macau abuts. As noted by Sassen, "the growth of a global economy has brought with it an institutional infrastructure that facilitates cross-border flows and represents, in that regard, an enabling environment for these alternative circuits."[56] In this instance, the growth of the global economy is manifested in the increased competitiveness, not of different countries, but of different parts of one contiguous region, that is, Macau in competition with Hong Kong and the Pearl Delta Region, especially Zhuhai. To compete with a Pearl Delta Region that has an ample supply of cheap labor, Macau has to ensure its own pool of equally cheap labor. In this context, Macau's laissez-faire immigration policies form an institutional infrastructure that enables alternative circuits of undocumented workers to supply Macau with competi-

Nicole Constable

Indonesian domestic workers enjoying a day off in Hong Kong's Victoria Park, June 2005. Drawing on their shared experience, Indonesian domestic workers in Hong Kong have engaged in civic actions in support of Indonesian domestic workers in Macau.

tively low-cost labor. At the same time, Macau does not acknowledge any state responsibility toward undocumented migrant workers.

The experiences of the sixty-six undocumented Indonesian migrants we interviewed can be understood as part of the metaphorical tip of a much larger iceberg. Although the scope of our project does not cover the entire population of undocumented migrant workers in Macau, suffice it to note that the overwhelming majority of such workers are from Mainland China. While accurate statistics of this population are difficult to obtain, an indication of the proportions involved may be gleaned from the Macau secretary for security's report on crime statistics for the first quarter of 2007. In this period, "the police had repatriated 5,736 people from Macau, among them 366 illegal immigrants from the Mainland, 3,760 Mainland overstayers, and 368 overstayers of other nationalities."[57] It is noteworthy that, according to this report, the number of overstayers of other nationalities is lower than 10 percent of Mainland Chinese overstayers. Furthermore, if the information we obtained from our sixty-six respondents is valid, then the number repatriated represents only those who have been able to earn enough money to buy their air tickets. As our research did not extend to Mainland Chinese overstayers, we cannot say whether the laissez-faire policy of allowing overstayers to earn enough money to pay for their passage home applies to them as well. If it is indeed the case that Macau's immigration policies form an institutional infrastructure that enables alternative circuits of undocumented workers to supply competitively cheap labor to Macau, then it would follow logically that Mainland Chinese overstayers would not be treated more strictly than overstayers of other nationalities, given that the former constitutes the main source of the desired cheap labor. This is a potential area for further research.

The advantages of this flexible labor pool of undocumented migrant workers accrue primarily to the host country, which can keep or kick the workers out at will. For the undocumented workers themselves, whether the advantages outweigh the problems is highly dubious, as the information obtained from our respondents indicates. Most respondents had gone to Macau to find jobs without having to return to Indonesia and go through the labor camps again before leaving for another term of overseas work. This change from their initial aim to their current wish simply to earn enough money to buy an air ticket home reveals the depth of their disillusionment as undocumented overstayers in Macau.

Our analysis of undocumented Indonesian migrants in Macau as an example of the "counter-geographies of globalization" is supported by the evident reluctance of the Indonesian government to intervene in behalf of these stranded workers or to maintain an official presence in Macau to help them. However, increased pressure from migrant worker activists beginning in August 2007 pushed the Indonesian Consulate in Hong Kong to open an office in Macau on 2 December 2007 for 2.5 hours each Sunday. Eni Lestari, Pilar's spokesperson, insisted that the services the Indonesian Consulate in Hong Kong offers are inadequate to meet the needs of the estimated six thousand Indonesian migrants working in Macau.[58]

Undocumented migrant workers we interviewed live in constant fear of being apprehended. Their daily desperate struggle to find work and earn income led one respondent to engage in commercial sex work, which she said began when she was hired to work in a spa. Others have depended on boyfriends or girlfriends, and while most of our respondents do not engage in sex work, their general attitudes were empathetic toward those in similar situations who have chosen to do sex work. Their comments included:

"It is natural because they also need to survive."

"Because of conditions, they are forced to perform that kind of work; otherwise no choice for them."

"They are forced to do that for survival."

"They are forced to do so since they need money to go home."

Anecdotal accounts have emerged from the field about babies born to Indonesian women in Macau, who are sold to agents acting for foreign adoptive parents, but these accounts are as yet unverified.

Conclusion

This article on women's labor migration from Indonesia has revealed at least two problems with research on "migrant flows" that focus exclusively on professional and skilled workers and with discourses of, as Ong has argued, "worlding" global nodes where, oblivious to feminist concerns, women disappear in a generic milieu of autonomous beings in postmodernist lexicons of "migrant corridors." As we have illustrated, such theories are flawed because they pretend that sexual politics do not have an impact on differently sexed bodies. Another fallacy has been the invisibility of the state as a very powerful actor in shaping migrant flows.

As this article points out, the Indonesian government defines its women migrants as being in need of protection *as women.* Thus it subjects the women to a range of oppressive practices, beginning even before they leave Indonesia, and gives its agents carte blanche to incarcerate migrant workers and put them into debt bondage. It is precisely to avoid this sort of exploitation, cast as state-endorsed "protection," that women migrant workers have been motivated to seek alternative routes to continuing with overseas employment after their contracts end, hoping to avoid the punitive system of job recruitment based on Indonesia's one-door exit policy. In the words of one migrant activist, the protection that they seek is protection from the exploitation by the Indonesian government.

Feminist socialism that takes into account gender–class, as well as the historical and material bases of women's exploitation, is a critical perspective that holds to account different regimes of treatment based on the fact of sexed bodies. In every aspect of Indonesian women's labor migration, gender is key. It is key in the way women have been defined as "oppress-able" (and for their own good) by anti-women Indonesian policies of labor export that ultimately place control in the hands of private operators. It is key in the fact that because they are women, they are "employable" as foreign domestic workers and therefore "admissible" into Hong Kong on that basis. It is key that their presence as domestics in Hong Kong acts to buffer the gender system of women's subordination in the domestic sphere where they replace local women as service staff in their homes. It is key that as a class of poor foreign women, they are discriminated against by the Hong Kong government, which by its two-week rule reduces their opportunity of seeking new employers, a rule more rigorously applied to them than to any other category of foreign workers in Hong Kong.[59] As Macau expands to become the playground of Mainland China, gender is key when women's livelihood vulnerabilities lead to their absorption into commercial sex services because official assistance is absent from both the Macau and Indonesian governments.

Our wider research on Indonesian labor migration to Hong Kong and other destinations reveals a tendency on the part of the Indonesian government to support the labor agencies even when it is evident that agencies blatantly exploit migrant workers. This tendency seems to be rooted in structural dysfunctionalities of the Indonesian state, which are neither accidental nor incidental, but result rather from a coincidence of private interests views of governance and capitalist agendas in systemic globalization, in which the state plays key restructuring roles. These dysfunctionalities fit the pattern described by Sassen:

> Growing numbers of traffickers and smugglers are making money off the backs of women and many governments are increasingly dependent on their remittances. A key aspect here is that through their work and remittances, women enhance the government revenue of deeply indebted countries and offer new profit-making possibilities to "entrepreneurs" …who can now operate their illegal trade globally. These survival circuits

are often complex, involving multiple locations and sets of actors consti-tuting increasingly global chains of traders and "workers." A central point...is that it is through these supposedly rather value-less economic actors — low-wage and poor women — that key components of these new economies have been built. Globalization plays a specific role here in a double sense, contributing to the formation of links between sending and receiving countries, and, secondly, enabling local and regional practices to become global in scale.[60]

There is thus a dovetailing of interests: on the one hand, the interests of the Macau state to enhance its regional competitiveness by allowing the emergence of a flexible labor supply of undocumented migrant workers and, on the other hand, the interest of a deeply indebted Indonesian state to generate foreign ex-change from the remittances of migrant workers, regardless of the personal costs borne by these workers. The result is a counter-geography of globalization that connects the villages of east and central Java, where the majority of Indone-sian migrant workers come from, to Indonesian towns and cities where labor re-cruitment "entrepreneurs" are based, to Jakarta as the seat of the Indonesian government, then to destination sites of labor migration, both legal and undoc-umented, such as Hong Kong and Macau. While this particular counter-geogra-phy of globalization is regional in scope, its reverberations are global, as the des-tination sites of labor migration extend far beyond to include the Middle East and elsewhere. The existence of such a counter-geography, built on colluding interests, indicates a pervasive system of the global subjugation of an underclass of transients, who support the mutually implicating economies of what may su-perficially appear as disparate sites. On the contrary, we suggest that these seemingly disparate sites should be understood metaphorically as the peaks of submerged landmasses that are actually connected under water.

ACKNOWLEDGMENTS: This article is an output of project no. 9360114, which was fully sup-ported by the Faculty of Humanities and Social Sciences, City University of Hong Kong.

Notes

Preface – Constable

1.   Indonesians commonly use only one name.
2.   Konigsberg 2008, A23.
3.   Eltman 2008.
4.   Kessler 2008.
5.   Konigsberg 2008, A23.
6.   Andolan 2008.
7.   Domestic Workers United 2008.
8.   See Stasiulis and Bakan 2002; Stasiulis and Bakan 2003; and Pratt 2004 on difficulties Canadian live-in caregivers experience.
9.   Sim and Wee 2009.
10. Constable 1997; 2007.
11. Parreñas 2001a, Lan 2006, Gamburd 2000. See also Gulati 1993.
12. Adams and Dickey 2000; Huang et al. 2005.
13. GCC countries include Saudi Arabia, Kuwait, Bahrain, Oman, Qatar, and the United Arab Emirates (UAE). In these articles we use the terms "West Asia" and the "Middle East" interchangeably to include regions such as Yemen and Lebanon that are not included in "the Gulf."
14. More than 8 million Filipinos and over 1.5 million Indonesians are currently overseas. According to the Philippine Overseas Employment Administration (POEA 2006) of the over 1.2 million overseas contracts that were processed in 2006 alone, 30 percent were for domestic or household worker contracts. The top ten destination countries for Filipino migrants in 2006 were Saudi Arabia, the UAE, Hong Kong, Kuwait, Qatar, Taiwan, Singapore, Italy, the United Kingdom, and South Korea (in descending order). Of all Filipino migrants deployed in 2006 28 percent went to Asia and 58 percent went to the Middle East (POEA 2006). Of the total reported "permanent, temporary, and irregular" Filipino migrants as of December 2006, the POEA reports 1.2 million in East and South Asia, and 1.8 million in West Asia (POEA, Table 29). In 2006, 5,720 Filipinos were deployed to Jordan, 792 to Yemen, 99,212 to the UAE, 5053 to Israel, 96,929 to Hong Kong, 39,025 to Taiwan, 2,802 to Macau, and 28,369 to Singapore (POEA 2006). Over 800,000 Sri Lankan women work overseas as migrant workers, the majority of them in GCC countries. Over 100,000 Sri Lankan women go abroad to work each year. Of the 70,000 foreign domestic workers in Jordan, 35,000 are from Sri Lanka (20,000 from Indonesia and 15,000 from the Philippines). Of the total 1.5 million Sri Lankans working abroad, Frantz states that 900,000, or 60 percent, are domestic workers (see Frantz and Gamburd, this volume). In 2004, over 1.5 million documented Indonesians were working overseas according to the Asian Migrant Centre (AMC 2005). The AMC migrant yearbook reported the top ten destination countries of Indonesian migrant workers in 2004 (in descending order) as Saudi Arabia, Malaysia, Taiwan, Hong Kong, Kuwait, Singapore, South Korea, Brunei, Jordan, and Qatar; the top ten destinations of Sri Lankan workers that year were Saudi Arabia, Kuwait, the UAE, Qatar, Lebanon, Jordan, Bahrain, Oman, Cyprus, and the Maldives.
15. Liebelt (this volume) applies the notion of "working class cosmopolitanism," which she borrows from Pnina Werbner 1999. Said (1984) uses the term "contrapuntal" in referring to exiled people; Constable (1999) applies that concept and that of "double vision" to migrant domestic workers.

164

16. Liebelt, this volume.
17. See de Regt, this volume, and de Regt 2009.
18. Rollins 1990, Constable 2007, Lan 2006.
19. See Sim and Wee 2009; Hsia 2009.
20. Ong, 2006.
21. See Gamburd, Constable, Sim and Wee, Hsia, in this volume.
22. See Massey 1994.
23. The more desired regions are not devoid of problems. See, for example, Stasiulis and Bakan 2002; Stasiulis and Bakan 2003; and Pratt 2004.
24. See de Regt, this volume and 2009; see Lan 2006 on employers and recruiters' perspectives on hierarchies of workers.
25. Parreñas 2001a.
26. See Constable 2007 on Hong Kong; Lan 2003 and 2006 on Taiwan.
27. Ong 1999; see also Ong 2006.

Chapter 1 – Liebelt

1. See, for example, Constable 1997; Parreñas 2001a; Stasiulis and Bakan 2005.
2. Werbner 1999.
3. See, for example, Ehrenreich and Hochschild 2003; Mills 2003.
4. While the Philippine government speaks of about 1.2 million documented "Overseas Filipino workers" (OFW) for 2006 (see http://www.poea.gov.ph/html/statistics.html [accessed 30 July 2008]), NGOs generally speak of 8 million Filipinos overseas. (See, for example, the website of Migrante International at http://migrante.tripod.com/ [accessed 7 November 2007]).
5. The central importance of remittances for domestic consumption and the Philippine currency is generally recognized (Mellyn 2003), a reality the Philippine Central Bank also acknowledges. In May 2007 the Philippine Central Bank announced that the remittances of OFW remained above the $1 billion mark for the eleventh straight month (see Bangko Sentral ng Pilipinas Media Release, 15 May 2007: http://www.bsp.gov.ph/publications/media.asp?id=1574 [accessed 30 July 2008]).
6. See, for example, Bello 2005, 11; Tyner 2004; on the Contemplacion case see Hilsdon 2000, 176f.
7. Gonzales 1998, 42f. For more recent data, see the statistics of the Philippine Overseas Employment Administration at http://www.poea.gov.ph/html/statistics.html (accessed 15 September 2008).
8. Eviota 1992.
9. Choy 2003.
10. According to POEA statistics, 279,767 OFW entered the Middle East in 1998 (33.6 percent out of a total of 831,643), as compared to 285,564 in 2003 (33.0 percent out of 867,969). Source: http://www.poea.gov.ph/html/statistics.html (accessed 20 July 2008).
11. Kav LaOved 2006.
12. Due to an international outcry and the intervention of the Philippine government, which apparently wished no repetition of the "Contemplacion fiasco," Sarah Balabagan was later released (see Hilsdon 2000).
13. Source: http://www.poea.gov.ph/Country/Kuwait.htm (accessed 20 July 2008).
14. Liebelt 2007.
15. In Israel, the social and class background of Filipina migrants is rather diverse. This is arguably the outcome of both a relatively unregulated flow of Filipino migrants to Israel prior to 1995 and a direct effect of Israeli recruiting policies, which apparently do not ascribe too much importance to regional origin or educational attainment as a criterion for selection (Liebelt 2007).
16. Kemp and Raijmann 2000; Willen 2007. A similar restriction, the so-called kafala system, exists in Arabic-speaking countries that employ Filipino domestic workers. See the forthcoming articles by Constable and Hsia for similar restrictions in Hong Kong.

17. It has been stated that many female migrant workers in Asian countries such as Hong Kong, Singapore, or Malaysia are not interested in becoming citizens (Ong 2006, 214; Constable 2009). Yet, they apparently do want social and legal entitlements that in many cases come only with legal citizenship or permanent residency. Filipinos' knowledge of the unavailability of these legal statuses and citizenship rights in Asia, so I was told in interviews with domestic workers in Israel, was one of the major reasons why many of them decided to migrate on, toward the "West," where, they hoped, these rights would be easier to acquire.

18. Constable 1997; Glick-Schiller and Fouron 2001; Gmelch 1992; Hondagneu-Sotelo 2001; Parreñas 2001a.

19. Ong 1993, quoted in Ong and Nonini 1997, 23.

20. The names of interview partners have been replaced with pseudonyms throughout this article.

21. Named after a small town in Luxembourg where in 1985 twenty-nine states (twenty-five European Union states as well as Iceland, Norway, Liechtenstein, and Switzerland) signed an agreement in order to facilitate free movement of persons within the area. A common Schengen visa allows its holders freedom of travel within "Schengen-land."

22. See, for example, Constable 1999.

23. Parreñas 2001b, 1140.

24. A spread made from mashed chickpeas, popular throughout the Middle Eastern world.

25. In Israel, single parents of minor children are normally not deported in spite of their illegality, due to protection under international law (see Hammer 1999).

26. According to the 2000 census, 92.5 percent of the Philippine population is Christian. Of these, an estimated 80.9 percent belong to the Roman Catholic Church (https://www.cia.gov/library/publications/the-world-factbook/geos/rp.html [accessed 20 July 2008]).

27. Karagiannis and Glick-Schiller 2006.

28. Wourms 1992.

29. Raijman and Kemp 2004, 176f.

30. Transcript from Pastor Albert's sermon on 22 September 2007.

31. Constable 1999, 224.

32. Parreñas 2001a, 3.

33. Pessar and Mahler 2003, 837.

34. Werbner 1999, 34.

35. Rapport and Stade 2007; Werbner 2008.

36. Personal interview with Lyna, 13 June 2005.

37. Lorenzo et al., for example, quote a report by the Philippines Hospital Association, according to which an estimated 80 percent of all public-sector doctors in 2004 were currently training or had already re-trained to become nurses (2007, 1410).

38. Stasiulis and Bakan 2005.

Chapter 2 – de Regt

1. While churches are not officially recognized in Yemen, and promoting a religion other than Islam is forbidden by law, non-Muslims are allowed to practice their religion, albeit under restricted circumstances. Church services always take place in the basements of private houses.

2. Yemeni women almost always cover themselves from head to toe when they enter public spaces and foreigners sometimes adapt their style of dress to this.

3. Yemen has a Human Development Index of 153 (out of 177 countries worldwide).

4. In 1990 the People's Democratic Republic of Yemen of former South Yemen and the Yemen Arab Republic of former North Yemen united into the Republic of Yemen. The capital, Sana'a, is located in former North Yemen.

5. See de Regt 2008.

6. See also Destremau 2002, 335.

7.   This research was part of the research program "Migrant Domestic Workers: Trans-national Relations, Families and Identities" at the International Institute of the Study of Islam in the Modern World (ISIM) in Leiden and the Amsterdam School for Social Science Research (ASSR) in Amsterdam. Periods of fieldwork were July–September 2003, August 2004–March 2005, and November–December 2005.

8.   See my article in *Signs* (de Regt 2009). A summary of this article can be found in de Regt 2007b.

9.   At the time of the research there were no recruitment agencies in Yemen with an official license from the Yemeni Ministry of Social Affairs and Labor. Two recruitment agencies that used to bring Ethiopian women to Yemen lost their licenses because of human rights violations.

10.   Historic links between Yemen and Ethiopia are strong, characterized by trade connections and mutual migration flows.

11.   The expatriate community in Yemen is large, consisting of embassy staff, people working for international and nongovernmental organizations, and oil company employees.

12.   See de Regt 2009.

13.   See also Hansen 1989.

14.   A strict system of social stratification based on notions of descent and maintained through endogamous marriage patterns characterized Yemeni society in the past. According to this system the population could be divided into five status groups, determining to a large extent the work someone performed. Service providers were one of the low social status groups.

15.   See Destremau 2002, 331, and de Regt 2008.

16.   See de Regt 2008.

17.   All Yemenis are Muslim with the exception of a very small minority of Jews.

18.   During my research I formed a support group of people concerned with the rights of domestic workers. One of the members of this group established a nongovernmental organization in order to improve the working conditions of domestic workers in Yemen. In addition, the Directorate General for Working Women of the Yemeni Ministry of Social Affairs and Labor, which is supported by the International Labor Organization, now pays more attention to domestic workers. See my report about the situation of domestic workers in Yemen for the ILO (de Regt 2006).

19.   The interview was conducted in November 2004.

20.   Being the least developed country in the Middle East, Yemen is the recipient of large sums of development aid, channeled through international, bilateral, and nongovernmental organizations. As a result, there is a large community of expatriate development workers residing in Yemen and employing migrant domestic workers.

21.   In May–July 1994 Yemen experienced a short civil war, mainly between the armies of former North Yemen and former South Yemen. Most expatriates left the country during the war.

22.   Government control of residence status is relatively weak in Yemen and migrants often overstay their tourist visas. In order to prevent the presence of undocumented migrants, the Yemeni government regularly announces a stricter control of the residence status of foreigners. Yet, there have never been any large-scale arrests and deportations. The most important problem undocumented migrants face is that they have to pay a penalty (US$0.85 per day) for the period they have resided in Yemen without a visa or residence permit. The result is that undocumented migrants cannot leave the country without paying high fines.

23.   Hondagneu-Sotelo 1994; Hagan 1998; Castles 2002; Beyene 2005.

24.   Hondagneu-Sotelo 1994; Beyene 2005.

25.   Hondagneu-Sotelo 1994.

26.   Constable 1997; Parreñas 2001a.

27.   Constable 1997; Parreñas 2001a.

28.   See Moors and de Regt 2008.

29. From 1993 to 1997, I worked as an anthropologist in a health care development project in Hodeidah, partly funded by the Dutch Ministry of Foreign Affairs.
30. The interview with Ayesha was conducted in January 2005.
31. Liebelt, this volume, argues that migrant domestic workers often move on and on rather than back and forth between sending and receiving country. The reasons why Asian migrant women may go to Yemen instead of to another country in or beyond the Middle East are varied.
32. Indian women commonly migrate on false passports or by bribing authorities, in particular after 2006 when the Indian government announced an age ban on migration of women under thirty (see Pattadath 2008).
33. India and Yemen have a bilateral agreement that governs labor migration between the two countries.
34. According to the Indian Embassy, around 10,000 Indians were living in Yemen in 2004, the majority of them employed in the health sector and for companies and hotels.
35. According to the data I received from the Labor Office in Sana'a eighty-seven Indonesian women were registered as domestics in 2004. Yet, this figure is likely to be higher because not all migrant workers are registered.
36. Yemeni merchants, in particular from the Hadramawt in former South Yemen, traveled to Indonesia in previous centuries and there are many families of Yemeni ancestry in Indonesia, and of Indonesian descent in Yemen (see Freitag and Clarence-Smith 1997).
37. This comment, however, may have been influenced by the presence of Fadl, in whose company it may have been difficult to be more critical about her life in Yemen.
38. See Robinson 2000.
39. In some countries the presence of mobile phones has made a big difference, enabling domestic workers to be in contact with each other.
40. See Anderson 2000; Jureidini and Moukarbel 2004.
41. Unfortunately, I was unable to obtain statistics about the number of Filipinas, Indian, and Sri Lankan women employed in the past twenty years. The government labor offices in Sana'a and Hodeidah could only provide me with statistics of the number of migrant domestic workers employed in the year of my field research (2004–2005).
42. In 2004, there were only eighteen Sri Lankan women registered as domestic workers at the labor office in Sana'a and only two at the labor office in Hodeidah.
43. Bakan and Stasiulis 1995, 323.
44. Constable 1997, 35.
45. Ibid., 37.
46. Lan 2003b; 2006.
47. Jamila has employed eight Filipina domestic workers over the past twenty years. While more families employed Filipinas in Hodeidah in the 1980s and 1990s, nowadays Jamila's two domestic workers are the only Filipinas in town.
48. See Jureidini and Moukarbel 2004, and Frantz, this volume.

Chapter 3 – Frantz

1. Hazaimeh 2008.
2. This calculation is based on data from the Jordanian Department of Statistics (2002/2003), which estimates that there are 806,000 households in the country.
3. The World Bank considers Jordan a "lower middle income country," with a per capita GDP of US$4,700 in 2007.
4. According to the Ministry of Labor, 300,000 foreigners held work permits in 2007, and another 100,000 worked illegally. Roughly 70 percent of migrant workers in Jordan are Egyptian. Jordan Times, May 29, 2007. These figures do not include Iraqi refugees, whose numbers are significant given Jordan's total population of 6 million in 2007.
5. Chammartin 2004.

6. Brochmann 1993, 63.
7. Ibid., 64. Pakistan banned the migration of women domestic workers below the age of forty-five in 1979; Bangladesh followed suit in 1983 (Shah et al. 1991, 483). India imposed a similar ban, allowing only women above the age of thirty to emigrate as maids (Shah et al. 1991). All three countries imposed minimum wage restrictions for domestic workers. This sharply contrasts with Sri Lanka, which has imposed no restrictions on the emigration of domestic workers (ibid.).
8. Samath 2007. Detailed descriptions of the official and unofficial migration process from Sri Lanka are provided in Gamburd 2000, chapters 2 and 3; Brochmann 1993, 66–70; and Eelens et al. 1992, Ch. 3.
9. Zilfi 2004, 4. One exceptional study of the history of servants in the region is Judith Tucker's social history of nineteenth-century Egypt, which draws on such primary source material to document women's expanding employment as domestic servants (Tucker 1985, 92–93).
10. Humphrey 1991, 54.
11. Regarding employer preferences for foreign housemaids over locals, see Moors 2007, 220–21.
12. Interview, October 2006.
13. Humphrey 1991, 55.
14. Hazaimeh 2008. The Sri Lankan Bureau of Foreign Employment estimated that there were a total of 77,558 Sri Lankans employed in Jordan as of 2007 (SLBFE 2008). This figure reflects documented migrants registered with the Bureau and is probably lower than the number actually present. According to a survey conducted at Colombo airport, 55 percent of migrants leaving for foreign employment had not registered with the SLBFE and hence would not be reflected in its records (SLBFE 2005, 2).
15. Similar nationality-based hierarchies of domestic workers have been noted elsewhere, for example in Qatar (Nagy 1998), Lebanon (Jureidini and Moukarbel 2004, 586), Taiwan (Lan 2006), and Hong Kong (Constable 2007).
16. Interview, December 2006.
17. Two studies of poverty conducted by the Ministry of Social Development in 1987 and 1993 suggest that income inequality has increased since the mid 1980s (Shteiwi 1996, 423).
18. Beal 1998.
19. Department of Statistics 2007, 2. In 2004, the average household size in Amman was smaller, at five persons (Department of Statistics 2006, 19).
20. Ghazwi 1985, 215. The transition from extended to nuclear households in Jordan has also been noted by Kawar (2000, 10).
21. Ghazwi 1985, 334–35.
22. Ibid., 219.
23. Othman 1974.
24. Noting increasing preferences for nuclear households in Taiwan, Lan (2000, 11) described a similar motivation amongst Taiwanese women who hire domestic workers in lieu of residing with in-laws.
25. Interview, February 2007. Pseudonyms have been used throughout to protect individual privacy.
26. Samih Erzallah, Ministry of Social Development, interview, Amman, Jordan, 7 June 2007. Several elderly employers of foreign maids confirmed in interviews that they had received these subsidies.
27. Examples are Anderson 2000, 1; Enloe 2000, 179; Gregson and Lowe 1994, Ch. 4.
28. World Bank 2005, 6.
29. While skeptical of the notion that domestic workers are hired in response to growing numbers of women working outside the home, Anderson (2001, 27) has suggested that employing domestic workers gives middle-class mothers more "quality time" with their children, something now commonly believed to be necessary for child development. This also appears to be the case in Jordan.
30. Interview, November 2006.

31. Interview, February 2007.
32. Interview, February 2007.
33. Forte 2001, 231.
34. Gill 1994, 51.
35. Longva 1997, 94.
36. Ibid., 101.
37. Silvey 2004, 146.
38. Longva 1997, 91.
39. Jureidini and Moukarbel 2004, 596.
40. Also excluded from the 1996 Labor Code are agricultural workers, gardeners, cooks, and civil servants (Solidarity Center 2005, 14).
41. Foreign workers who dare to strike face deportation. In 2006, 175 Bangladeshi garment factory workers led a protest against a factory in Jordan's free trade zone where they had been working sixteen-hour days for less than fifty cents an hour. Their request for more pay and better working conditions was refused, and the leaders of the protest were beaten by police, detained, and deported (Iritani 2006).
42. Brochmann 1993, 71; Sriskandarajah 2002, 293. While Muslims constitute only 7 percent of the Sri Lankan population, Muslim women comprise 22 to 23 percent of migrant housemaids (Gamburd 2000, 40).
43. Korale 1986, 217.
44. SLBFE 2007.
45. Dias and Jayasundere 2004, 166.
46. The term "cohorts" is borrowed from Rofel (1999), who used it in her study of Chinese women factory workers to describe distinct groups of women with divergent life experiences and memories who, hence, constructed their identities and conceptions of modernity in different ways.
47. This lack of a sense of migrant communal identity and a rejection of the term "community" also has been remarked upon by Hage (2005) with reference to the Lebanese diaspora.
48. Interview, April 2007.
49. 'Atiyat 2006. Freelance, live-out work is usually illegal under the terms of the kafala system.
50. Samath 2004.
51. These embassy figures on runaways were reported by an NGO called the Friends of Women Workers in Jordan in a study entitled, "Migrant Women Workers in Jordan: The Case of Runaways," published in 2007. Excerpts are available at http://www.mfasia.org/mfaResources/Migrantpercent20Womenpercent20Workerspercent20inpercent20Jordan.pdf (accessed 12 June 2008).
52. Marecek 2000.
53. It is worth mentioning that in terms of grassroots activism and cooperation, Sri Lankan domestic workers in Amman are less organized than Filipinos, who have formed twenty communal associations comprising a federation with more than eight hundred members. These associations have elected officials, by-laws, and a constitution, and hold annual general assembly meetings. They organize regular athletic events and entertainment and provide material support to migrants in distress.
54. Qayum and Ray 2003, 537; Rollins 1990, 81; Anderson 2000, 31.
55. Interview, March 2007.
56. Interview, March 2007.
57. Interview, May 2007.
58. Interview, December 2007.
59. For example, a Sunday Times article (11 November 2007) told the story of Mallika, who worked for thirteen years in Saudi Arabia without pay. Twenty percent of the Sri Lankan domestic workers interviewed for a recent Human Rights Watch report (2007, 40) reported that they did not receive their full salaries.
60. For example by Tellis-Nayak (1983) of Christian servants in South India, Muttarak (2004) of Thai housemaids, and Gill (1994) of domestic workers in Bolivia. I am

grateful to Martha Mundy for reading an earlier version of this essay and helping to refine my thinking about patron-client relations.

61. Scott 1972, 3.
62. Similarly, Jureidini and Moukarbel (2004) have suggested that most Sri Lankan domestic workers in Lebanon work under conditions akin to "contract slavery."
63. For a discussion of these trends in Sri Lanka, see Gombrich and Obeyesekere 1988, and Stirrat 1992.
64. Some of the evangelical Christian groups operating in Amman are not officially recognized. In 2007, the Jordanian authorities deported or refused residence permits to a number of expatriate church leaders for illegal missionary activities. I have not named the churches I attended in order to avoid causing problems for them with the authorities.
65. A Sri Lankan Pentecostal pastor interviewed in Amman reported that he had baptised thirty new members during the course of the preceding year. Interview, June 2008. This compares to the handful of new members who have been baptized by the Sri Lankan Roman Catholic priest in Amman.
66. Despite the existence of the contract, escalating reports of abuse and inadequate legal protections prompted the Philippines to temporarily ban the deployment of housemaids to Jordan in January 2008.
67. See, for example, the on-line edition of the Unifem newsletter, June 2003, p. 2: http://www.unifem.org/news_events/currents/currents200306.doc (accessed 17 July 2008).
68. On the widespread use of wasta in Jordan and how it is generally regarded as an unfair but essential element of social interaction, particularly in dealings with the government or business, see Loewe et al. 2008.
69. For example, the average sentence for honor killings in Jordan is a mere seven and a half months, which, as Zuhur (2005, 403) has noted, reinforces the idea that certain types of punishment against women are acceptable.

Chapter 4 – Gamburd

1. I have studied labor migration from Sri Lanka to the Middle East since 1992 (Gamburd 2000, 2005). The data for this paper were gathered during fieldwork done in Sri Lanka (1992–2005) and the United Arab Emirates (2004). Data include statistical information from the Sri Lanka Bureau of Foreign Employment (SLBFE 2006), as well as qualitative interviews with government bureaucrats, migrant women, and activists in labor unions, migrant worker associations, and international organizations.
2. SLBFE 2006, 57.
3. In 2005, the migrants made up 15 percent of the labor force and 16 percent of the total number of employed people (ibid., 88).
4. Ibid.
5. Ibid., 89.
6. Ibid., 6. Domestic servants are known in Sri Lanka in both English and Sinhala as "housemaids," though their duties exceed those traditionally covered by the term.
7. Jayaweera, Dias, and Wanasundera 2002, 1; SLBFE 2006, 57; Weerakoon 1998, 109.
8. Ong 2006.
9. Rostow 1960; Frank 1966.
10. Escobar 1988; Miyoshi 1993.
11. Gledhill 2007.
12. Chang 2000.
13. Khalaf and Alkobaisi 1999. I use "the Middle East," "West Asia," "Gulf Cooperation Council (GCC)," and "the Gulf" interchangeably to refer to a varied and diverse region with many cultural traditions. This rich complexity gets lost in many Sri Lankan accounts of migration, where migrants are said to work in "Arabia," "the Middle East," or merely "abroad."
14. Ehrenreich and Hochschild 2002; Decena, Shedlin, and Martinez 2006; Harrison 1997.

15. Gamburd 2008; Nicholson 2006.
16. Freeman 2001.
17. Collier and Yanagisako 1987.
18. Gamburd 2000, 2005.
19. Rahman, Yeoh, and Huang 2005, 255; Lan 2003a.
20. Mundlak 2005.
21. Longva 1997.
22. Hugo 2005, 76; Sebastian and Raghwan 2000, 2.
23. Human Rights Watch 2007, 68; Ilolex 2005.
24. Gamburd 2000.
25. Anderson 2002, 112; Constable 2002, 135; Parreñas 2001a, 179.
26. Lynch 2007.
27. See Hugo 2005, 83, regarding Saudi Arabia; Ruhunage 2004, regarding the UAE; and Leonard 2003, 134, 153, regarding the UAE and Kuwait.
28. Lan 2005, 227.
29. Wee and Sim 2005, 193.
30. Sorensen 2005, 4.
31. Ilolex 2005. The International Labor Organization (ILO) plays a role in regulating transnational labor relations. The ILO has several conventions that cover migrant workers. ILO Convention C97 (Migration for Employment Convention (Revised) 1949 suggests, among other things, that migrants should be subject to the same rules and regulations government labor for citizens, including pay, days off, minimum working age, and the right to join unions and bargain collectively. None of the GCC countries has ratified this Convention; neither has Sri Lanka. In the Asia–Pacific region, only New Zealand and Malaysia have ratified Convention No. 97 (Sebastian and Raghwan 2000, i–ii). ILO Convention C143, Migrant Workers (Supplementary Provisions) Convention 1975 suggests that states should respect basic human rights of migrants, that they should police illegal migration, and that they should prosecute manpower traffickers. Neither Sri Lanka, nor any of the main sending countries of domestic labor, nor any of the GCC labor-receiving countries has ratified this convention (Ilolex 2005). ILO conventions provide an international framework of standards, but are not enforceable. In addition, they do not apply to countries that have not ratified them.
32. Weerakoon 1998, 107.
33. Leonard 2003, 145.
34. Guest workers make up high percentages of populations in GCC countries including UAE (75–81 percent), Kuwait (64–66 percent), and Qatar (70–77 percent) (Kapiszewski 2006, 4; Leonard 2003, 136–37; Nagy 2006, 119).
35. Kapiszewski 2006, 4; Khalaf and Alkobaisi 1999, 272; Leonard 2003: 133.
36. Kapiszewski 2006, 4.
37. Khalaf 1992, 65–66; Winkler 2005, 10.
38. Andrew Gardner, personal communication.
39. Addleton 1991; Looney 1992.
40. Khalaf 1992, 72.
41. Khalaf and Alkobaisi 1999, 294; Longva 1997.
42. Foucault 1979; Rose 1999.
43. Khalaf and Alkobaisi 1999: 274.
44. Leonard 2003, 133.
45. Qurtoba Services 2004.
46. See also, Rahman, Yeoh, and Huang 2005, 242–43.
47. Leonard 2003, 133; Winkler 2005, 18.
48. Kapiszewski 2006, 6; Winkler 2005, 18.
49. Kapiszewski 2006, 5.
50. Khalaf and Alkobaisi 1999, 284.
51. An international branch of the American Federation of Labor and Congress of Industrial Organizations (AFL-CIO), ACILS has been active in Sri Lanka for roughly

twenty years (with a hiatus between 1988 and 1993, during the peak of civil unrest in the southern parts of the island) (Conklin 2004).

52. Soysa 2004; Wijesiri 2004.
53. Wijesiri 2004.
54. Actform was formed in 1999 and has been active since 2001 (Perera 2004).
55. Actform 2003a, 2003b, 2004.
56. IOM has been active in Sri Lanka since 1990 and set up an office there in 2002 (Yapa 2004).
57. Iredale 2003; Nonnenmacher et al. 2003.
58. Conklin 2004; Witharana 2004.
59. Conklin 2004.
60. Jayawardena and de Alwis 2002, 257.
61. Jayawardena 1973.
62. ACILS is a local branch of the AFL-CIO. MSC is affiliated with Sri Lanka's National Workers' Congress and the All Ceylon Federation of Free Trade Unions (Witharana 2004). Locally, the Ceylon Workers Congress, the plantation workers' trade union, does some organizing on behalf of their constituents who have migrated abroad (Wijesiri 2004).
63. Conklin 2004.
64. Bass 2004.
65. Hewamanne 2008.
66. Conklin 2004.
67. Shinozaki 2005, 7–8.
68. Gamburd 2008, 12–13.
69. Jayaweera 2002a, 16, 19.
70. Jayaweera 2002b, 102–4.
71. Goonasekere 2002: 55; WHO 2005. Compare the situation in the United States, where women make up between 15 and 20 percent of most representative legislative bodies.
72. Jayaweera 2002b, 137.
73. Jayawardena and de Alwis 2002, 257.
74. Sunday Times 2008.
75. DGMF 1998, 7; emphasis added.
76. Ibid., 7.
77. Afsar 2005, 129.
78. Conklin 2004.
79. Afsar (2005) makes a similar point about Bangladesh. She notes that the government organ regulating migration, the Ministry of Expatriate Welfare and Overseas Employment (MEWOE), is quite small relative to the needs of migrants, operates on a very small budget, and receives a low priority among government programs. Bangladesh has only a few overseas labor attachés, and most migrants are unaware of available diplomatic services abroad. Afsar suggests that "greater efforts and commitment on the part of the government are needed to transform safe migration from rhetoric to reality" (2005: 127).
80. Conklin 2004; Fernando 2004.
81. Sebastian and Raghwan 2000, 4; Weerakoon 1998, 114.
82. Khalaf 1992: 58.
83. Malik 2004.
84. Financial Times Information 2004.
85. Ruhunage 2004.
86. Wee and Sim 2005, 184.
87. Ibid., 197.
88. Ibid., 194. See also Constable 2009.
89. Constable 2007.
90. Wee and Sim 2005, 198.
91. Rahman, Yeoh, and Huang 2005, 251.
92. Ibid., 241–42.

93. Constable 2009; Sim and Wee 2009.
94. Briones, personal communication.
95. Andall 2005, 16.
96. Wagner 2005, 10.
97. Hess 2005, 3.
98. Lutz 2008.
99. Wee and Sim 2005, 177; Liebelt 2008.
100. Hugo 2005, 84.
101. Asis 2005, 44.
102. Wee and Sim 2005, 197–98.
103. Lan 2005, 226; Lan 2006; Rahman, Yeoh, and Huang 2005, 251.
104. SLBFE 2006, 1, 57. In 2005, housemaids made up 54 percent of the total migrants and 91 percent of the female migrants (SLBFE 2006, 6). The majority of female migrants are between twenty-five and forty-five years of age (SLBFE 2006, 56). SLBFE figures indicate that approximately 720,000 of the estimated 800,000 Sri Lankan women working abroad are working as domestic servants in the Gulf (SLBFE 2006, 57).
105. Asis 2005, 25.
106. Asis notes that Filipinos gather at public spaces such as "Lucky Plaza in Singapore, Chongshan North Road in Taipei, [and] Central in Hong Kong" (2005: 37) and socialize at the Catholic Church in many labor-receiving countries (2005: 45). All the notable gathering places mentioned by Asis are in Asian, not Middle Eastern, countries.
107. Asis 2005, 25; SLBFE 2004, 23.
108. Asis 2005, 28.
109. IPS 2004, ix.
110. Thompson 1963.
111. Asis 2005, 25; Wee and Sim 2005, 195.
112. McKay 2005, 310.
113. Parreñas 2001a, 19.
114. Gunatillake and Perera 1995, 43.
115. Weerakoon 1998, 102.
116. Emerging ethnographic data (Gamburd 2008) suggests that a second generation, the educated daughters of Middle East migrants, are taking jobs outside the Middle East, for example as care-providers in Israel or seamstresses in Italy. This suggests that in the next ten years, Sri Lanka's migrant profile (and hopefully its laborers' empowerment abroad) may undergo a shift for the better.
117. Constable 2007, 32.
118. Ibid., viii.
119. Gamburd 2008; Wanasundera 2001.
120. Asis 2005, 44–45. Hugo (2005, 69) makes similar claims about the Indonesian government's lack of "commitment to protect Indonesian workers in foreign nations." Roughly 42 percent of Indonesian migrants go to Saudia Arabia and the UAE, while 58 percent go to Asian destinations, particularly Malaysia and Singapore (Hugo 2005, 60). Hugo suggests that the Philippines has done more than Indonesia has in sending labor attachés to destination countries and working for bilateral and multilateral labor agreements. Both countries' governments could support NGO activities in destination countries if the local governments limit the powers of diplomatic officials. But here again, NGO activity is more accepted in Asian than in Middle Eastern destinations.
121. Ortner 2006.

Chapter 5 – Lyons

1. See Chin 2003; Ford 2004; Gurowitz 1999; Gurowitz 2000; Law 2003; Law and Nadeu 1999; Lyons 2005b; Lyons 2007b; Piper 2003; Sim 2003a; Weekley 2004.
2. Ford 2006; Piper 2006.
3. Ford and Piper. 2007; Piper and Uhlin 2002.

4.   See Ball and Piper 2002; Moghadam 2005.
5.   Ong 2006, 215.
6.   Desai 2005, 328.
7.   This project examines the role of nongovernmental organizations and local and transnational networks that have developed in Singapore and Malaysia to address the rights of female domestic workers. The organizations under study include faith-based groups, service-oriented groups, advocacy groups and networks, training and support centers, embassies, government departments, and trade unions.
8.   Ford and Piper 2007.
9.   Piper and Uhlin, eds. 2004.
10.   Keck and Sikkink 1998, 3.
11.   See Della Porta and Tarrow 2005.
12.   See Swider 2006; and Hsia 2009.
13.   Piper 2005.
14.   Hsia 2009.
15.   Constable 2009.
16.   Lyons 2007c.
17.   MOM 2007.
18.   Almenoar and Tan 2004.
19.   Yeoh et al. 2004.
20.   Lyons and Gomez 2005.
21.   Lyons 2000.
22.   Perera and Ng 2002.
23.   Parliamentary Debates Republic of Singapore: Official Report 2004, 37.
24.   Ho 2000, 186.
25.   Lyons and Gomez 2005.
26.   The ISA was introduced during British rule and allows arrest and detention without trial for up to sixty days and unlimited extensions beyond the initial detention.
27.   Rodan 1993, 92.
28.   Mauzy and Milne 2002, 130.
29.   Haas 1989, 59.
30.   Huang et al., eds. 2005.
31.   See Hilsdon 2000.
32.   See Lyons 2005b.
33.   Gee and Ho, eds. 2006; Lyons 2005b.
34.   Comment made by a member of TWC2 executive, interview with the author, April 2006.
35.   TWC2 2008b.
36.   TWC2 2008a.
37.   Interview with John Gee, February 2006.
38.   This campaign was launched in November 2007 and spearheaded by a coalition comprised of five NGOs working in the field of migrant worker activism: Asia Pacific Forum on Women, Law and Development (APWLD); Asia Pacific Mission for Migrants (APMM); CARAM Asia; Global Alliance against Trafficking in Women (GAATW); and Mekong Migration Network (MMN).
39.   Ford and Piper 2007.
40.   MFA has long acknowledged the problems of working in Singapore and the difficulties that civil society groups face in working with transnational and international organizations. MFA's decision to partner with the state-supported National Trade Union Congress (NTUC) is a strategic move on its part to ensure that migrant worker issues are placed on the national agenda. The strength of this partnership may be another factor in TWC2's decision to join MFA. NTUC's involvement constitutes de facto support for its activities by the ruling party.
41.   HOME 2008.
42.   Statement made in an interview with the author by a member of TWC2, June 2008. Unlike TWC2, which has a limited service role, HOME has much to lose. Its women's shelter, for example, houses over one hundred women.

43. HOME 2008.
44. Interview April 2006.
45. SMS 2008.
46. HOME became a member of MFA a year earlier than TWC2, and given the nature of continued rivalry between the two organizations, this in itself may have been another motivating factor in TWC2's decision to join in 2007.
47. MFA 2008.
48. TWC2 2008a.
49. Lyons 2005a.
50. Ong 2006.
51. It appears that Ong includes in her description of "NGOs" employment agencies and their affiliated training centers. Although these may fit the broad definition of CSOs, few scholars would describe these as NGOs.
52. Ong 2006, 21.
53. Ong 2006, 217.
54. See Lyons 2007a.
55. Yee 2008.
56. Ferree 2006, 14.
57. It is important to recognize that the Catholic Church is not a monolithic entity. Lew is involved with the Scalabrini Sisters in the Philippines and, through them, with the Scalabrini lay movement. She distances herself from the Catholic Archdiocese in Singapore.
58. See Lyons 2005b.
59. Interview April 2006.
60. For a discussion of how similar fears have shaped the development of the women's rights movement, see Lyons 2000.
61. Lyons 2004.

Chapter 6 – Hsia

1. Ford 2004.
2. Sim 2003a.
3. Petras 1999.
4. For example, see Constable 1997; Sim 2003a; and Law 2002. This confusion between NGOs and grassroots organizations results in NGOs, especially mega NGOs, receiving the credit for work that grassroots migrants organizations themselves have done.
5. Parreñas 2001a.
6. See Lyons 2009.
7. Cheng 2003; Lan 2003b.
8. Cheng 2004; Tierney 2002.
9. Evans 2000.
10. Brecher et al. 2000.
11. Freire 1970.
12. Porta and Tarrow 2005.
13. Evans 2000, 240.
14. Smith 1994, 25.
15. Law 2002.
16. Constable 1997; Law 2002; Sim 2003a; Ford 2004.
17. Other coalitions or networks are composed of NGOs alone or of a mixture of NGOs and grassroots migrant organizations, such as the Coalition of Migrants Rights, initiated by the Asian Migrants Center.
18. Law 2002; Sim 2003a.
19. Law (2002) briefly notes AMCB's existence, but doesn't analyze the organization in depth.
20. The interviews were done between March 2007 and June 2008. All these interviews were done in Hong Kong. Additionally, between March 2007 and July 2008, I attended several protest actions organized by the AMCB, its member organizations

and local organizations to observe how the AMCB's member organizations relate to each other and how the AMCB relate to the local organizations.

21. The Hong Kong government uses the term "Foreign Domestic Helpers (FDH)," but in this paper I use "Migrant Domestic Workers (MDWs)," the term widely used in international human rights discourse.
22. Hong Kong Government, 2004a, 2005.
23. Hong Kong Government, 1997, 2001, 2002, 2003, 2004, 2005.
24. Sim 2003b.
25. See Constable 2009.
26. Sim 2003b.
27. Ibid.
28. APMM, 2003.
29. Migrant organizations involved in the initial formation of AMCB include ASL, Feona, FOT, Indonesian Group (an informal association), TWA, and Unifil.
30. APMM 2003.
31. Ibid.
32. AMCB was the first migrant organization to launch campaigns against wage cuts. Later on, other migrant organizations staged their own protests against such policy.
33. See Constable 2007.
34. Other migrant organizations support the levy. See http://www.apmigrants.org/papers/CMR_Joint_Position_Paper_on_Wage&Levy.htm. Unifil once issued a statement against this position: see http://www.apmigrants.org/papers/07.htm. (Both accessed 4 July 2008.)
35. Under the maternity protection provision, pregnancy is not a basis for the termination of a contract. Migrant workers who have been terminated for this reason have the right to file a case and, if successful, can get extra benefits outside the contractual obligations of the employer. Proponents of the abolition pushed for a more "flexible" arrangement between the employer and the migrants in such cases.
36. The numbers of participants in this anti-WTO protest and previously mentioned campaigns are all based on head counts by AMCB member organizations and its partners. Protesters mobilized by other migrant organizations are not included.
37. APMM 2003.
38. I attended the IMA founding assembly and was present for Lestari's election. The AMCB's achievements were mentioned several times throughout the meeting as an inspiration to grassroots migrant movement.
39. The forum was co-organized by APMM, AMCB, and Panap.
40. APMM 2005.
41. See Constable 2009.
42. Ong 2006.
43. Law 2007.
44. Though the laws do not discriminate against migrants, migrants are discriminated against in practice and as a result of immigration policies. For example, it is an unwritten policy rather than the law that prevents MDWs from applying for residency. Though migrants are entitled to join unions, union leaders who volunteer to work at the unions need to prove to the immigration officers that their employers allow them to do so, because the policy does not permit MDWs to work outside the employer's house.
45. There are still many restrictions on protests. While some local activists like to challenge these regulations, migrant organizations make sure to apply for permits, abide by restrictions, and maintain friendly relationships with the police, so that migrant workers will not be terminated or deported.
46. The CTU had not yet been established; an education center was set up as a platform of different unions.
47. Ho 2000, 191.
48. Freire 1970.

49. In 1982, President Ferdinand Marcos issued Executive Order No. 857 (EO-857), popularly known as "Forced Remittance," that decrees that all overseas contract workers (OCW) had to remit 50 to 70 percent of their total earnings (depending on which category the workers belongs to: seafarers, professionals, construction workers, or domestic helpers). The bill also prohibits the use of non-banking channels and restricts OCW to remit only through government-authorized channels. OCWs who cannot produce proof of remittance in the required amounts face punitive acts such as losing their rights to renew their contracts, renew their passports, cancelation of working contracts, or being eliminated from the list of eligible workers for overseas employment. Since migrant workers spend a part of their salary in the host country, remitting such a large percentage of their salary is not easy. Such punitive provisions forced Filipino migrant workers to borrow money from financing agencies and remit the money through banks for them to have remittance receipts as proof.

50. APMMF 2000, 4.
51. KMP 1994.
52. Filipino migrants started to be organized in early 1980s. See Bultron 2006.
53. For details, see: http://www.bayan.ph/about_bayan_the_alliance.htm (accessed 5 December 2008).
54. Bultron 2006.
55. Law 2002.
56. Touraine 1988.
57. Hsia 2006.

Chapter 7 – Constable

1. Sassen 2000, 2001.
2. Ong 2006.
3. Foreign domestic workers (who work full-time for one employer and are "live in") did not criticize the use of the levy to retrain local women since local workers (who work part-time and hourly) do not compete for the same market. Foreign domestic workers objected primarily to the fact that a HK$400 cut had been imposed on the monthly minimum legal wage of foreign domestic workers in 2003 on the basis that employers struggled to afford to pay such high wages, and then only three months later a HK$400 levy was imposed on the supposedly struggling employers. As such, the employers broke even, the local women stood to gain, and the foreign domestic workers were the "losers."
4. See Constable 1997 on Filipina domestic workers in Hong Kong, and 2007 for a discussion of the wider changes since 1997 including the influx of Indonesian workers. In December 2005 I was accompanied by my 15-year-old son/photographer, Peter Constable Alter. A migrant worker friend invited us to join this protest and reserved space for us on the bus.
5. Hong Kong Government, email communication, 2005. Beginning with the oil boom of the 1970s and 1980s, Indonesian women went mainly to work as domestic servants in the Middle East, but by the 1990s labor exportation had expanded to include other regions of Asia (Blackburn 2004, 190).
6. See also Hsia, and Sim and Wee, this volume.
7. Blackburn 2004,189.
8. Robinson 2000.
9. Mufti 1996, cited in Blackburn 2004,189.
10. These stereotypes of Filipinas versus Indonesians are widespread. See Lan 2006 for a discussion of such stereotypes in Taiwan.
11. Blackburn 2004, 191.
12. The live-in rule is more strictly enforced than it was in the early 1990s.
13. One notable change since the late 1990s is the decrease in domestic worker monthly salaries from HK$3870 (about US$490) in 1998, to HK$3270 (US$420) in 2003. Small wage increases, including a raise of HK$50, were introduced in summer 2005 for newly signed contracts. Another change is that workers previously

had the option of arranging their own employment, but they are now required to use an employment agency. As noted earlier, the HK$400 levy is also new.

14. Evans 2005.
15. HKPA 2005.
16. Sim 2003a and b; see also Hsia, this volume.
17. Employment agencies have recently begun to sponsor their own shelters. These are less popular among workers and for obvious reasons do not serve the same consciousness-raising purpose.
18. See Hsia (this volume) for a discussion of the history and organization of the AMCB.
19. Bakhtin 1984.
20. I am grateful to Donald Nonini for drawing my attention to the idea of comparative advantage and to Michele Gamburd for pushing me further. See also Robinson 2000, 253; Vasudevan 2005, 4.
21. Ruwich 2005.
22. Sassen 2001.
23. Ong 2006.
24. Ong 2006, 110; 112–13.
25. See Castles and Davidson 2000, 94–96 on the rights of legal residents in Europe referred to as "quasi-citizens," "margizens," or "denizens"; see also Soysal 1994.
26. Ong 1999.
27. As Sassen (2001) writes, "the centrality of place in a context of global processes engenders a transnational economic and political opening in the formation of new claims and hence in the constitution of entitlements, notably rights to place, and, at the limit, in the constitution of new forms of 'citizenship' and a diversity of citizenship practices." For broad definitions of citizenship, see also Geertz 1973; Rosaldo 1994; Verdery 1998; Ku and Pun 2005.
28. Ong 1999, 2006.
29. Newendorp 2008; see also Ku 2001.
30. See Tiwari and Solnit 2005.
31. For example, Guarnizo et al. 2003, 1214.
32. See Lyons 2009 for a deeper discussion of transnational alliances and organizing.
33. In particular, the "march" in which Korean protestors, mainly farmers, processed from Causeway Bay to Wanchai by walking three steps then bowing their foreheads all the way to the ground, kowtowing an ancient Buddhist rite, moved some of the local observers to tears and others to join the protests, to donate food or water, or to display banners or signs of support. Many news reports commented on both the criticism voiced by locals and their heartfelt support (e.g., Ruwich 2005).
34. Ehrenreich and Hochschild 2004; Lan 2006; Parreñas 2001a, 2005.
35. For example, Hsia 2009; Law 2002; Piper 2005; Sim 2003a; Yamanaka and Piper 2005.
36. H. Lee (2006) argues that in the case of mainland Chinese women who work for foreigners in China, the home is a quasi-public sphere in which cosmopolitan subjectivities are forged. In Hong Kong, many Chinese employers' homes are viewed far less positively and the public sphere in which their political subjectivities are forged are outside of their workplaces.
37. Guarnizo et al. 2003, 1239.
38. Gupta and Ferguson 1992.
39. Freeman 2001.
40. Ku and Pun 2005; So 2005; Tiwari 2002; Wong 2003; Tsang 2003; Taipei Times 2003; Lin 2003; Knight 2003; IMWU 2005.
41. Lee, C.K. 2000, 2002.

Chapter 8 – Sim and Wee

1. UN Habitat, State of the World's Cities, 2006–2007.
2. For an excellent discussion of discourses and definitions on world/global cities, see Short et al. 1999.

3.   Ibid.
4.   Ong and Roy 2008, 2.
5.   See, for example, Jansen and Piermartini 2004, 3, where trade negotiations for the transnational movement of people (under Mode 4 of the WTO agreements) recognize a very restricted category of persons, such as intra-corporate transfers of high-level personnel and business visitors. Developing countries have stressed the need to expand the coverage to other categories, including low-skilled workers in trade negotiations.
6.   Centers of wealth and power concentration today have historical precedents in ancient cities that were centers of governance and powerhouses of their day in trade and learning.
7.   Ong and Roy 2008.
8.   Wee and Sim 2004, 2005.
9.   Choi 2004, 2.
10.   Manpower needs and wages survey: Manufacturing, hotels, restaurants and banking and insurance, Statistics and Census Service, Macau Government, various years, cited from Choi 2004, 4.
11.   See, for example, Chan 1999.
12.   Choi 1999, 2.
13.   Government of Macau, 25 April 2008.
14.   Short and Kim's term (1999, 57).
15.   Choi 2004, 5.
16.   Ibid.
17.   Choi 2004, 1.
18.   "Gender-class" was coined by Varda Burstyn (1985, 49, cited in Knuttila and Kubik 2000, 169) to describe how as Marxist concepts illuminate economic class relations, the use of the word "man" to describe humanity obscured women's realities through another set of class relations, related to gender.
19.   Burstyn 1985, 55, cited in Knuttila and Kubik 2000, 170.
20.   Ursel 1986, 153, cited in Knuttila and Kubik 2000, 186.
21.   We have put the word "race" within quotation marks to highlight that "race" is a social construction, not a biological fact. As the American Anthropological Association Statement on "Race" declares, "In the United States both scholars and the general public have been conditioned to viewing human races as natural and separate divisions within the human species based on visible physical differences. With the vast expansion of scientific knowledge in this century, however, it has become clear that human populations are not unambiguous, clearly demarcated, biologically distinct groups. Evidence from the analysis of genetics (e.g., DNA) indicates that most physical variation, about 94 percent, lies within so-called racial groups.... Today scholars in many fields argue that 'race'; as it is understood in the United States of America was a social mechanism invented during the eigthteenth century to refer to those populations brought together in colonial America: the English and other European settlers, the conquered Indian peoples, and those peoples of Africa brought in to provide slave labor." (See American Anthropological Association 1998.)
22.   Wee and Sim 2004, 2005.
23.   For example, research carried out by Vivienne Wee et al. (in the "Women's Empowerment in Muslim Contexts" project) documents a positive correlation between land ownership and the relative lack of women's migration from Sumatra, Indonesia, and the high rates of labor migration by women from Java and their lack of land ownership.
24.   Sassen 1988, 18.
25.   Choi 2004.
26.   Parreñas 2001a, 448.
27.   Rosewarne 1998, 2001, cited in Choi 2004, 8.
28.   CARAM International et al. 2002, 7.
29.   Ministry of Justice (Japan), cited in AMC and MFA 2003, 173.

30. Ministry of Justice Immigration Office (Korea), cited in AMC and MFA, 2003, 187.
31. AMC and MFA 2000, 231; 2002–3, 187.
32. National Police Administration of Taiwan, cited in AMC and MFA, 2003, 261.
33. AMC and MFA 1999, 195; 2002–3, 260. While these figures are drawn from NGO sources and may in some cases be overstated, some of these figures are drawn from government sources, such as the National Police Administration in Taiwan; but in any case, these preliminary reports provide an entry into hitherto relatively uncharted waters.
34. Chiu 1999, 95; Skeldon 1995, 310.
35. Hong Kong Immigration Department, cited in AMC and MFA 1999, 112. See http://www. info.gov.hk/immd/english/facts.htm cited in Chiu 1999, 95 (accessed 6 December 2008).
36. SCMP, 27 August 2004.
37. APWLD 2003. 12 March. This is one discriminatory practice amongst others targeted at foreign domestic versus other foreign employees in Hong Kong, e.g., rights to residency and sectoral mobility.
38. While in these centers the prospective migrant workers are not allowed to return home to visit their families or to leave the premises for any other reason, even to buy their toiletries.
39. Legco Paper No. 3150/93–94, 30 May 1994, cited in Hong Kong Human Rights Monitor 1996/97.
40. Sim 2008.
41. AMC and MFA 1999, 12.
42. Ibid., 112.
43. Our research in other sites supports this analysis as we have also found cases of Hong Kong agencies creating short-term flexible labor pools of this type in various parts of China, such as Shenzhen and other parts of Guangdong.
44. Wee and Sim 2004.
45. There is empirical validity in these views as a relevant category used in Indonesian economic statistics is discouraged workers, i.e., "jobless workers who want jobs but do not look for one because they do not believe a job is available for them" (Suryadarma et al. 2005, 3). "In 2003…discouraged workers made up around a third of the official BPS open unemployment number of 9.5 million workers.… In terms of gender, females form the majority of discouraged workers" (Ibid., 10–12). Indonesian migrant workers are recruited mostly from this category of discouraged workers. Also see Jakarta Post, 17 July 2003, and South China Morning Post, 20 October 2006.
46. Further study needs to be undertaken to collect data on the economic activities of this community.
47. Sim forthcoming.
48. Suara, 23 February 2007.
49. ATKI was established on 1 October 2000. Its main objective is to assert and defend the rights and welfare of Indonesian migrant workers in Hong Kong. See http://gaatw.net/GAATW percent20Reports/Delhi percent20paper-revised-Eni_pdf.pdf (accessed 15 May 2008).
50. An Islamic charity; see http://www.dompetdhuafa.org/home_eng.php (accessed 15 May 2008).
51. Pilar (United Indonesians against Overcharging) was founded on 1 April 2007.
52. For more about civic actions by migrant workers in Hong Kong, see Constable 2009.
53. Ong and Roy 2008.
54. Sassen 2002, 274.
55. Ibid., 256, 274.
56. Ibid., 274.
57. Government Information Bureau, 22 May 2007.
58. This figure does not include the unknown numbers of undocumented workers in Macau. Ibid.

59. This rule has never been applied to migrant workers in professional categories.
60. Sassen 2002, 255. See also Sassen 1991, 1996.

❑

References

Actform. 2003a. *Tharani: Newsletter of the Action Network for Migrant Workers (Actform)*. First quarter. Ratmalana: Navamaga Printers.

———. 2003b. *Tharani*. Second quarter. Ratmalana: Navamaga Printers.

———. 2004. *Handbook for Migrant Workers* (Sinhala-language publication). Colombo: Actform.

Adams, Kathleen M., and Sara Dickey. 2000. *Home and hegemony: Domestic service and identity politics in South and Southeast Asia*. Ann Arbor: University of Michigan Press.

Addleton, Jonathan S. 1991. The impact of the Gulf War on migration and remittances in Asia and the Middle East, *International Migration* 29 (4): 509–26.

Afsar, Rita. 2005. Conditional mobility: The migration of Bangladeshi female domestic workers. In Huang et al., eds. 2005. 115–45.

Almenoar, Maria, and Theresa Tan. 2004. Minimum age for maids raised from 18 to 23. *The Straits Times*.

AMC and MFA. 1999. *Asian migrant yearbook 1998: Migration facts, analysis and issues*. Hong Kong: Asian Migrant Centre and Migrant Forum in Asia.

———. 2000. *Asian migrant yearbook 2002–3: Migration facts, analysis and issues*. Hong Kong: Asian Migrant Centre and Migrant Forum in Asia.

———. 2003. *Asian migrant yearbook 2002–3: Migration facts, analysis and issues 2001–2002*. Hong Kong: Asian Migrant Centre and Migrant Forum in Asia.

American Anthropological Association. 1998. Statement on "Race." http://www.aaanet.org/stmts/ racepp.htm (accessed 29 November 2008). 17 May.

Ananta, Aris, ed. 2004. *International migration in Southeast Asia: Challenges and impacts*. Singapore: Institute of Southeast Asian Studies.

Andall, Jacqueline. 2005. Change and continuity in the Italian domestic work sector. Paper presented at the conference "Migration and Domestic Work in Global Perspective," 26–29 May 2005. The Netherlands Institute of Advanced Studies, Wassenar.

Anderson, Bridget. 2000. *Doing the dirty work? The global politics of domestic labour*. London: Zed Books.

———. 2001. Just another job? Paying for domestic work. *Gender and Development* 9 (1): 25–33.

———. 2002. Just another job? The commodification of domestic labor. In Ehrenreich and Hochschild, eds. 2002. 104–14.

Andolan, 2008. Action alert: Domestic workers protest tomorrow in New York. http:// www.passtheroti.com/?=720 (accessed 22 July 2008).

APWLD (Asia Pacific Forum on Women, Law and Development). 2003. Specific groups and individuals: Migrant workers. [Statement submitted to United Nations Economic and Social Council]. http://www.unhchr.ch/Huridocda/Huridoca.nsf/(Symbol)/E.CN.4.2003.NGO.122.En?Opendocument (accessed 28 April 2004). 12 March.

Asia Pacific Mission for Migrant Filipinos (APMMF). 2000. *A brief guide in organizing migrants*. Hong Kong: APMMF.

Asia Pacific Mission for Migrants (APMM). 2003. *Evaluation report: Asian Migrant Coordinating Body,* Hong Kong: APMM.

———. 2005. *News Digest: Monthly Newsletter for the Asia Pacific Mission for Migrants,* November–December.

Asian Migrant Centre (AMC). 2005. *Asian migrant yearbook 2005 statistics.* http://www.asian-migrants.org/index.php?option+com_content&task+category&sectionid=3&id=47&Itemid=30 (accessed 31 July 2008).

Asis, Maruja M.B. 2005. Caring for the world: Filipino domestic workers gone global. In Huang et al., eds. 2005. 21–53.

'Atiyat, Farah. 2006. Owners of domestic worker recruitment agencies demonstrate today. *Al-Ghad,* 2 May. (Arabic)

Bakan, Abigail B., and Daiva K. Stasiulis. 1995. Making the match: Domestic placement agencies and the racialization of women's household work. *Signs: Journal of Women in Culture and Society* 20 (2): 303–35.

Bakhtin, Mikhail. 1984. *Rabelais and his world.* Bloomington: Indiana University Press.

Ball, Rochelle, and Nicola Piper. 2002. Globalisation and regulation of citizenship: Filipino migrant workers in Japan. *Political Geography* 21: 1013–34.

Bass, Daniel. 2004. *A place on the plantations: Up-country Tamil ethnicity in Sri Lanka.* PhD diss. (Department of Anthropology, University of Michigan).

Beal, Anne. 1998. *Consumerism and the culture of consumption: Class, national identity, and gender among Jordanian elites.* PhD diss. (University of Chicago).

Bello, Walden. 2005. *The anti-development state: The political economy of permanent crisis in the Philippines.* London: Zed Books

Beyene, Joyet. 2005. *Women, migration and housing: A case study of three households of Ethiopian and Eritrean female migrant workers in Beirut and Naba'a.* Masters thesis (American University of Beirut).

Blackburn, Susan. 2004.*Women and the state in modern Indonesia.* Cambridge: Cambridge University Press.

BLIB.TV. 2008. Researching governance in challenging environments the big issue for DFID. http://r4d.blip.tv/file/840889/ (accessed 5 June 2008). 4 April.

Brecher, Jeremy, Tim Costello, and Brendan Smith. 2000. *Globalization from below: The power of solidarity.* Cambridge, Mass.: South End Press.

Brochmann, Grete. 1993.*Middle East avenue: Female migration from Sri Lanka to the Gulf.* Oxford: Westview Press.

Bultron, Ramon. 2006. The struggle and development of migrants movement: The Philippine experience. Paper presented at the 3rd International Conference on Transborder and Diaspora: Governance, Survival and Movements, in Taipei, Taiwan, 7–8 October 2006. Organized by the Graduate Institute for Social Transformation Studies, Shih Hsin University, Taipei.

Burstyn, Varda. 1985. Masculine domination and the state. In Varda Burstyn and Dorothy E. Smith. *Women, class, family and the state.* Toronto: Garamond.

Caram Indonesia, KOPBUMI, Komnas Perempuan. 2002. *Indonesian migrant workers: Systematic abuse at home and abroad.* An Indonesian Country Report to the UN Special Rapporteur on the Human Rights of Migrants. Kuala Lumpur.

Castles, Stephen. 2002. Migration and community formation under conditions of globalization. *International Migration Review* 36 (4): 1143–68.

Castles, Stephen, and Alastair Davidson. 2000. *Citizenship and migration: Globalization and the politics of belonging*. New York: Routledge.

Chammartin, Gloria Moreno-Flores. 2004. Women migrant workers' protection in Arab League States. In Simel Esim and Monica Smith, eds. *Gender and migration in Arab states: The case of domestic workers*. Beirut: International Labour Organisation (ILO).

Chan, Sau San. 1999. Labour importation and unemployment in Macau. *Journal of Macau Studies* 12: 40–51 (in Chinese).

Chang, Grace. 2000. *Disposable domestics: Immigrant women workers in the global economy*. Cambridge, Mass: South End Press.

Cheng, Shu-Ju Ada. 2003. Rethinking the globalization of domestic service: Foreign domestic, state control, and the politics of identity in Taiwan. *Gender and Society* 17 (2): 166–86.

Cheng, Shu-Ju Ada. 2004. Right to mothering: Motherhood as a transborder concern in the age of globalization. *Journal of the Association for Research on Mothering* 6 (1): 135–44.

Cheung, S.Y.L., and S.M.H. Sze, eds. 1995. *The other Hong Kong report 1995*. Hong Kong: The Chinese University Press.

Chin, Christine B.N. 2003. Visible bodies, invisible work: State practices toward migrant women domestic workers in Malaysia. *Asian and Pacific Migration Journal* 12 (1–2): 49–73.

Chiu, Stephen W.K. 1999. Hong Kong (China): Economic changes and international labour migration. *OECD Proceedings: Labour Migration and the Recent Financial Crisis in Asia*. Paris: OECD. 85–110.

Choi, Alex H. 2004. Migrant workers in Macao: Labour and globalisation. Working Paper Series No. 66. Southeast Asia Research Centre, City University of Hong Kong.

Choy, Catherine Ceniza. 2003. *Empire of care: Nursing and migration in Filipino American history*. Manila: Ateneo de Manila University Press.

Collier, Jane, and Sylvia Yanagisako. 1987. Toward a unified analysis of gender and kinship. In Jane Collier and Sylvia Yanagisako, eds. *Gender and kinship: Essays toward a unified analysis*. Palo Alto, Calif.: Stanford University Press. 14–50.

Conklin, William. 2004. Interview. 5 February 2004. American Center for International Labor Solidarity. Colombo, Sri Lanka.

Constable, Nicole. 1997. *Maid to order in Hong Kong: Stories of Filipina workers*. Ithaca, N.Y., and London: Cornell University Press.

———. 1999. At home but not at home: Filipina narratives of ambivalent returns. *Cultural Anthropology* 14 (2): 203–28.

———. 2002. Filipina workers in Hong Kong homes: Household rules and relations. In Ehrenreich and Hochschild. 2002. 115–41.

———. 2007. *Maid to order in Hong Kong: Stories of migrant workers*. Ithaca, N.Y.: Cornell University Press.

———. 2007. 2d ed. *Maid to order in Hong Kong: Stories of Filipina workers*. Ithaca, N.Y.: Cornell University Press.

———. 2009. Migrant workers and the many states of protest in Hong Kong. *Critical Asian Studies* 41 (1): 143–64.

Curley, Melissa G., and Wong Siu-lun, eds. 2008. *Security and migration in Asia: The dynamics of securitisation*. London: RoutledgeCurzon.

de Regt, Marina. 2006. Mapping study on women domestic workers in Yemen. Unpublished report. Beirut: International Labour Organization

———. 2007a. Ethiopian women in the Middle East: The case of migrant domestic workers in Yemen. Paper presented at the Africa Studies Centre, Leiden, The Netherlands, 15 February.

———. 2007b. Migrant domestics and religious closeness in Yemen. *ISIM Review* 20: 50–51.

———. 2008. Employing migrant domestic workers in urban Yemen: A new form of social distinction. *Hawwa: Journal of Women of the Middle East and the Islamic World* 6 (2). November. 154–75.

———. 2009. Preferences and prejudices: Yemeni employers' views on domestic workers. *Signs: Journal of Women in Culture and Society* 32 (3): 559–81.

Decena, Carlos Ulises, Michele G. Shedlin, and Angela Martinez. 2006. Los hombres no mandan aqui: Narrating immigrant genders and sexualities in New York. *Social Text* 24 (3): 36–54.

della Porta, Donatella, and Sidney Tarrow. 2005 (2004). *Transnational protest and global activism*. Lanham, Md.: Rowman and Littlefield.

Department of Statistics (Hashemite Kingdom of Jordan). 2002–2003. *Household Expenditures and Income Survey 2002/2003*. Department of Statistics, Hashemite Kingdom of Jordan.

———. 2006. *Social Trends in Jordan. Issue No. 1*. Department of Statistics, Hashemite Kingdom of Jordan.

Department of Statistics (Hashemite Kingdom of Jordan). 2007. Jordanian mothers: Facts and figures. Press release, 21 March. Department of Statistics, Hashemite Kingdom of Jordan.

Desai, Manisha. 2005. Transnationalism: the face of feminist politics post-Beijing. *International Social Science Journal* 57 (184): 319–30.

Destremau, Blandine. 2002. L'Émergence d'un Marché du Travail Domestique au Yémen: Une Étude sur Sana'a. *Revue Tiers Monde* XLIII (170): 327–51.

DGMF (Deputy General Manager [Finance]). 1998. Report on the study tour made by the delegation to Kuwait and United Arab Emirates (September 20th–September 30th 1998). Sri Lankan Bureau of Foreign Employment. 6 October. Photocopy.

Dias, Malsiri, and Ramani Jayasundere. 2004. Sri Lanka: The anxieties and opportunities of out-migration. Ch. 6. In Pong-Sul Ahn, ed. *Migrant workers and human rights: Out-migration from South Asia*. Geneva: International Labor Organization (ILO).

Dickey, Sara, and Kathleen M. Adams. 2000. Introduction: Negotiating homes, hegemonies, identities, and politics. In Kathleen A. Adams and Sara Dickey, eds. *Home and hegemony: Domestic service and identity politics in South and Southeast Asia*. Ann Arbor: University of Michigan Press. 1–29.

Dickinson, James, and Bob Russell, eds. 1985. *Family, economy and state*. Toronto: Garamond.

Domestic Workers United. 2008. Domestic Workers United: Programs and history. www.domesticworkersunited.org/programs.php (accessed 22 July 2008).

Eelens, F., T. Schampers, and J.D. Speckmann, eds. 1992. *Labour migration to the Middle East: From Sri Lanka to the Gulf.* London: Kegan Paul International.

Ehrenreich, Barbara, and Arlie Hochschild, eds. 2004 (2002, 2003). *Global woman: Nannies, maids, and sex workers in the new economy.* New York: Metropolitan Books.

Eltman, Frank. 2008. Mahinder Sabhnani, NY millionaire who tortured housekeepers, sentenced to prison. *The Huffington Post,* 27 June. www.huffing tonpost. com/2008/06/27/mahender-sabhnani-ny-mill_n_109709.html?view=print (accessed 22 July 2008).

Enloe, Cynthia. 2000. *Bananas, beaches and bases: Making feminist sense of international politics.* Berkeley and Los Angeles: University of California Press.

Escobar, Arturo. 1988. Power and visibility: Development and the invention and management of the third world. *Cultural Anthropology* 3(4): 428–43.

Evans, Peter. 2000. Fighting marginalization with transnational networks: Counter-hegemonic globalization. *Contemporary Sociology* 29 (1): 230–41.

———. 2005. Hegemonic globalization: Transnational social movements in the contemporary global political economy. In Thomas Janoski, Alexander Hicks, and Mildred Schwartz, eds. *Handbook of political sociology.* Cambridge: Cambridge University Press. 655–70.

Eviota, Elisabeth Uy. 1992. *The political economy of gender: Women and the sexual division of labour in the Philippines.* London: Zed Books.

Fernando, KODD. 2004. Interview. 14 January. Deputy general manager information technology, Sri Lankan Bureau of Foreign Employment. Colombo, Sri Lanka.

Ferree, Myra Marx. 2006. Globalization and feminism: Opportunities and obstacles for activism in the global arena. In Myra Marx Ferree and Aili Mari Tripp, eds. *Global feminism: Transnational women's activism, organizing and human rights.* New York: New York University Press. 3–23.

Financial Times Information. 2004. Migrant worker rights group gets licence in Bahrain. Financial Times Information. http://web.lexis-nexis.com/universe/document?_m=38e988085ba38a4b127a5b6e11774822&_docnum=7&wchp=dGLbVtz-zSkVA&_md5=342df4a4cb939afd936cd7334 96c1157. Posted 31 December 2004 (accessed 27 February 2005).

Ford, Michele. 2004. Organizing the unorganizable: Unions, NGOs, and Indonesian migrant labour. *International Migration* 42 (5): 99–119.

———. 2006. Migrant labor NGOs and trade unions: A partnership in progress? *Asian and Pacific Migration Journal* 15 (3): 299–318.

Ford, Michele, and Nicola Piper. 2007. Southern sites of female agency: Informal regimes and female migrant labour resistance in East and Southeast Asia. In J. Hobson and L. Seabrooke, eds. *Everyday politics of the world economy.* Cambridge: Cambridge University Press. 63–80.

Forte, Tania. 2001. Shopping in Jenin: Women, homes and political persons in the Galilee. *City and Society* 13 (2): 211–43.

Foucault, Michel. 1979. *Discipline and punish.* New York: Vintage.

Frank, Andre Gunder. 1966. The development of underdevelopment. *Monthly Review* 18: 17–31.

Freeman, Carla S. 2001. Is local: Global as feminine: Masculine? Rethinking the gender of globalization. *Signs: Journal of Women, Culture, and Society.* Special issue on gender and globalization. 26 (4): 1007–37.

Freire, Paulo. 1970. *Pedagogy of the oppressed.* New York: Continuum.

Freitag, Ulrike, and W.G. Clarence-Smith, eds. 1997. *Hadrami traders, scholars and statesmen in the Indian Ocean, 1750s–1960s.* Leiden: Brill.

Gamburd, Michele R. 2000. *The kitchen spoon's handle: Transnationalism and Sri Lanka's migrant housemaids.* Ithaca, N.Y., and London: Cornell University Press.

———. 2005. Lentils there, lentils here: Sri Lankan domestic labour in the Middle East. In Huang et al., eds. 2005. 92–114.

———. 2008. Milk teeth and jet planes: Kin relations in families of Sri Lanka's transnational domestic servants. *City and Society* 20 (1): 5–31.

———. 2009. Protecting Sri Lankan migrant workers: Obstacles and challenges. *Critical Asian Studies* 41 (1): 61–88.

Gardezi, Hassan H. 1995. *The political economy of international labour migration.* Montreal: Black Rose Books.

Gee, John, and Elaine Ho, eds. 2006. *Dignity overdue.* Singapore: John Gee and Elaine Ho.

Geertz, Clifford. 1973. The integrative revolution: Primordial sentiments and civil politics in the new states. In *The interpretation of culture: Selected essays.* New York: Basic Books. 255–310.

Ghazwi, Fahmi Salim. 1985. *Modernisation and social change in family life in Jordan, 1961–1981.* PhD diss. (University of Virginia, Dept. of Sociology).

GHK (Government of Hong Kong). 1997. Foreign domestic helpers. *Hong Kong yearbook 1997.* GHK, Hong Kong.

———. 2001. Imported workers. *Hong Kong yearbook 2001*, GHK, Hong Kong.

———. 2002. Imported workers. *Hong Kong yearbook 2002*, GHK, Hong Kong.

———. 2003. Imported workers. *Hong Kong yearbook 2003*, GHK, Hong Kong.

———. 2004. Entry of foreign domestic helpers. *Hong Kong yearbook 2004.* GHK, Hong Kong.

———. 2005. Imported workers. *Hong Kong yearbook 2005*, GHK, Hong Kong.

Gill, Lesley. 1994. *Precarious dependencies: Gender, class and domestic service in Bolivia.* New York: Columbia University Press.

Gledhill, John. 2007. Neoliberalism. In David Nugent and Joan Vincent, eds. *A companion to the anthropology of politics.* Oxford: Blackwell Publishing. 332–48.

Glick Schiller, Nina, and Georges E. Fouron. 2001. *Georges woke up laughing: Long-distance nationalism and the search for home.* Durham, N.C., and London: Duke University Press.

Gmelch, George. 1992. *Double passage: The lives of Caribbean migrants abroad and back home.* Ann Arbor: University of Michigan Press.

Gombrich, Richard, and Gananath Obeyesekere. 1988. *Buddhism transformed: Religious change in Sri Lanka.* Princeton, N.J.: Princeton University Press.

Gonzales, Joaquin L. 1998. *Philippine labour migration. Critical dimensions of public policy.* Singapore: Institute of Southeast Asian Studies.

Goonasekere, Savitri. 2002. Constitutions, governance and laws. In Swarna Jaya-weera, ed. *Women in post-independence Sri Lanka*. New Delhi: Sage. 41–78.

Government Information Bureau (Macau). 2007. Macau crime on the rise. http://macaudailyblog.com/macau-news/macau-crime-on-the-rise/ (accessed 15 May 2008). 22 May.

Government of Macau. 2008. Principal statistical indicators. http://www.dsec.gov.mo/index.asp? src=/english/indicator/e_piem_indicator.html (accessed 1 July 2008). 25 April.

Gregson, Nicky, and Michelle Lowe. 1994. *Servicing the middle classes: Class, gender and waged domestic labour in contemporary Britain*. London: Routledge.

Guarnizo, Luis Eduardo, Alejandro Portes, and William Haller. 2003. Assimilation and transnationalism: Determinants of transnational political action among contemporary migrants. *American Journal of Sociology* 108 (6): 1211–48.

Gulati, Leela. 1993. *In the absence of their men: The impact of male migration on women*. New Delhi: Sage Publications.

Gunatillake, Godfrey, and Myrtle Perera, ed. 1995. *Study of female migrant worker* [sic]. Colombo: Marga Institute (Sri Lanka Centre for Development Studies), World Bank, and Ministry of Policy Planning and Implementation.

Gupta, Akhil, and James Ferguson. 1992. Space, identity and the politics of difference. *Cultural Anthropology* 7 (1): 6–23.

Gurowitz, Amy. 1999. Mobilizing international norms: Domestic actors, immigrants, and the Japanese state. *World Politics* 51 (3): 413–45.

———. 2000. Migrant rights and activism in Malaysia: Opportunities and constraints. *Journal of Asian Studies* 59 (4): 863–88.

Haas, Michael. 1989. The politics of Singapore in the 1980s. *Journal of Contemporary Asia* 19 (1): 48–77.

Hagan, Jacqueline Maria. 1998. Social networks, gender and immigrant incorporation: Resources and constraints. *American Sociological Review* 63: 55–67.

Hage, Ghassan. 2005. A not so multi-sited ethnography of a not so imagined community. *Anthropological Theory* 5 (4): 463–75.

Hammer, Leonard. 1999. Migrant workers in Israel: Towards proposing a framework of enforceable customary international human rights. *Netherlands Quarterly of Human Rights* 171: 5–30.

Hansen, Karen. 1989. *Distant companions: Servants and employers in Zambia, 1900–1985*. Ithaca, N.Y.: Cornell University Press.

Harrison, Faye V. 1997. The gendered politics and violence of structural adjustment. In Louise Lamphere, Helene Ragone, and Patricia Zavella, eds. *Situated lives: Gender and culture in everyday life*. New York: Routledge. 451–68.

Hazaimeh, Hani. 2008. Philippine government to lift ban on sending domestic helpers. *Jordan Times,* 6 April.

Hess, Sabine. 2005. Big sisters are better domestic servants?! Au pair as live-in domestic work. Paper presented at the conference "Migration and Domestic Work in Global Perspective," 26–29 May 2005. The Netherlands Institute of Advanced Studies, Wassenar.

Hewamanne, Sandya. 2008. *Stitching identities in a free trade zone: Gender and politics in Sri Lanka*. Philadelphia: University of Pennsylvania Press.

Hilsdon, Anne-Marie. 2000. The Contemplacion fiasco: The hanging of a Filipino domestic worker in Singapore. In Anne-Marie Hilsdon et al., eds. *Human rights and gender politics: Asia-Pacific perspectives.* London and New York: Routledge. 172–92.

HKPA (Hong Kong People's Alliance). 2005. Hong Kong People's Alliance on WTO. http://www. hkpaowto.org.hk/eng/home/html (accessed 4 October 2007).

Ho, Denny Kwok Leung. 2000. The rise and fall of community mobilization: The housing movement in Hong Kong. In Stephen Wing Kai and Tai Lok Lui, eds. *The dynamics of social movement in Hong Kong.* Hong Kong: Hong Kong University Press. 185–208.

Ho, Kai Leong. 2000. *The politics of policy-making in Singapore.* Oxford: Oxford University Press.

HOME. 2008. *About us.* http://www.home.org.sg/aboutus.asp (accessed 12 January 2008).

Hondagneu-Sotelo, Pierrette. 1994. Regulating the unregulated? Domestic workers' social networks. *Social Problems* 41 (1): 50–64.

———. 2001. *Doméstica: Immigrant workers cleaning and caring in the shadows of affluence.* Berkeley, Los Angeles, and London: University of California Press.

Hong Kong Human Rights Monitor. 1996/1997. The two-week rule. http://www. hkhrm.org.hk/english/reports/enw/enw0796d.htm (accessed 25 May 2008).

Hsia, Hsiao-Chuan. 2006. The making of immigrants movement: Politics of differences, subjectivation and societal Movement. *Taiwan: A Radical Quarterly in Social Studies* 61: 1–71. In Chinese.

———. 2009. The making of a transnational grassroots migrant movement: A case study of Hong Kong's Asian Migrants' Coordinating Body *Critical Asian Studies* 41 (1): 113–41.

Huang, Shirlena, Brenda S.A. Yeoh, and Noor Abdul Rahman, eds. 2005. *Asian women as transnational domestic workers.* Singapore: Marshall Cavendish Academic.

Hugo, Graeme. 2005. Indonesian international domestic workers: Contemporary developments and issues. In Huang et al., eds. 2005. 54–91.

Human Rights Watch. 2007. Exported and exposed: Abuses against Sri Lankan domestic workers in Saudi Arabia, Kuwait, Lebanon and the United Arab Emirates. *Human Rights Watch* 19 (16c). November.

———. 2008. *"As if I am not human": Abuses against Asian domestic workers in Saudi Arabia.* New York: Human Rights Watch.

Humphrey, Michael. 1991. Asian women workers in the Middle East: Domestic servants in Jordan. *Asian Migrant* 4 (2): 53–60.

Ilolex. 2005. Database of International Labour Standards. http://www.ilo.org/ilolex/ english/conv disp1.htm. Geneva: ILO. Updated 17 March (accessed 25 November 2005).

IMWU (Indonesian Migrant Workers Union). 2005. Indonesian Consulate should fulfill its responsibility as protector of Indonesian citizens. http://www.mfasia. org/mfaStatements/Statement 14-IMWU-Kotkiho.html (accessed 3 March 2006).

Institute of Policy Studies (IPS). 2004. *Sri Lanka: State of the economy 2004.* Colombo: Institute of Policy Studies.

Iredale, Robyn. 2003. *Asian labour ministerial consultations, Sri Lanka, 1–3 April 2003: International labour migration in Asia: Trends, characteristics, policy and interstate cooperation*. Colombo: International Organization for Migration.

Iritani, Evelyn. 2006. Group accuses Jordan of failing to enforce labor rights: The nation is not living up to promises in a trade agreement with the US, the organization alleges. *Los Angeles Times,* 16 October.

Jakarta Post. 2003. 70 percent of job-seekers underpaid, overqualified. 17 July.

Jansen, Marion, and Roberta Piermartini. 2004. The impact of mode 4 on trade in goods and services. World Trade Organization, Economic Research and Statistics Division, Staff Working Paper ERSD-2004-07. November.

Jayawardena, Kumari. 1973. *The origins of the left movement in Sri Lanka*. Colombo: Sanjiva Books.

Jayawardena, Kumari, and Malathi de Alwis. 2002. The contingent politics of the women's movement in Sri Lanka after independence. In Swarna Jayaweera, ed. *Women in post-independence Sri Lanka*. New Delhi: Sage. 245–77.

Jayaweera, Swarna. 2002a. Fifty years since political independence: An overview. In Swarna Jayaweera, ed. *Women in post-independence Sri Lanka*. New Delhi: Sage. 15–40.

———. 2002b. Women in education and employment. In Swarna Jayaweera, ed. *Women in post-independence Sri Lanka*. New Delhi: Sage. 99–142.

Jayaweera, Swarna, Malsiri Dias, and Leelangi Wanasundera. 2002. *Returnee migrant women in two locations in Sri Lanka*. Colombo: Cenwor.

Jureidini, Ray, and Nayla Moukarbel. 2004. Female Sri Lankan domestic workers in Lebanon: A case of "contract slavery"? *Journal of Ethnic and Migration Studies* 30 (4): 581–607.

Kapiszewski, Andrzej. 2006. Arab versus Asian migrant workers in the GCC countries. Paper presented at the "United Nations Expert Group Meeting on International Migration and Development in the Arab Region." United Nations Secretariat. Beirut, Lebanon, 15–17 May.

Karagiannis, Evangelos, and Nina Glick-Schiller. 2006. Contesting claims to the land: Pentecostalism as a challenge to migration theory and policy. *Soziologus* 56 (2): 137–71.

Kav LaOved. 2006. *Collection of job-brokers' fees from Filipino migrant caregivers in Israel*. Report, September 2006. Tel Aviv: KLO.

Kawar, Mary. 2000. Gender and generation in household labor supply in Jordan. *West Asia and North Africa Regional Paper 43*. Cairo: Population Council.

Keck, Margaret E., and Kathryn Sikkink. 1998. *Activists beyond borders: Advocacy networks in international politics*. Ithaca: Cornell University Press.

Kemp, Adriana, and Rebecca Raijman. 2000. "Foreigners" in the Jewish state: The new politics of labour migration in Israel. *Israeli Sociology* 31: 79–110. [Hebrew]

———. 2003. Christian Zionists in the Holy Land. Evangelical churches, labour migrants, and the Jewish state. *Identities: Global Studies in Culture and Power* 10: 295–318.

Kessler, Robert E. 2008. Wife in Muttontown slave case sentenced to 11 years. Newsday.com. 27 June. http://www.newsday.com/news/local/crime/ny-lislav2757431 65jun27,0,3651872,printstory (accessed 22 July 2008).

Khalaf, Sulayman N. 1992. Gulf societies and the image of unlimited good. *Dialectical Anthropology* 17: 53–84.

Khalaf, Sulayman, and Saad Alkobaisi. 1999. Migrants' strategies of coping and patterns of accommodation in the oil-rich Gulf societies: Evidence from the UAE. *British Journal of Middle Eastern Studies* 26 (2): 271–98.

Kilusang Magbubukid ng Pilipinas (KMP). 1994. Development divergence: Reformism in the Philippine NGO community. *Peasant Update Philippines*. September: 3–7 and 14–15.

Knight, Alan. 2003. Free speech in China: An analysis of press coverage of the Article 23 debate. www.ejournalism.au.com/knight2.pdf (accessed 2 February 2006).

Knuttila, Murray, and Wendee Kubik. 2000. *State theories: Classical, global and feminist perspectives*. New York: Zed Books.

Konigsberg, Eric. 2008. Couple's downfall culminating in sentencing in slavery case. *New York Times*, 23 June.

Korale, R.B.M. 1986. Migration for employment in the Middle East: Its demographic and socioeconomic effects on Sri Lanka. Ch. 12. In Fred Arnold and Nasra M Shah, eds. *Asian labor migration: Pipeline to the Middle East*. Boulder, Colo., and London: Westview.

Ku, Agnes S. 2001. Hegemonic construction, negotiation and displacement: The struggle over right of abode in Hong Kong. *International Journal of Cultural Studies* 4 (3): 259–78.

Ku, Agnes S., and Ngai Pun, eds. 2005. *Remaking citizenship in Hong Kong: Community, nation, and the global city*. London and New York: RoutledgeCurzon.

Lan, Pei-Chia. 2000. Bargaining with patriarchy: Taiwanese women hiring migrant domestic workers. *Anthropology of Work Review* 21 (3): 9–14.

———. 2003a. Negotiating social boundaries and private zones: The micropolitics of employing migrant domestic workers. *Social Problems* 50 (4): 525–49.

———. 2003b. Political and social geography of marginal insiders: Migrant domestic workers in Taiwan. *Asian and Pacific Migration Journal* 12 (1–2): 99–125.

———. 2005. Surrogate family, disposable labour and stratified others: Transnational domestic workers in Taiwan. In Huang et al., eds. 2005. 210–32.

———. 2006. *Global Cinderellas: Migrant domestics and newly rich employers in Taiwan*. Durham, N.C.: Duke University Press.

Law, Lisa. 2002. Sites of transnational activism: Filipino non-governmental organizations in Hong Kong. In Brenda S.A. Yeoh, Peggy Teo and Shirlena Huang, eds. *Gender politics in the Asia-Pacific region*. London and New York: Routledge. 205–22.

———. 2003. Sites of transnational activism: Filipino non-government organisations in Hong Kong. In Brenda S.A. Yeoh, Peggy Teo, and Shirlena Huang, eds. *Gender politics in the Asia-Pacific region*. London: Routledge. 205–21.

Law, Lisa, and Kathy Nadeau. 1999. Globalization, migration and class struggles: NGO mobilization for Filipina domestic workers. *Kasarinlan* 14 (3-4): 51–68.

Law, Wing-sang. 2007. *Re-theorizing colonial power*. Hong Kong: Oxford University Press. In Chinese.

Lee, Ching Kwan. 2000. The revenge of history: Collective memories and labor protests in northeastern China. *Ethnography* 2 (1): 217–37.

———. 2002. From the specter of Mao to the spirit of the law: Labor insurgency in China. *Theory and Society* 31 (2): 189–228.

Lee, Haiyan. 2006. Nannies for foreigners: The enchantment of Chinese womanhood in the age of millennial capitalism. *Public Culture* 18 (3): 507–29.

Leonard, Karen. 2003. South Asian workers in the Gulf: Jockeying for places. In Richard Warren Perry and Bill Maurer, eds. *Globalization under construction: Governmentality, law, and identity*. Minneapolis: University of Minnesota Press. 129–70.

Li, F.L.N., A.M. Findlay, and H. Jones. 1998. A cultural economy perspective on service sector migration in the global city: The case of Hong Kong. *International Migration* 36 (2): 131–57.

Liebelt, Claudia. 2007. *Caring for the "Holy Land": Transnational Filipina domestic workers in the Israeli migration regime*. PhD diss. (Institute of Social Anthropology, Martin-Luther University Halle-Wittenberg, Germany).

———. 2008. On sentimental Orientalists, Christian Zionists, and working class cosmopolitans: Filipina domestic workers' journeys to Israel and beyond. *Critical Asian Studies* 40 (4): 567–608.

Lin, Paul. 2003. Why is Regina so smug these days? AFAR: Association for Asian Research. 27 July 2003. http:www.asianresearch.org/articles/1477.html (accessed 2 February 2006).

Loewe, Markus, Jonas Blume, and Johanna Speer. 2008. How favoritism affects the business climate: Empirical evidence from Jordan. *Middle East Journal* 62 (2): 259–76.

Longva, Anh Nga. 1997. *Walls built on sand: Migration, exclusion and society in Kuwait*. Boulder, Colo., and Oxford: Westview Press.

Looney, R.E. 1992. Manpower options in a small labour-importing state: The influence of ethnic composition on Kuwait's development. *International Migration* 30 (2): 175–200.

Lorenzo, Fely M.E., et al. 2007. Nurse migration from a source country perspective: Philippine country case study. *Health Services Research* 42 (3). Part II: 1406–18.

Lutz, Helma, ed. 2008. When home becomes a workplace: Domestic work as an ordinary job in Germany? In *Migration and domestic Work: A European perspective on a global theme*. Burlington, Vt: Ashgate Publishing. 43–60.

Lynch, Caitrin. 2007. *Juki girls, good girls: Gender and cultural politics in Sri Lanka's global garment industry*. Ithaca, N.Y.: Cornell University Press.

Lyons, Lenore. 2000. The limits of feminist political intervention in Singapore. *Journal of Contemporary Asia* 30 (1): 67–83.

———. 2004. *A state of ambivalence: The feminist movement in Singapore*. Leiden: Brill Publishers.

———. 2005a. *Making citizen babies for papa: Feminist responses to reproductive policy in Singapore*. Copenhagen: Asia Research Centre Copenhagen Discussion Papers.

———. 2005b. Transient Workers Count Too? The intersection of citizenship and gender in Singapore's civil society. *Sojourn: Journal of Social Issues in Southeast Asia* 20 (2): 208–48.

———. 2007a. A curious space in-between: The public/private divide and gender-based activism in Singapore. *Gender, Technology and Development* 11: 27–51.

———. 2007b. Dignity overdue: Women's rights activism in support of foreign domestic workers in Singapore. *Women's Studies Quarterly* 35 (3-4): 106–22.

———. 2007c. L'organisation au service des droits des travailleurs migrants: Le militantisme transnational à Singapour et en Malaisie. *Lien Social et Politiques* 58 (Autumn): 57–71.

———. 2009. Transcending the border: Transnational imperatives in Singapore's migrant worker rights movement. *Critical Asian Studies* 41 (1): 89–112.

Lyons, Lenore, and James Gomez. 2005. Moving beyond the ob markers: Rethinking the space of civil society in Singapore. *Sojourn: Journal of Social Issues in Southeast Asia* 20 (2): 119–31.

Malik, A. 2004. Bahrain human rights group dissolved. Associated Press. http://web. lexis-nexis. com/universe/document?_ m=4025f9a98e2483581f3870d28c6032 b8&_docnum=2&wchp=dGLbVtz-zSkVA&_md5=d8ea084d65e9ad0d4cc 0f85dc8d10e68. Posted 29 September 2004 (accessed 27 February 2005).

Marecek, Jeanne. 2000. Am I a woman in these matters? Notes on Sinhala nationalism and gender in Sri Lanka. In T. Mayer, ed. *Gender ironies of nationalism: Sexing the nation*. London: Routledge.

Massey, Doreen. 1994. *Space, place and gender.* Minneapolis: University of Minnesota Press.

Mauzy, Diane K., and R.S. Milne. 2002. *Singapore politics under the People's Action Party*. London: Routledge.

McKay, Deirdre. 2005. Success stories? Filipina migrant domestic workers in Canada. In Huang et al., eds. 2005. 305–38.

Mellyn, Kevin. 2003. Worker remittances as a development tool: Opportunity for the Philippines. Report for the Asian Development Bank. Manila: Asian Development Bank, 13 June. Source: www.adb.org/documents/reports/consultant/ worker_remittances_phi.pdf (accessed 24 September 2008).

MFA. 2008. *Asian Domestic Workers Assembly.* http://www.mfasia.org/mfaResources/ADWA2007. html (accessed 12 January).

Mills, Mary Beth. 2003. Gender and inequality in the global labor force. *Annual Review of Anthropology* 32: 41–62.

Miyoshi, Masao. 1993. A borderless world? From colonialism to transnationalism and the decline of the nation-state. *Critical Inquiry* 19 (4): 726–51.

Moghadam, Valentine M. 2005. *Globalizing women: Transnational feminist networks*. Baltimore and London: The Johns Hopkins University Press.

MOM. 2007. *Singapore Yearbook of Manpower Statistics.* http://www.mom.gov. sg/publish/etc/medialib/mom_library/mrsd/yb_2007.Par.45234.File.tmp/2007Year Book_LFtable1_1.xls (accessed 5 February).

Moors, Annelies. 2007. Paid domestic labor: Central Arab states, Egypt and Yemen. In Suad Joseph, ed. *Encyclopedia of women and Islamic cultures.* Vol. 4. *Economics, education, mobility and space*. Leiden: Brill Academic Publishers.

Moors, Annelies, and Marina de Regt. 2008. Migrant domestic workers in the Middle East. In Marlou Schrover et al., eds. *Illegal migration and gender in a global and historical perspective.* Amsterdam: IMISCOE. 151–70.

Mundlak, Guy. 2005. Recommodifying time: Working hours of "live-in" domestic workers. In Joanne Conaghan and Kerry Rittich, eds. *Labour law, work and family: Critical and comparative perspectives.* Oxford: Oxford University Press. 125–56.

Muttarak, Raya. 2004. Domestic service in Thailand: Reflection on conflicts in gender, class and ethnicity. *Journal of Southeast Asian Studies* 35 (3): 503–29.

Nagy, Sharon. 1998. "This time I think I'll try a Filipina": Global and local influences on relations between foreign household workers and their employers in Doha, Qatar. *City and Society* 10 (1): 83–103.

———. 2006. Making room for migrants, making sense of difference: Spatial and ideological expressions of social diversity in urban Qatar. *Urban Studies* 43 (1): 119–37.

Newendorp, Nicole. 2008. *Uneasy reunions: Immigration, citizenship, and family life in post-1997 Hong Kong.* Palo Alto, Calif.: Stanford University Press.

Nicholson, Melanie. 2006. Without their children: Rethinking motherhood among transnational migrant women. *Social Text* 24 (3): 13–33.

Nonnenmacher, Sophie, et al. 2003. *Asian labour migration ministerial consultations, Sri Lanka, 1–3 April 2003: Compendium on labour migration policies and practices in major Asian labour sending countries.* Colombo: International Organization for Migration.

Ong, Aihwa. 1993. On the edge of empires. Flexible citizenship among Chinese in diaspora. *positions* 1 (3): 745-78.

———. 1999. *Flexible citizenship: The cultural logics of transnationality.* Durham, N.C.: Duke University Press.

———. 2006. *Neoliberalism as exception: Mutations in citizenship and sovereignty.* Durham, N.C.: Duke University Press.

Ong, Aihwa, and Ananya Roy. 2008. Concept paper: Inter-referencing Asia: Urban experiments and the art of being global. Paper presented at the SSRC conference, "Inter-Asian Connections," Dubai. 21–23 February.

Ong, Aiwha, and Donald M. Nonini, eds. 1997. *Ungrounded empires: The cultural politics of modern Chinese transnationalism.* New York and London: Routledge.

Ortner, Sherry B. 2006. *Anthropology and social theory: Culture, power, and the acting subject.* Durham, N.C.: Duke University Press.

Othman, Ibrahim. 1974. Changing family structure in urban Jordan. Unpublished study prepared for UNESCO, Amman.

Parliamentary Debates, Republic of Singapore: Official Report. 2004. *Part IV of First Session of Tenth Parliament* 77 (18). Singapore.

Parreñas, Rhacel Salazar. *See* Salazar Parreñas.

Pattadath, Bindulakshmi. 2008. Gender, mobility and the state: Multiple engagements. Paper presented at the Amsterdam School for Social Science Research, University of Amsterdam, 13 May.

Perera, Leon, and Tisa Ng. 2002. Foreign funding: Managing conflicting views. In Constance Singam, Tan Chong Kee, Tisa Ng, and Leon Perera, eds. *Building social space in Singapore: The working committee's initiative in civil society activism*. Singapore: Select Publishing. 93–96.

Perera, Viola. 2004. Interview. 1 December. Coordinator, Action Network for Migrant Workers. Nawala, Sri Lanka.

Pessar, Patricia R., and Sarah J. Mahler. 2003. Transnational migration: Bringing gender in. *International Migration Review* 37 (3): 812-46.

Petras, James. 1999. NGOs: In the service of imperialism. *Journal of Contemporary Asia,* 29 (4): 429–40.

Philippine Overseas Employment Administration (POEA). 2006. *OFW global presence: A compendium* of overseas employment statistics, 2006. http://www. poea.gov.ph/stats/2006Stats.pdf (accessed 31 July 2008).

Pilar [United Indonesians Against Overcharging] and Gammi [Indonesian Migrant Muslim Alliance]. 2008. Delay means more abuses. Indonesian migrants hit consulate for slow actions on demands. Press release. 13 April.

Piper, Nicola. 2003. Feminization of labor migration as violence against women: International, regional, and local nongovernmental organization responses in Asia. *Violence against Women* 9 (6): 723–45.

———. 2005. Rights of foreign domestic workers: Emergence of transnational and transregional solidarity? *Asian and Pacific Migration Journal* 14 (1-2): 97–119.

———. 2006. Migrant worker activism in Singapore and Malaysia: Freedom of association and the role of the state. *Asian and Pacific Migration Journal* 15 (3): 359–79.

Piper, Nicola, and Anders Uhlin. 2002. Transnational advocacy networks and the issue of female labor migration and trafficking in East and Southeast Asia: A gendered analysis of opportunities and obstacles. *Asian and Pacific Migration Journal* 11 (2): 171–96.

Piper, Nicola, and Anders Uhlin, eds. 2004. *Transnational activism in Asia: Problems of power and democracy*. London: Routledge.

Portes, Alejandro. 2000. Globalization from below: The rise of transnational communities. In Don Kalb et al., eds. *The ends of globalization: Bringing society back in*. Lanham, Md.: Rowman and Littlefield. 253–70.

Pratt, Geraldine. 2004. *Working feminism*. Philadelphia: Temple University Press.

Qayum, Seemin, and Raka Ray. 2003. Grappling with modernity: India's respectable classes and the culture of domestic servitude. *Ethnography* 4 (4): 520–55.

Qurtoba Services. 2004. Interview with Qurtoba Services Manpower Recruitment Agency, Ajman, UAE, 9 November.

Rahman, Noor Abdul, Brenda S.A. Yeoh, and Shirlena Huang. 2005. "Dignity overdue": Transnational domestic workers in Singapore. In Huang et al., eds. 2005. 233–61.

Raijman, Rebecca, and Adrianna Kemp. 2004. Consuming the Holy Spirit in the Holy Land: Evangelical churches, labor migrants and the Jewish state. In Kalman Applbaum and Yoram S. Carmeli, eds. *Consumption and market society in Israel*. Oxford and New York: Berg. 163–83.

Rapport, Nigel, and Ronald Stade. 2007. A cosmopolitan turn — or return? *Social Anthropology* 15 (2): 223–35.

Robinson, Kathryn. 2000. Gender, Islam and nationality: Indonesian domestic servants in the Middle East. *In* Kathleen M. Adams and Sara Dickey, eds. *Home and hegemony: Domestic service and identity politics in South and Southeast Asia*. Ann Arbor: University of Michigan Press. 249–82.

Rodan, Garry. 1993. Preserving the one-party state in contemporary Singapore. In Kevin Hewison, Richard Robison, and Gary Rodan, eds. *Southeast Asia in the 1990s: Authoritarianism, democracy, and capitalism*. St. Leonards: Allen and Unwin. 76–108.

Rofel, Lisa. 1999. *Other modernities: Gendered yearnings in China after socialism*. Berkeley and Los Angeles: University of California Press.

Rollins, Judith. 1990. Ideology and servitude. In Roger Sanjek and Shellee Colen, eds. *At work in homes: Household workers in world perspective*. Washington, D.C.: American Ethnological Society Monograph Series No. 3, American Anthropological Association.

Rosaldo, Renato. 1994. Cultural citizenship and educational democracy. *Cultural Anthropology* 9 (3): 402–11.

Rose, Nikolas. 1999. Powers of freedom: Reframing political thought. Cambridge: Cambridge University Press.

Rosewarne, Stuart. 1998. The globalization and liberalization of Asian labour markets. *World Economy* 21 (3): 71–84.

Rostow, Walter W. 1960. *The stages of economic growth*. Cambridge: Cambridge University Press.

Ruhunage, L.K. 2004. Interview, 11 November. Counsellor (Employment and Welfare), Consulate General of the Democratic Socialist Republic of Sri Lanka, Dubai, UAE.

Ruwich, John. 2005. Protests puzzle free trade poster child Hong Kong. Reuters Alertnet. 15 December. http://www.alertnet.org/printable.htm?URL=thenews/newsdesk/HKG296554.htm (accessed 13 January 2006).

Said, Edward W. 1978. *Orientalism*. New York: Pantheon Books; London: Routledge and Kegan Paul; Toronto: Random House.

———. 1984. Reflections on exile. *Granta* 13: 157–72.

Salazar Parreñas, Rhacel. 2001a. *Servants of globalization*. Palo Alto, Calif.: Stanford University Press.

———. 2001b. Transgressing the nation-state: The partial citizenship and "imagined (global) community" of migrant Filipina domestic workers. *Signs* 26 (4): 1129–54.

———. 2005. *Children of global migration: Transnational families and gendered woes*. Palo Alto, Calif.: Stanford University Press.

Samath, Feizal. 2004. Jordan: Sri Lankan women workers seek new relationships. Inter-Press Service, 28 May.

———. 2007. Lankan housemaids seek higher wages overseas. *Sunday Times,* 21 November.

Sassen, Saskia. 1988. *The mobility of labour and capital: A study in international investment and labour flow*. Cambridge: Cambridge University Press.

———. 1996. New employment regimes in cities. *New Community* 22: 579–95.

———. 2000 (1991). *The global city*. Princeton, N.J.: Princeton University Press.

———. 2001. The global city: Strategic site/new frontier. Globalization: A Symposium. New Delhi, India. July 2001. http://www.india-seminar.com/2001/503/503%20saskia%20sassen. htm (accessed 15 March 2006).

———. 2002. Women's burden: Counter-geographies of globalization and the feminization of survival. *Nordic Journal of International Law* 71: 255–74.

SCMP (*South China Morning Post*). 2004. Magistrates "too lenient on illegal bosses"; Sentence review highlights cases where punishment guidelines are being ignored by lower court. 27 August.

———. 2006. Wait of expectation. 20 October.

Scott, James C. 1972. Patron–client politics and political change in Southeast Asia. *The American Political Science Review* 66 (1): 91–113.

Sebastian, Michael, and Raghwan, eds. 2000. *Asia Pacific regional trade union symposium on migrant workers, 6–9 December 1999, Kuala Lampur, Malaysia*. Geneva: ILO.

Shah, Nasra, Sulayman Al-Qudsi, and Makhdoom Shah. 1991. Asian women workers in Kuwait. *International Migration Review* 25 (3): 464–86.

Shinozaki, Kyoko. 2005. Keeping women on the move: Transnational "families" in the Philippines' politics of reproductive labor migration. Paper presented at the conference "Migration and Domestic Work in Global Perspective, 26–29 May 2005. The Netherlands Institute of Advanced Studies, Wassenar.

Short, John Rennis, and Yeong-Hyun Kim. 1999. *Globalization and the city*. Harlow: Longman.

Shteiwi, Musa. 1996. Class structure and inequality in the city of Amman. In Jean Hannoyer and Seteney Shami, eds. *Amman: The city and its society*. Beirut: Centre d'Études et de Recherches sur le Moyen-Orient Contemporain (CERMOC).

Silvey, Rachel. 2004. Transnational migration and the gender politics of scale: Indonesian domestic workers in Saudi Arabia. *Singapore Journal of Tropical Geography* 25 (2): 141–55.

Sim, Amy. 2003a. Organising discontent: NGOs for Southeast Asian migrant workers in Hong Kong. *Asian Journal of Social Science* 31 (3): 478–510.

———. 2003b. The cultural logic of transnational activism: Indonesian domestic workers in Hong Kong. Paper presented at the Third International Convention of Asia Scholars. 19–22 August 2003. Singapore.

———. 2008. The cultural economy of illegal migration: Migrant workers who overstay in Hong Kong. In Curley and Wong, eds. 2008, 120–47.

———. Forthcoming. The sexual economy of desire: Girlfriends, boyfriends and babies among Indonesian women migrants in Hong Kong. *Sexualities*.

Sim, Amy, and Vivienne Wee. 2009. Undocumented Indonesian workers in Macau: The human outcome of colluding interests. *Critical Asian Studies* 41 (1): 165–88.

Skeldon, Ronald. 1995. Immigration and population issues. In S.Y.L. Cheung and S.M.H Sze, eds. *The other Hong Kong report 1995*. Hong Kong: The Chinese University Press.

Smith, M.P. 1994. Can you imagine? Transnational migration and the globalization of grassroots politics. *Social Text* 39: 15–33.

SMS. 2008. *About us*. http://www.solidaritas.org/aboutus.asp (accessed 12 January 2008).

So, Alvin. 2005. One country, three systems? State, nation, and civil society in the making of citizenship in the Chinese triangle of Mainland-Taiwan-Hong Kong.

In Agnes S. Ku and Ngai Pun eds. *Remaking citizenship in Hong Kong: Community, nation, and the global city*. New York: Routledge. 235–53.

Solidarity Center. 2005. *Justice for all: The struggle for worker rights in Jordan*. Washington, D.C.: The American Center for International Labor Solidarity (Solidarity Center). http://solidarity.timberlakepublishing.com/files/JordanFinal.pdf (accessed 17 July 2008).

Sorensen, Ninna Nyberg. 2005. Transnational family life across the Atlantic: The experience of Colombian and Dominican migrants in Europe. Paper presented at the conference "Migration and Domestic Work in Global Perspective, 26–29 May 2005. The Netherlands Institute of Advanced Studies, Wassenar.

Soysa, David. 2004. Interview. 3 February 2004. Migrant Services Centre. Dehiwela, Sri Lanka.

Soysal, Yasemin Nuhoglu. 1994. *Limits of citizenship: Migrants and postnational membership in Europe*. Chicago: University of Chicago.

Sri Lankan Bureau of Foreign Employment (SLBFE). 2004. *Statistical handbook on migration, 2003*. Colombo, Sri Lanka: Research Division, SLBFE.

———. 2005. Departures for foreign employment by sex, 1986–2004. In SLBFE Research Division, *Annual statistical report of foreign employment, 2004*. Battaramulla, Sri Lanka.

———. 2006. *Statistical handbook on migration, 2005*. Colombo, Sri Lanka: Research Division, SLBFE.

———. 2007. Total departures for foreign employment by country, 2002–2006. In SLBFE Research Division, *Annual statistical report of foreign employment, 2006*. Battaramulla, Sri Lanka.

———. 2008. Estimated stock of Sri Lankan overseas contract workers by country and sex 2007. In SLBFE Research Division, *Annual statistical report of foreign employment, 2007*. Battaramulla, Sri Lanka.

Sriskandarajah, Dhananjayan. 2002. The migration-development nexus: Sri Lanka case study. *International Migration* 40 (5). Special issue 2: 283–307.

Stasiulis, Daiva, and Abigail Bakan. 2002. Negotiating the citizenship divide: Foreign domestic worker policy and legal jurisprudence. In R. Jhappan, ed. *Women's legal strategies in Canada: A friendly assessment*. Toronto: University of Toronto Press. 237–94.

———. 2005 (2003). *Negotiating citizenship: Migrant women in Canada and the global system*. Toronto, Buffalo, and London: Toronto University Press.

Stirrat, R.L. 1992. *Power and religiosity in a post-colonial setting: Sinhala Catholics in contemporary Sri Lanka*. Cambridge: Cambridge University Press.

Suara. 2007. At last Macau is opened. 23 February.

Sunday Times. 2008. Crisis is averted over housemaids. The *Sunday Times* Online, Sunday, 13 January. http://www.sundaytimes.lk/080113/FinancialTimes/ft 326.html (accessed 17 January 2008).

Suryadarma, Daniel, Asep Suryahadi, and Sudarno Sumarto. 2005. The measurement and trends of unemployment in Indonesia: The issue of discouraged workers. Working paper from SMERU Research Institute. Available at SSRN: http://ssrn.com/abstract-861464. July.

Swider, Sarah. 2006. Working women of the world unite? Labor organizing and transnational gender solidarity among domestic workers in Hong Kong. In

Myra Marx Ferree and Aili Mari Tripp, eds. *Global Feminism: Transnational women's activism, organizing and human rights*. New York: New York University Press. 110–40.

Taipei Times. 2003. Cabinet secretaries resign. *Taipei Times* 17 July, p.1. http://www.taipeitimes.com/News/front/archives/2003/07/17/2003059718 (accessed 2 February 2006).

Tellis-Nayak, V. 1983. Power and solidarity: Clientage in domestic service. *Current Anthropology* 24 (1): 67–79.

Thompson, Edward Palmer. 1963. The making of the English working class. New York: Pantheon Books.

Tierney, Robert. 2002. Foreign workers and capitalist class relations in Taiwan: A study of economic exploitation and political isolation. *Bulletin of Labor Research* (Cheng-Chi University) 12: 125–65.

Tiwari, Pranjal. 2002. Hong Kong faces new "national security" legislation. Znet. http://www.zmag.org/content/print_article.cmf?itemID=2520&sectionID=1 (accessed 2 February 2006).

Tiwari, Pranjal, and David Solnit. 2005. Kong yee sai mau: The battle of Hong Kong. Znet.http://www.zmag.org/content/print_article.cfm?itemID=9399&section ID=1 (accessed 2 February 2006).

Touraine, Alain. 1988. *Return of the actor.* Minneapolis: University of Minnesota Press.

Tsang, Steve. 2003. Crisis in Hong Kong. *China Review.* http://www.gbcc.org.uk/iss 26analysis.htm (accessed 2 February 2006).

Tucker, Judith. 1985. *Women in nineteenth-century Egypt*. Cambridge: Cambridge University Press.

TWC2. 2008a. *Our objectives.* http://twc2.org.sg/site/who-we-are/mission.html (accessed 12 January 2008).

———. 2008b. *Vision.* http://twc2.org.sg/site/who-we-are/vision.html (accessed 12 January 2008).

Tyner, James A. 2004. *Made in the Philippines: Gendered discourses and the making of migrants.* London and New York: Routledge.

UN Habitat. 2006. *State of the world's cities*, 2006–2007. New York: United Nations.

Ursel, Jane. 1986. The state and the maintenance of patriarchy: A case study of family, labour and welfare legislation in Canada. In Dickinson and Russell, eds. 1985.

Vasudevan, Ramaa. 2004. The gospel of free trade. In *Gloves off.* May 2004. http://www.glovesoff. org/features/vasudevan_freetrade.html (accessed 20 April 2006).

Verdery, Katherine. 1998. Transnationalism, nationalism, citizenship and property: Eastern Europe since 1989. *American Ethnologist* 25 (2): 291–306.

Wagner, Heike. 2005. The instruction and the placement of female Ecuadorian domestic workers in a Catholic parish in Madrid. Paper presented at the conference "Migration and Domestic Work in Global Perspective. 26–29 May 2005. The Netherlands Institute of Advanced Studies, Wassenar.

Wanasundera, Leelangi. 2001. *Migrant women domestic workers: Cyprus, Greece and Italy*. Colombo: Cenwor.

Wee, Vivienne, and Amy Sim. 2004. Transnational labour networks in female labour migration: Mediating between Southeast Asian women workers and international labour markets. In A. Ananta, ed. *International migration in Southeast Asia: Challenges and impacts*. Singapore: Institute of Southeast Asian Studies. 166–98.

———. 2005. Hong Kong as a destination for migrant domestic workers. In Huang et al., eds. 2005. 175–209.

Weekley, Kathleen. 2004. Saving pennies for the state: A new role of Filipino migrant workers? *Journal of Contemporary Asia* 34 (3): 349–64.

Weerakoon, Nedra. 1998. Sri Lanka: A caste case study of international female labour migration. In S. Sta. M. Amparita, J.J. Balisnono, R. Plaetevoet, and R. Selwyn, eds. *Legal protection for Asian women migrant workers: Strategies for action*. Makati City, Philippines: Ateneo Human Rights Center. 97–118.

Werbner, Pnina. 1999. Global pathways: Working class cosmopolitans and the creation of transnational ethnic worlds. *Social Anthropology* 7 (1): 17–35.

———, ed. 2008. *Anthropology and the new cosmopolitanism: Rooted, feminist and vernacular perspectives*. Oxford and New York: Berg.

WHO (World Health Organization). 2005. *Core indicators 2005: Health situation in the South-East Asia and Western Pacific Regions*. Geneva: WHO.

Wijesiri, Dudley. 2004. Interview. 3 February 2004. Migrant Services Centre. Dehiwela, Sri Lanka.

Willen, Sarah S. 2007. Toward a critical phenomenology of "illegality": State power, criminalization, and abjectivity among undocumented migrant workers in Tel Aviv, Israel. *International Migration* 45 (3): 8–38.

Winkler, Onn. 2005. Was it worth it? A reexamination of the cost/benefit balance of the inter-Arab labor migration. Paper presented at the conference "Transnational Migration: Foreign Labor and Its Impact in the Gulf." Bellagio, Italy. 20–24 June.

Witharana, Manori. 2004. Interview. 5 February 2004. American Center for International Labor Solidarity. Colombo, Sri Lanka

Wong, Benson Wai-kwok. 2003. People's power in power? Hong Kong's political development and the July rally. *Online Journal of the Austrian Association of Asian Studies*. http://www.eastasia. at/vol2_1/article03p.htm (accessed February 2, 2006).

World Bank. 2005. *The economic advancement of women in Jordan: A country gender assessment*. Social and Economic Development Group, MENA Region. May.

Wourms, Michael. 1992: *The J.I.L. love story*. El Cajon, Calif.: Christian Services Publishing.

Yamanaka, Keiko, and Nicola Piper. 2005. Feminized migration in East and Southeast Asia: Policies, actions and empowerment. United Nations Research Institute for Social Development. Occasional Paper 11.

Yapa, Kanti. 2004. Interview. 3 February 2004. IOM (International Organization for Migration). Colombo, Sri Lanka.

Yee, Yeong Chong. 2008. *Injured citizenship: Governmentality and civil society in Singapore*. Paper presented at the Eighth Asean Inter-University Conference, Manila, Philippines, 29–31 May.

Yeoh, Brenda S.A., et al. 2004. Diasporic subjects in the nation: Foreign domestic workers, the reach of the law and civil society in Singapore. *Asian Studies Review* 28 (1): 7–24.

Zilfi, M.C. 2004. Servants, slaves, and the domestic order in the Ottoman Middle East. *Hawwa* 2 (1): 1–33.

Zuhur, Sherifa. 2005. Law: Criminal-Arab States. In Suad Joseph, ed. *Encyclopedia of women and Islamic cultures*. Vol. 2: *Family, law and politics*. Leiden: Brill Academic Publishers.

❏

Contributors

Nicole Constable is professor of anthropology at the University of Pittsburgh. She is the author of *Christian Souls and Chinese Spirits: Hakka Identity in Hong Kong* (University of California Press, 1994), *Maid to Order in Hong Kong* (Cornell University Press, 1997, 2007), and *Romance on a Global Stage: Pen Pals, Virtual Ethnography, and Mail Order Marriages* (University of California Press, 2003), and the editor of *Guest People: Hakka Identity in China and Abroad* (University of Washington Press, 1996) and *Cross-Border Marriages: Gender and Mobility in Transnational Asia* (University of Pennsylvania Press, 2005). Email: ncgrad@pitt.edu.

Elizabeth Frantz is a doctoral candidate in social anthropology at the London School of Economics and Political Science. Her current research concerns migrant domestic workers in the Arab world. It examines the causes and consequences of women's migration from the perspective of a host country, Jordan, and the sending country of Sri Lanka. She has also done fieldwork on the experiences of Palestinian refugees in Egypt and asylum policies in Turkey and the UK. Her interests include forced and free labor, kinship and gender, forms of inequality, migration and development in the Arab world and South Asia. Email: E.A.Frantz@lse.ac.uk.

Michele R. Gamburd, a cultural anthropologist, is currently a professor in the Anthropology Department at Portland State University in Portland, Oregon. Topics of study include the migration of labor from Sri Lanka to West Asia (the Middle East), the use and abuse of alcohol, and the aftermath of the 2004 Indian Ocean tsunami. She is the author of *The Kitchen Spoon's Handle: Transnationalism and Sri Lanka's Migrant Housemaids* (Cornell University Press, 2000) and *Breaking the Ashes: The Culture of Illicit Liquor in Sri Lanka* (Cornell University Press, 2008), and co-editor (with Dennis McGilvray, University of Colorado at Boulder) of *Tsunami Recovery in Sri Lanka: Ethnic and Regional Dimensions* (Routledge, 2010). Email: gamburdm @pdx.ed.

Hsiao-Chuan Hsia is professor at the Graduate Institute for Social Transformation Studies, Shih Hsin University, Taipei. As the first scholar studying marriage migration issues in Taiwan, her first book is titled *Drifting Shoal: The "Foreign Brides" Phenomenon in Capitalist Globalization* (Taishi, 2002; in Chinese). As an activist her concerns are the empowerment of immigrant women and the making of im/migrant movement in Taiwan. Email: hsiaochuan.hsia@gmail.com.

Claudia Liebelt completed her PhD in social anthropology in Halle (Germany) and is now a research assistant at the Research Institute of Law, Politics and Justice at Keele University (UK). Her research interests are in urban anthropology, gender, migration, and the anthropology of religion. Her recent work investigates Filipina care workers' making of sacred geographies in Israel as part of a comparative research project on sociality, caring, and the religious imagination in the Filipino diaspora (the "Footsteps" project, funded by the AHRC Diaspora, Migration and Identities Programme, PI Prof. Pnina Werbner). She has published on the Filipino diaspora, female migration, and migrant domestic workers in Israel. Email: claulie@gmx.net.

Lenore Lyons is research professor in Asian Studies at the University of Western Australia. A leading scholar on the feminist movement in Singapore, her work has appeared in a number of edited collections as well as journals including *International Feminist Journal of Politics, Critical Asian Studies, Asian Studies Review, Asia Pacific Viewpoint,* and *Citizenship Studies*. Her book *A State of Ambivalence: The Feminist Movement in Singapore* (Brill Academic Publishers, Leiden) was published in 2004. She recently completed a major study of citizenship, identity, and sovereignty in the Riau Islands of Indonesia (with Michele Ford, University of Sydney) and is currently working on a study of migrant worker activism in support of female domestic workers in Malaysia and Singapore. Email: lenore.lyons@uwa. edu.au.

Marina de Regt is a cultural anthropologist specializing in gender, labor, and migration in the Middle East, in particular in Yemen. In 2003 she received her PhD degree from the University of Amsterdam for her dissertation on women health workers in Yemen (published in book form in 2007 by Syracuse University Press: *Pioneers or Pawns? Women Health Workers and the Politics of Development in Yemen*). She is currently working as coordinator of the South-South Exchange Programme for Research on the History of Development (SEPHIS) at the International Institute of Social History in Amsterdam. Email: mre@iisg.nl.

Amy Sim is a cultural anthropologist with the Department of Sociology at the University of Hong Kong. Her areas of research include women's labor migration from Indonesia to Hong Kong, the Indonesian labor export system, undocumented migration, labor organizing, the institutional development of civil space, women's leadership, activism, sexuality and issues of identity among migrant women workers in Hong Kong. Email: asim@hku.hk.

Vivienne Wee is associate professor at the Department of Asian and International Studies and associate director of the Southeast Asia Research Centre, City University of Hong Kong. She currently directs a Research Programme Consortium on "Women's empowerment in Muslim contexts: Gender, poverty and democratisation from the inside out," a five-year research program covering China, Indonesia, Iran, Pakistan, and cross-border contexts. Trained as an anthropologist, she has wide-ranging research interests in religion and ideology, nation-state evolution, ethnicity and ethno-nationalism, gender and development, as well as labor migration. Email: v.wee@ cityu.edu.hk.

❏

Index

*For Product Safety Concerns and Information please contact
our EU representative GPSR@taylorandfrancis.com Taylor & Francis
Verlag GmbH, Kaufingerstraße 24, 80331 München, Germany*

T - #0179 - 270225 - C0 - 246/174/13 - PB - 9780415509497 - Gloss Lamination